CW00537472

THE CONSTABLES
OF HORLEY MILL

A True Saga of a Family
from the Surrey and Sussex Borders
during the 19th Century

James Constable (1749–1838) known as 'The Old Gentleman'

THE
Constables
OF HORLEY MILL

Claire Constable

First published in Great Britain in 2001
by Surrey Mills Publishing Ltd.
PO Box 24
Tunbridge Wells North TN5 6BQ

British Cataloguing in Publication Data
A catalogue record for this book is
available from the British Library.

ISBN 0 9540359-0-9

Editor Christine Davis
Design Mónica Bratt

Printed and bound in Great Britain
by the Amadeus Press
Cleckheaton, West Yorkshire
BD19 4TQ

To the memory of my grandmother,
Clara Maud Maybury Grece

Contents

Illustrations

Introduction

THIS IS THE STORY OF the Constable family from Horley in Surrey. The family appears to have been part of the close-knit milling community strung along the river Mole; they had lived in the area for at least five hundred years. For nearly three hundred years they lived at Horley Mill and, according to family hearsay, they possessed deeds dated back to the reign of King John (1167-1216). The names Thomas and William crop up time and time again although it is mere fantasy to imagine that Thomas atte mulle and William atte mulle, who occupied the mill in 1309, were family members. However, this story begins many years later in 1797, at the end of the French Revolution, and ends in 1838 with the death of James Constable, known as 'The Old Gentleman'. It is clear from the articles in his possession that James Constable Sr. held strong republican views. He had pictures on his walls of the radicals, Thomas Paine and Thomas 'Clio' Rickman and, among his correspondence, letters from Thomas Paine, the writer and politician William Cobbett, the reformer Joel Barlow and the poet Percy Bysshe Shelley.

Daniel, the eldest son, was a radical reformer and a self-professed wanderer. He also possessed practical skills; he and his younger brothers dismantled and rebuilt the family watermill soon after his return from America in 1808. James became a country gentleman, Mildred emigrated to the wilds of Indiana,

William, the artist, accompanied Daniel on a 17,000 mile adventure to America and later became a successful surveyor and well-known photographer, Charles ran the family mills and Susanna cared for her parents and faithfully kept her journal. There is happiness and heartbreak, success and failure.

The old oak chest stood in the hall for very many years. This story has been woven from its contents: a collection of old letters, journals, daguerreotypes and photographs, old newspapers and a scrapbook of cuttings recording all memorable family incidents. The family appear to had a sense of history, which encouraged them to preserve personal documents through the years. At least one person in every generation became aware of the importance of the growing record, and added his or her own contribution, however small.

My research has led me far and wide. On each trip I am rewarded with yet more information for the growing archive. I have taken the liberty of modernising the punctuation in the original letters, purely to make them easier to read. However, it is now time to tell the story, hopefully as interesting to read as it was to write.

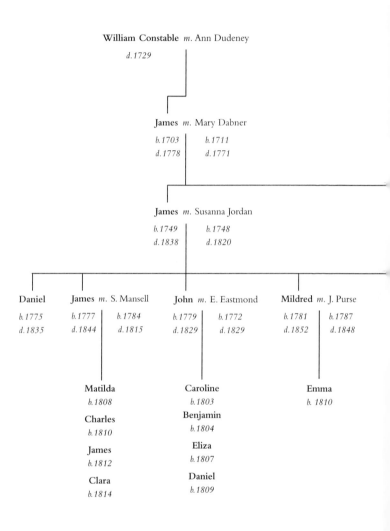

William Constable *m*. Ann Dudeney
d.1729

James *m*. Mary Dabner
b.1703 *b.1711*
d.1778 *d.1771*

James *m*. Susanna Jordan
b.1749 *b.1748*
d.1838 *d.1820*

Daniel **James** *m*. S. Mansell **John** *m*. E. Eastmond **Mildred** *m*. J. Purse
b.1775 *b.1777* *b.1784* *b.1779* *b.1772* *b.1781* *b.1787*
d.1835 *d.1844* *d.1815* *d.1829* *d.1829* *d.1852* *d.1848*

Matilda Caroline Emma
b.1808 *b.1803* *b.1810*

Charles Benjamin
b.1810 *b.1804*

James Eliza
b.1812 *b.1807*

Clara Daniel
b.1814 *b.1809*

THE
Constable
FAMILY TREE

Daniel *m.* Elizabeth Sewell
b. 1751   *b. 1751*
d. 1803   *d. 1834*

William *m.* J. Mott   **Benjamin**   **Charles** *m.* J. Charman   **Richard**   **Susanna** *m.* H. Grece
b. 1783   *b. 1786*   *b. 1785*   *b. 1786*   *b. 1796*   *b. 1789*   *b. 1790*   *b. 1799*
d. 1861   *d. 1829*   *d. 1806*   *d. 1867*   *d. 1863*   *d. 1795*   *d. 1879*   *d. 1851*

Lavinia   **Clair James**
b. 1828   *b. 1831*

Fanny
b. 1830

Cast of Major Characters

JAMES CONSTABLE (1749-1838). Known by one and all as The Old Gentleman. During his long life he lived only in two houses, barely two hundred yards apart. He was born at The Mill House, Horley Mill and died at Tedhams where he had established a well known and well patronised store. He fathered nine children, seven of whom lived to adulthood. He was a freethinker and among his friends he counted the radicals, Thomas Paine and Thomas 'Clio' Rickman.

DANIEL CONSTABLE (1775-1835). Daniel started the well known store of Hanningtons in Brighton in 1802. He sold this in 1806 and sailed to America where he spent two years exploring the New World. Upon his return he helped rebuild the family watermill before becoming a partner in a wholesale tea and drug business in Southwark. He was a religious dissenter and a radical in his political views.

JAMES CONSTABLE JR (1777-1844). James Jr. bought a run-down business in Storrington, Sussex, which he turned into a successful shop with a branch at Findon. He fathered four children, overcame the tragic death of his young wife and acquired much property. Matilda, his elder daughter, was a great favourite of her Uncle William. James, his younger son, emigrated to America where he made a fortune.

JOHN CONSTABLE (1779-1829). After a difficult start John moved to Cobham where he ran a successful business. He and his wife died young, within days of each other. After their parents' death their four children, Caroline, Benjamin, Eliza and Daniel all emigrated to America with varying success.

MILDRED CONSTABLE (1781-1852). Mildred spent her youth helping out with her brothers' families before marrying John Purse and emigrating to the wilderness of Indiana. They had one daughter named Emma. Mildred remained in America for the rest of her life apart from one year during which she returned to England.

WILLIAM CONSTABLE (1783-1861). William was a partner in Daniel's venture in Brighton. He then accompanied Daniel to America. After rebuilding the watermill he became a surveyor and was responsible for many feats of engineering including a suspension bridge and a tunnel. At a time when most people of his age were taking things easy he started the Photographic Institute in Brighton and photographed many worthies of the time, including Prince Albert.

CHARLES CONSTABLE (1786-1867). Charles stayed at home and looked after the family mills. He became a pillar of the local community, becoming High Constable for the Reigate Hundred. He and his family were much involved in fighting for the redemption of the Corn Laws. His two daughters, Lavinia and Fanny, were playmates of their cousin, Clair James.

SUSANNA CONSTABLE (1790-1879). Susanna also spent her youth helping out first with her brothers' families and then nursing her parents. She married Henry Grece, a local farmer and fuller's earth merchant. They had one son named Clair James. For many years Susanna kept daily journals describing her life and the countryside around her.

Map of Surrey and Sussex

DISTANCE CHART

Horley Mill to London . . . . 22 miles

London to Mitcham . . . . .9 miles

Mitcham to Reigate . . . . .13 miles

Reigate to The Mill . . . . .4 miles

The Mill to Rusper . . . . .5 miles

The Mill to Storrington . . . . .19 miles

The Mill to Brighton . . . . .25 miles

Rusper to Storrington . . . . 16 miles

Storrington to Brighton . . . . 18 miles

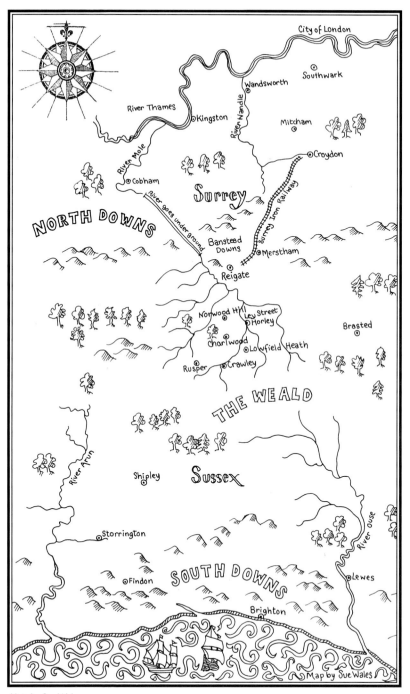

Map by Sue Wales

CHAPTER ONE

The Family

THERE HAS BEEN A watermill on the river Mole at Ley Street in Surrey for centuries. There are tales that the original waterwheel was once horizontal but time has obliterated any trace if that were so. The river derives its name from Mulle, meaning Mill, while Ley Street is a Saxon term meaning a straight track between villages. Horley Mill together with the Mill House, an adjoining property called Tedhams, cottages and surrounding land, had belonged to a family by the name of Constable for nearly three hundred years. The family also owned a farm called Spikemead (sometimes known as Harebrains) at Lowfield Heath, about three miles further up the river. Spikemead stood on the edge of the heath facing the windmill, which also formed part of the Constable property.

The hamlet of Ley Street has long been swallowed up in the urban sprawl of Horley. In the nineteenth century it was set in a quiet landscape of ancient lanes, winding streams, thick hedgerows and dense woods. It boasted a church, an inn or two, a manor house, the watermill at Ley Street and a few scattered farms and cottages. The land from Ley Street to the church was open commonland. Tedhams (later known as The Old Mill House) stands overlooking the lane which winds over the river. Originally it was a mediaeval hall house with the garden running almost to the river's edge. A row of lime trees, pleached each spring, formed a green screen from the road. In the garden there was once a sunken millstone (now moved to another local garden), a remnant of the Mill described by William Cobbett in his *Rural Rides*, as 'the very prettiest flour mill I have ever seen'. Also facing onto the lane, adjoining the garden wall, was a cottage known as Tedhams Cottage.

Tedhams was converted into four houses in 1970. These are now known as Old Mill House, Bell House, Wisteria Cottage and Garden Cottage. At first glance the building looks Victorian with bay windows and a slate roof but the white façade hides the timber-framed house beneath. Entering the massive oak front door, by the ancient japonica and wisteria, the Great Parlour was on the right. This was a big rectangular room with an inglenook fireplace stretching nearly the

Upstairs corridor at Tedhams
c. 1950

length of one wall. The fireback bore the arms of Elizabeth I, dated 1571. On the left of the front door was the family parlour. At the rear was the big kitchen, dominated by an American range, complete with the original cast iron water pump. It is not difficult to imagine the family and servants dining at a long oaken table here. There was another small room of a later date off the Great Parlour, perhaps used as an office, with two large rooms beyond which formed the original shop. There was a spacious pantry and a scullery leading to a two-storeyed wing (possibly a stable block). The staircase, built around the chimney in the Great Parlour, led to a long corridor, which stretched from one end of the house to the other, with eight rooms altogether on either side.

By the late eighteenth century Horley Mills consisted of a large wheat and corn mill, together with a separate malt mill, a house for the miller and cottages for the workers. According to a report drawn up by the Surrey Domestic Buildings Research Group, 'the Millers appear to have been prosperous and it is not difficult to imagine them living at the Mill House and keeping up with the latest fashions'. According to a contemporary report it was a busy mill which drew trade from a large area.

If Ley Street has been swallowed up by Horley it has been lightly treated. The village of Lowfield Heath is no more, apart from the church standing forlornly among the hangars and buildings of Gatwick Airport. Spikemead, which also originally belonged to the Jordan family, is a rectangular Elizabethan farmhouse. It once stood at the end of an avenue of fruit trees, forming a square with its thatched barns and stables. The name Spikemead comes from a curious spike-shaped field bordering the river. The land in front of the house was originally common heathland, which ran eastwards to the windmill, the village and the London/Brighton turnpike.

In 1704 William Constable was witness to a grant of land to Thomas Dabner, with permission to erect a windmill on Norwood Hill (in the neighbouring parish of Charlwood). William had married Ann Dudeney of Charlwood and their son, James, had been born the year before. Some years later James was apprenticed to a lapidarist from whom he learnt to carve stone. He was subsequently employed as the resident millwright at Horley Mill, owned by the Dabner family.

Horley Mill had been in the occupation of the Dabner family since 1696; one Ephraim Dabner was recorded as having kept a fine team of horses to draw the wagons. James fell in love with Mary Dabner and in 1737 they married at Guildford, obviously with her family's blessing since her brother was to leave James some land in his will. Shortly after this James moved a post mill from Horsham Common to Lowfield Heath (a post mill is a windmill with the entire body turning on an upright post in order to catch the wind). This must have been a Herculean task with oxdrawn wagons, even although he presumably waited until the summer sun had dried the sticky wealden clay into a dusty flatness. This post mill was particularly tall to compensate for the exceedingly flat area. According to G. Coomber's excellent book on local mills, 'It was a skilled job to build and maintain a mill in working order, and a good millwright could command a premium wage and good working conditions. They possessed what would later be thought of as engineering skills, and it is no coincidence that many millwrights set up engineering businesses in the 19th century.' (This mill has now been moved to Charlwood where it has been expertly restored.)

James and Mary were childless for the first twelve years of their marriage but must have been more than delighted when two sons finally arrived, James Jr. in 1749, and Daniel in 1751. Five years later, after the death of Mary's parents, James astutely bought out Mary's brothers and sisters thus becoming the owner of Horley Mill. James was not only astute but he was also a hard worker as ten years later, in 1766, he was able to buy the adjoining property, known as Tedhams (later known as The Old Mill House). James was also fortunate in his choice of a wife; their son, James Jr. was often to speak in glowing terms of the untiring industry of his mother.

James Jr. made several improvements to Tedhams, including a new porch on which he carved his initials and the date, 1772. At this time he was already courting Susanna Jordan from the neighbouring village of Charlwood. According to family rumour James and Susanna eloped to Scotland on horseback, with Susanna riding pillion. Although it may be a romantic notion to imagine them thundering through the night their marriage was actually solemnised at St Andrew by the Wardrobe, Blackfriars, on 27 January, 1773. Whatever happened in the church on the day they were married remains unknown but certainly James was not to set foot inside another church for the next fifty years. He remained a freethinker. (Since 1753 Parliament had decreed that all marriages must be performed by a clergyman. It was possible, though, to be married in Scotland at a civil ceremony and many dissenters preferred this option.)

Susanna Jordan came from a similar well established yeoman family, described in *The Free Men of Charlwood* (1951) written by Ruth Sewill and Elizabeth Lane:

> probably typical of many throughout England, who lived quietly on their estates, respected by their neighbours and, though taking a great part in local affairs, were not ambitious to become famous in the outside world. They reached their greatest eminence in early Stuart days, by which time they had been living in the village for at least 300 years.

Several years later, upon the death of their father in 1778, James Jr. and Daniel inherited the watermill, together with The Mill House, Tedhams, Spikemead and the windmill. Daniel had married Elizabeth Sewell two years previously. He had run the watermill for many years but now retired to live at Pictstones (now known as Hookwood Manor), which he had inherited through his maternal uncle. Although Daniel and Elizabeth were to remain childless, James and Susanna had nine children, all but one living to adulthood. Daniel, James, John, Mildred, William, Benjamin, Charles, Richard and Susanna were born at neat two-year intervals between 1775 and 1790. Daniel was already apprenticed by the time Susanna was born. The children were taught at home during their early years, afterwards they briefly attended school. Certainly William and Charles attended school in Oxted while Susanna, at least, went to Reigate. It was usual at that time for pupils to board during the week, returning home at weekends. Given their father's views on religion it is likely that their schools were run by freethinkers such as William Godwin.

In the eighteenth century most communities boasted a mill powered either by wind or water. Although the squire and the vicar held sway in local communities the miller also played an important role. The mill was a gathering place for the local people and was undoubtedly a hotbed of gossip. Many mills had shops on the premises, the forerunners of the village shop. There was a shop attached to Tedhams, which, under James Jr.'s capable hands, grew into a large enterprise employing over sixty people. On top of the house there is still a bell which was rung to summon the employees, and was also used to warn of fire in the neighbourhood. The shop sold everything needed by the local people, including flour from the mill and bread from the bakery attached to the shop. There were silks and worsteds to be bought, or shirts and dresses made by the dressmaker, trousers and jackets by the tailor. Boots and shoes were manufactured on the premises; building materials wcre also available, and furniture (including coffins) was made in the carpenters' shop. Other funeral services were provided alongside all manner of goods and services necessary for daily living. This, it should be remembered, was in the days before any sort of transport was available, apart from the horse. One of William's early childhood memories was of collecting the small pieces of left-over woven fabric, called thrums, and binding them together to make twine for fastening the parcels sent out from the shop, a task he found most tedious. His father, James, obviously an entrepreneur, also ran a wheelwright's shop in one of the barns at Spikemead.

One sadness was the death of Richard, in 1795, aged just six years old. Perhaps he succumbed to typhoid or smallpox, always a fear in early childhood at this time, or perhaps he accidentally drowned in the mill race. The rushing waters of the mill must have provided an endless attraction for the children – and an endless worry for their mother.

A verse written in the front of the family Bible is attributed to James Constable Jr.:

The Man of Independent Mind

Bold is the man and adamant his heart,
That dares from custom's beaten track depart.
The sneers of friends and calumny of foes
And scorn and hate of all he undergoes.
Despising these, fair nature is his guide,
Conscious of truth and reason on his side.
Fell superstition ne'er disturbs his rest,
Nor is his mind with groundless fears oppressed;
Those cruel fears that plague mankind through life
Black fair Nature's plan, and fill the world with strife.

CHAPTER TWO

Family Life

CLEARLY, DESPITE THE prosperity in which they had been raised, a family of eight children was bound to drain family coffers and it was incumbent upon the boys, once their education was complete, to seek a living. The use of steam was growing and James Constable could no doubt see the threat to traditional milling. His own venture into the infant retail trade had been very successful, which is probably why he decided to apprentice his sons to the drapery trade. His plan was to set them up in businesses of their own as soon as they had gained some experience. The family was clearly literate and intelligent and, although their formal education was brief, they had obviously been well taught at home. Since both the Constable and Jordan families were known dissenters, originally Quakers, they were precluded from entrance to university, commissions in the armed forces and public office.

The detailed nature of Daniel's, William's and Susanna's journals, together with extensive family correspondence, paintings, daguerreotypes and photographs, gives us a vivid description of the younger generation of Constables. Daniel and

William were described by a contemporary as being tall and good looking, and Daniel himself talks about his 'narrow phiz'. Daniel left a detailed journal of this early part of his life and from this, and family correspondence, it is known that in 1797, now aged twenty-two, he was employed as an assistant to a linen draper, Daniel Hack, who was a prominent Quaker citizen of Brighton. James, aged twenty, was working in London; John, eighteen, apprenticed in Caterham, Surrey; and Mildred, sixteen, was being taught the art of millinery. William was fourteen and had just been apprenticed to Henry Browne, a wholesale and retail linen draper who lived in Lewes, Sussex. In a letter to his parents soon after he left home he showed his innate sensitivity in his concern over his dog:

> I hope you will take care of poor old Trimmer [named after Sarah Trimmer, the author of *New and Comprehensive Lessons*, probably used in the Constable schoolroom]. I think he derives still more enjoyment than pain from living which is a sufficient reason why he should continue to exist.

Benjamin, twelve, was not as robust as his brothers and sisters and was taught at home, while Charles, eleven, was probably at school in Oxted. Susanna, aged seven, was also now at school in Reigate.

At this time Napoleon, having defeated seven armies and captured some 160,000 prisoners, was riding high. England was recovering from the shock of the French Revolution, although there was also much sympathy for the new regime. For instance the Lunar Society of Birmingham, a group of talented men which included Joseph Priestley, were supporters of the French Revolution. In July 1789 Josiah Wedgwood wrote to Darwin: 'I know you will rejoice with me in the glorious revolution that has taken place in France.'

Under the threat of invasion from France, the militia companies were busy drawing for new recruits, particularly near the south coast. In October James wrote to his brother, Daniel:

Dear Dan'l,

Misfortunes still attend me. I was drawn for the Sussex Militia on Saturday, 21st inst. for the parish of Shipley. It will cost me at least twelve pounds to procure a substitute which will score my pocket but I know of no way to prevent it. I think it very unjust of their drawing from the old list that has been standing, I believe, more than twelve months and I have been from that parish more than six. Our laws are hard to be got at but I hope for regulation that they may be plain to man.

I walked about 30 miles yesterday for advice, to one Mr. Harry Goring of Wiston. He said we came from another district so he had nothing to do with it. If you can advise me to anything it will be acceptable. I offered twelve pounds for a substitute but have not had any as yet.

I am very well and hope this will find you the same. I was at Horsham on Sunday and John was there and all are well.

I have nothing particular more to acquaint you only that rough music is now playing up and down our street.

I am, your affectionate brother,

James Constable

Note: Shipley is a village south of Horsham, where James had served his apprenticeship. Peter Agate Brown lived at Kingsland (the house where Hilaire Belloc was to live for many years). Wiston, near Steyning, was the home of the Goring family; Charles Goring had planted the famous landmark, Chanctonbury Ring, some thirty years earlier. 'Rough music' was the term used for a noisy protest march with the participants literally making rough music by banging tins, etc.

It seems likely that James found a substitute to take his place in the militia.

It appears that Daniel and James enjoyed a good rapport and often spent time together. Although they were both merchants, milling was in their blood, and on one occasion they walked to Battersea and climbed the horizontal windmill: 'quite a curious sensation to be ascending such a building and whirling round with it'.

In February 1798 Daniel received a letter from his father in Horley:

> Dr. Daniel,
> Yours of the 5th I did not receive 'till last night. Before this you have mine of the 6th. I have nothing at present more to say.
> I am now this minute setting off to see little Sukey and carry her a few hogs puddings. Being much in a hurry Milley begs you'd excuse her this time but will take an opportunity ere long and cram together all the nonsense she can collect.
> Yr. affectionate father
> J. Constable

Note: Milley was Mildred, aged sixteen, little Sukey was Susanna, aged seven, already at school in Reigate, and the hogs puddings were made from pig's offal mixed with herbs and spices, no doubt made from pigs reared at the mill.

Daniel's real passion in life appears to have been politics and he was much influenced by the works of Joseph Priestley and Jean-Jacques Rousseau, among others. Having gained experience of the retail trade, he left his job at Hacks in the middle of April 1798 and moved to London, where he lodged in Southwark with Edward Rose, a cousin on the Dabner side. In his own words, he 'lounged' about and explored the city while ostensibly looking for a business to buy. It seems probable that he was connected with one of the reform societies. His journal has a code running through it and he makes curious comments. He may have run the Brighton branch of the Corresponding Society, much in the news at the time. The Corresponding Society's aim was to reform the system of government in place at that time, in which many peers held as many as a dozen seats, which were passed down from father to son. Voting at this time was confined to the favoured few. There were a number of so-called 'rotten boroughs' which were boroughs in name only; in other words, a complete farce.

Another cousin, Mary Whitbourn, some fifteen years older than Daniel, was a very close friend. The Whitbourn family came from Shalford, near Guildford, but Mary moved to London to live with her sister when their parents died. Mary was betrothed to Edward Rose, and formed part of the circle of friends Daniel had met through his father which included several prominent reformers such as Horne Tooke, Mary Wollstonecraft and John Thelwall. Daniel recorded one day meeting C. J. Fox at the Castle Inn. Fox was the famous liberal politician, son of the first Lord Holland who was, for twenty years, the political opponent of Pitt the Younger.

On 29 April, 1798, Daniel recorded in his journal:

> Fine day, set out in the morn for Harley Street. Mary and I then set out for a walk to Primrose Hill. The scene was truly beautiful but my mind was so unhinged with various reflections that I had no enjoyment. We went to see that truly good man, Clio Rickman; everything about his house bespeaks him a man of science and the philanthropist showed me the table where that best of men, the inimitable Thos. Paine wrote his sacred Rights of Man. Went to Purse.

Thomas 'Clio' Rickman, originally from Lewes, was a bookseller, writer and publisher, a friend, ardent disciple and biographer of Thomas Paine. He was also a reformer at a time when to express political differences openly, particularly of the liberal sort, was highly dangerous. Thomas Paine lodged with the Rickman family in Marylebone while writing *The Rights of Man* and used one of Clio Rickman's tables to write on. Clio had to flee to France, dressed as a woman, to avoid imprisonment for his connection with Paine. Mr. Purse was another member of this group and the father of John Purse, at this time ten years old, who was later to marry Mildred Constable.

No wonder Daniel's mind was unhinged. The Corresponding Society had run into deep trouble and several of their members had been arrested on charges of high treason. A bill had been brought into Parliament for suspending the Habeas Corpus Act, by which the government was enabled to detain all prisoners in custody as long as the convenience of the state rendered such a measure necessary. It may well be that, if Daniel was involved in one of the splinter groups of this society, once their papers were seized he was in a dangerous position. Possibly Clio was already urging Daniel to go to America, seen by the reformers as the Land of the Free, promising his young friend an introduction to Thomas Paine.

In May Daniel received a letter from his father in Horley:

Dr. Daniel,

The things you sent are returned with two new shirts and your mother desired you to send again in a month from this time. I have sent in the box two bills of £10 each on Mr. Sam'l Salaway, Tanner, Bermondsey St., Southwark, which I will thank you to present for payment and to pay a bill (when presented) which I have drawn on you, payable to Sam'l Scott or bearer of the above date at £16. 10s., and the remainder of the money keep till I come to town which perhaps may be next week.

At present I am not in a condition for travelling being lame from broken skin. We are all in good health at Horley and hope you are the same. Send us a line by return that we may know you received the things safe. If the box should not be delivered in the evening you had better make enquiry as sometimes the bookkeeper neglects sending out the things for a day or two.

I have nothing more at present but that we all join in love

and best wishes to you.

I am, yr. affectionate father,

J. Constable

Note: It seems that the young people sent their linen home for laundering and mending. Although there was a seamstress employed by the shop and no doubt maids to do the heavy work, Mrs. Constable must have been a busy person with all her children making demands on her time, quite apart from a large household to organise. Incidentally she was also well known for her excellent elderberry wine.

Daniel, still searching for a business, looked at various premises in London but found nothing exactly to his liking. One day he accidentally met his father at Clio's, not having known he was in London, and they spent the day together. As they were walking they met James Hack (Daniel Hack's brother from Chichester) and talked over the possibility of Daniel returning to Brighton. A few days later Daniel received another letter from his father:

Dr. Dan'l,

I was obliged to walk to Mitcham the other day, the Brighton coach, the only one that came that way, being quite full and by the time that I had transacted my business there the Ryegate coach was past. I had again to walk and only got a lift in a return chaise from The Tangier to Ryegate. I found myself tired when I got home which was about eight o'clock, however I now find no bad effects from the journey, my leg being now quite well. James was at Horley yesterday. He is quite well and happy in his situation.

Whenever you think it best to leave London you know you have a home at Horley where you are welcome.

Yr. affectionate father,

J. Constable

James Sr. was obviously an affectionate, easy-going man. He was now nearly fifty years old and the distance between Horley and Mitcham, about seventeen miles, must have been a good walk. (The Tangier Inn was a stopping place for the London coaches on Banstead Downs, famous for its elderberry wine.)

It is clear that Daniel, although he enjoyed himself in London, missed the open countryside. In early June he noted:

After dinner set out through the City, Downing St., Pall Mall, Carlton House to Cavendish Square and Harley St., drank tea and then Mary and I set out for Primrose Hill and never in my life did I see a more delightful scene. There was a large field of hay that had been left in large cocks the night before entirely spread over the whole field. I should think there were four or five hundred people of all ages, in the best of nature in all its lovely forms, all the shackles of society seemed thrown off for this innocent simplicity of nature.

Note: A haycock is a conical heap of hay.

Daniel finally decided to take his leave of London in July. He returned to Brighton to stay with his friend, Robert Wigney, spending a few days en route with his parents at Horley. He was happy to be back in Brighton and 'lounged' with his friends, going to the races and swimming in the sea.

On Sundays the young Constables often went home to Horley for the day, frequently accompanied by friends, to exchange news and visit their parents. The inglenook fireplace in the Great Parlour at Tedhams was well known as a corner for conversation, both of a political and social nature. Daniel, at this time, recorded that he was reading works by Rousseau, including *Reverie of the Solitary Walk*, *Emile* and *The New Heloise*. Clio Rickman visited in July and Daniel noted writing to Mary Whitbourn and going to the theatre to see the famous Mrs. Siddons. He recorded how he had a fight with Robert Wigney, his great friend: 'Wigney and self quarreled, blows ensued. Fought like tigers, he first tore my waistlet, then I his handkerchief, he again my handkerchief. Stopped half an hour after, shook hands and all was well.' Fortunately this fight did not seem to affect their friendship.

By December Daniel had still not succeeded in finding a business to buy, so he accepted the offer of a position with Messrs. Clarksons, linen drapers, in Kingston, a village about ten miles south-west of London. He travelled as far as Banstead Downs with James, where they took shelter from the bitter cold in the Tangier Inn and drank a pint of ginger beer. It is apparent, however, that he did not find Kingston much to his liking. He hankered after Brighton, and spent an hour one Sunday writing to Mr. Hack, presumably asking for his help in finding either a business to buy or a new position.

As is the case in most families, the children were very different from each other. Daniel was a bookworm as well as being passionate about politics. He delighted in spending his Sundays attending churches of different denominations such as Methodist, Presbyterian or Quaker Meeting Houses, and he often walked thirty miles or so afterwards. James, by his own admission, was not fond of the written word but loved outdoor life, particularly hunting and shooting. Apparently he had trained his dog to stay on the local common with his grazing horse, and to remain there, without food, until called home. If John kept a journal this has not survived, and little is known about him. He was the first of the family to marry. Mildred was highly strung, inclined to be a worrier, and took her role as elder daughter quite seriously. Benjamin was the musical one of the family. William, an artist and keen botanist, was also fascinated by the world of science and engineering. Charles was an excellent worker, but panicked when things went awry, while Susanna, intelligent and practical, possessed a keen sense of humour.

William was also on the lookout for a suitable position for his brother. In the middle of February he wrote:

Dear Bro'. Dan'l,
Your letter came safe to hand last week. I immediately made enquiry of Mr. Eyles concerning a situation for you but he informs me he intends to take an apprentice, if he can get one just to his mind. In case he cannot he says he will let me know. I wrote you on the subject today.
Our good mother sent me some sausages last week. Horley folk are all pretty well except Benjamin who is still pretty

poorly at times. As he is debarred playing the Flute he is now attempting the Violin.

I am happy to hear James likes his situation and I wish you could like yours better than you appear to do. For my part things go on about in the old track with me. I believe Drawbridge will continue with us some time except he can get into business for himself which he wishes to do. We live very comfortably and happy together, Mr. Browne being such a kind of man that he cannot be happy except those are happy around him.

Farewell,

Yours affectionately,

W. Constable

William at this time was well settled in his apprenticeship. The Brownes were family friends from Ditchling, and Henry Browne was a prominent citizen and High Constable of Lewes, as well as being a man of scientific interests. He had a private chemical laboratory and printing press, and was also something of an artist. He encouraged his young assistant's penchant for drawing and painting.

On the same day that Daniel received William's letter he received another from a Brighton friend, Robert Williams:

Friend Constable,

Yours I received and I know you expected to hear from me before this but really it has not been in my power to get an interview with Governor Hack, for he is so much taken up with parochial business that he has not entered my shop since you left Brighton. My brother and he fell into a conversation the other day and Dan'l told him he had received a letter from you and that you could not reconcile yourself to Kingston, and further that you wished to come to him again. He says neither of the young men suit him but he would not (as he told you) discharge them without some substantial plea. 'If he does come and live with me again, I shall turn over a new leaf, attending to books, politics, etc'.

I was in Wigney's shop yesterday and talking of you and your dislike of Kingston. Bob says you must come and live with them again the ensuing summer and he wishes you to inform him if you recollect settling a bill with old Martha Gunn for Blue Frieze? I think Wigney told me the sum was 10s. Bob carried in the bill and she said she had paid it, to you or somebody else.

I really think you will be at Hacks before long and you may depend on it, if anything transpires, that either of the young men is going to leave, I'll drop you a line. Smith desired me to tell you he has received a whole cargo of Mirabaud.

I am,

Yours sincerely,

R. Williams

Note: Daniel Hack was prominently associated with the public life of the growing community in Brighton, and became High Constable in 1803. He was particularly interested in providing education for the poor and he also campaigned for the abolition of slavery. Amongst many other achievements he extended the town to the north by developing Trafalgar Street. Billy was Robert Williams's brother, and their friend, John Smith, was a bookseller in Brighton. Martha Gunn, a well-known figure in Brighton, was familiarly known as 'the Priestess of the Bath'. She attended the bathing machines for the ladies of the town and achieved notoriety, according to the *Morning Herald*, for boasting that from the sale of her ducks (that is the ducking of her clients) she was often able to purchase a goose for dinner. A story was told that she often visited the kitchens at the Pavilion and that one day the Prince of Wales happened to notice that she had slipped a pat of butter into one of her capacious pockets. Talking all the while he managed to edge her nearer the stove, where the inevitable happened and she was 'much discomfited', to his considerable amusement.

Note: The 'cargo of Mirabaud' were translations from the original French of M. de Mirabaud called *The System of Nature* or *The Laws of the Moral and Physical World*.

On 1 June Daniel received a letter from Robert Williams, informing him that Mr. Hack would like him to write, saying when he could be at Brighton. Daniel immediately replied and the following day they met in London and strolled together in Temple Gardens; afterwards Daniel walked up Harley Street to have tea with Mary Whitbourn, who accompanied him to Hyde Park Corner to board the coach back to Kingston. No doubt Daniel was able to tell Mary that Napoleon claimed that 10,000 Greeks had joined him, and that he had planted the Tree of Liberty at Jerusalem and Gazo. Did Daniel tell Mary that everything was 'favourable to the truly great man'? At this stage Daniel, like many others, thought Napoleon a true hero. However, having taken his leave of Mary he was soon diverted.

1799 June 2. There was only one very nice little girl in the

coach so we got in a train of familiar chat and I found her
a most pleasing companion. I almost imperceptibly closed
my arms around her and in that happy position we went on
to Isleworth, with now and then a lovely embrace from her
sweet lips, far sweeter I never touched. She was about 18
and entirely free from that artful cunning which is often
exercised by the sex. In fact, I loved the girl and the rolling
of the coach, with so precious a charge in my arms were
moments of indescribable and heartfelt pleasure. Parted
from her at Isleworth and then had to walk to Kingston,
time near 11 p.m., past 12 o'clock when I got home. Could
not get indoors and slept at The Griffin.

Daniel makes no excuse for his behaviour with this unknown
girl; from his observation of familiar chat perhaps this was not
unusual. He obviously liked the opposite sex: 'Let the idiots prate
about morality but the smiles of a lovely female means more than
anything I hear from men', was a comment in his journal. Was he
something of a peacock, perhaps as a result of his knowledge of
the drapery trade? He records wearing a plaid cloak in order to
attract attention from the girls, loving it when they mistook him
for a Colonel or a Captain (was this a reference to Col. Despard's
Constitution Society?). It is apparent from his diary that he was
very disappointed when one Phoebe Elphick did not arrive to
spend the day with him as planned. On another occasion he was
looking forward to a few hours enjoyment with a girl of his
acquaintance called Betsy Ellis. They had planned tea in Hove
but she was taken ill: 'I was very sorry as I had quite set my heart
on it.' The following day he recorded spending the evening

looking after Betsy: 'But found nor favour nor pleasure from her.' He also had a long standing relationship with a certain Kay Holden, noting that she was very 'playful and funny' and that he would often like to go walking with her. This relationship eventually foundered as he wrote: 'acquitted myself honourably with K., had a difficult meeting, much mystery, etc.'

Daniel stayed in Kingston until the Messrs. Clarkson found a suitable replacement for him. One Sunday he and a friend hired a boat and set out for Oatlands, noting:

> All the exertions we could make were ineffectual to stem the current of the river and with much labour we almost made Ditton when we were overtaken by a heavy barge 150 tons burdened and had not the men stopped the horses the minute they did there was not a doubt but our boat would have been run over and ourselves drowned. It was quite a hair's breadth escape and, had we been actually in the water, we could not have been more frightened. We then lashed our boat to the barge and they towed us up to Walton. We admired the hospitality of the bargemen who gave us the most hearty welcome to their wholesale cheer which after our fright and fatigue we enjoyed much. Left our boat at Walton and walked on to Oatlands where we saw the Grotto which exceeded anything I could have thought. Back to Walton, got a bottle of ale, bread and cheese and got on board our boat and let her float with the stream while we ate our repast which we enjoyed much.

Note: The Shell Grotto to which he referred was built by

the Duke of Newcastle and consisted of several rooms, connected by passages, elaborately decorated with shells, corals, ammonites and crystals.

The end of June found Daniel packing his boxes and taking leave of Clarksons. He walked through the market gardens and fields of Putney and Fulham to the Horse Cellar, Piccadilly, where he had supper and spent an hour wandering up Bond Street. The following day he met his father and James, and spent two or three hours with them, accompanying James to buy a hunting watch. James Sr. and Daniel returned to Horley the next morning, taking the coach to Reigate and then walking home through the fields. A few days later Daniel returned to Brighton, happy to be back amongst his friends.

Although, as mentioned earlier, Daniel and his brothers all eventually went into business for themselves, in 1799 they were still employed and spent their spare time rambling over the downs, rowing and swimming in the sea, attending the theatre and opera, drinking and socialising with their friends. Daniel talks of 'lounging' on The Steine – originally a grassy area in Brighton where the fishermen dried their nets but by this time a smart promenade. Brighton was still a small town, where everybody knew everybody else. Clearly they had a wide circle of friends but they were still very united as a family, frequently visiting each other on the weekends when they did not return home to Horley. James, living and working in London, was visited by any member of the family who happened to be in the city. Sometimes Daniel and

William rowed up the river from Lewes, at other times they rowed out to sea. Mildred, by now eighteen, frequently met her brothers, and once Daniel recorded meeting her at Falmer, half way between Lewes and Brighton. They walked back together to Brighton, where he hired a single-horse chaise to take her to Cuckfield. Mildred was staying, at this time, with their uncle, Charles Packham, and his wife, who owned the watermill there; it was quite common for unattached daughters to make extended visits of several weeks to family members and friends.

One Sunday Daniel intended to meet James at the Friar's Oak in Handcross but it was too wet and he noted rather disconsolately, 'read nothing, learnt nothing'. This might have been more easily believed had he not already recorded that at the time he was reading *The Canterbury Tales* and Mary Wollstonecraft's *The Wrongs of Women*, and had also started to learn French in the evenings.

Daniel was definitely a thinker. He sought out friends who debated the issues of the day, shared the reformers' enthusiasms and followed the fortunes of the French philosopher, liberal and celebrated writer, Le Comte de Volney. He noted being much pleased at learning about a group of some twenty-four young men who shared his general philosophy. After all, the Constable sons had been brought up to admire Benjamin Franklin, known as the father of the American Constitution, and Thomas Paine, whose writing so inspired the revolutionary movement in America. Daniel's friend, Turton, fully shared Daniel's political views; it was he who invented the code that Daniel used in his journal. This was presumably so that any correspondence getting into the wrong hands would not be incriminating. William also used an early form of shorthand.

As mentioned earlier William had been apprenticed at the age of fourteen to Henry Browne of Lewes. In November, 1799, he wrote to Daniel:

Dear Bro'.,

I have this morn received the enclosed from bro'. John and I am happy he is pleased with his situation. We go on swingingly in the Brokery way. Our warehouse is nearly complete and it is I think, very well contrived both for convenience and show. Mr. B. a few days ago purchased a house in the neighbourhood, part of which he intends devoting to Brokery business.

I devote the greater part of my leisure hours to the study of drawing, hoping that with a little perseverance and, flattering myself I have something of a natural genius for that art, I may someday be tolerably proficient at it.

I remain, your affectionate bro'.

William

P.S. Our Company of Comedians are going to perform 'The Purse' or 'Benevolent Tar' at a Friends House next Christmas. I am to take the part of the Baron and Frank Gell, whom perhaps you may remember when at Brighton, takes Will Steady.

Note: Since Henry Browne was also a wholesale draper, presumably his brokery was for the buying and selling of cloth. William did become tolerably proficient in the art of drawing, but realised within the next few years that his talent was not sufficient to enable him to earn a living. Frank Gell became Sir Francis Gell, and it was to his legal firm that James' son was articled some twenty years later.

Clearly, their long time family friend, Thomas 'Clio' Rickman, was also influential. Clio must have been a fascinating person to these young, impressionable men. A kindly man, often drawn back to his native Lewes, Clio contributed a weekly column to the *Brighton Herald*, and on one occasion even took over as editor.

CHAPTER THREE

Business Ventures

IN THE DAWN OF the new century young James found an interesting business for sale. He wrote to Daniel on 6 May, 1800:

Dr. Bro'.,

I have this morning received a letter from our father saying that Mr. Hill, the Oilman, had written to him concerning a shop at Dover. I have since waited on Mr. H. He informs me that it is a grocers and that the man is going to retire. It stands in the heart of the market.

I will assure you that I am not in a hurry but if I could come at it comfortably I should have no objection in this line. There is not the hazard of a heavy stock and may be carried on with a little capital. If we should be blessed with a Peace that will be the first place. Make no dependence on this as it is all supposition. I know nothing of the terms but I hope for the advice of an experienced bro. the first opportunity.

If I continue here I think that you and I may do a little business together; that is in buying of wool. I will make some enquiries in the price and let you know. I wrote to a person about some Nankeen; I am to know the price as soon as any arrives – hope you will not lay in a large stock. I am going to see a round of Irish Linen which I can get lower than they were invoiced from Ireland; the reason is, some of them were shipped damp. I think I can make a good profit with many of our neighbours in that line. There are 19 rounds, begin at 1s. 7½d a run to 3s. 6d; that is, to me. If I were to go to any draper they would not let me have better cloth for 2/- than that at 1s. 7½d; this was brought for a sample. I think if they answer to what I have seen I will send you a few pairs of middling price.

We have no new news only they have been Poping at The George and I have heard that a great riot was in St. James Park. It is past nine and I want my supper; work is the order of the day.

From your affectionate bro. J. Constable.

Mildred is at Maidstone. Hat is placed to your account Horley, 16/- with box.

Note: The reference to 'Poping' is a reminder that the Catholic community was persecuted, as were the dissenters, neither being allowed to take public office nor to take commissions in the army or navy. Mildred had a great friend in Maidstone called Miss Ing, with whom she often went to stay. All the young Constables ran accounts with the Horley shop, which was inevitably to prove something of a problem in later years.

James, twenty-two, did not pursue the shop in Dover probably because he found a more suitable property. In June he bought a house and run-down shop in Storrington, Sussex. Storrington was a bustling village at the foot of the north side of the South Downs, some twenty miles from Brighton. He planned to renovate the house and to run the shop as a grocers and drapers.

Mildred, now aged nineteen, moved to Storrington to help her brother. This must have been a big adventure for the pair of them. James had apparently bought the premises without his elder brother seeing them as Daniel noted in his journal: 'July 20: Fine hot day, set out for Storrington ab't 6 o'clock. House and shop much better than I expected.' Although it was only twenty miles from Brighton to Storrington the route lay over the South Downs which are criss-crossed with many ancient paths. Daniel missed his way attempting to return home that evening: 'Got lost and wandered much out of my way, almost got to Worthing, did not get home till half past twelve, and completely tired.' Six months later, returning from another visit to Storrington to meet his father, he noted in his journal: 'When I had got on the Downs it was got quite dark, the wind blew a very heavy gale and I was soon lost. I determined to get back again to Storrington if possible which very fortunately I accomplished. I set out again through Steyning but never was I exposed to the elements in so tremendous an evening. It rained excessively all the way, the wind blew so hard that it was with difficulty I could keep my saddle, my horse frequently making a full stop, the climbing Beeding Hill was awful to a great degree, the rain driving so hard in my face as to be very painful.' Anyone familiar with the South Downs will know the sheer force of the wind driving off the sea. The top of the Downs is completely exposed to the elements being almost treeless and devoid of shelter. However, when the weather is fine there is no more beautiful place to be as Daniel also experienced on another occasion: 'I never had so pleasant a ride and the hills were beautiful.'

At Christmas time Charles, now fourteen, left school. It seems as if he might have been apprenticed to James as he, too, moved to Storrington. No doubt a young, strong, pair of hands was much appreciated and, no doubt, they all worked hard but also enjoyed themselves. During February Daniel walked twice to visit his siblings and, perhaps, to offer them his help. He noted in his journal: 'After tea self, Mildred, James and Charles took a walk on the Chantry Hill, very pleasant and a larger fleet of ships than I had ever seen.' As there was at this time an imminent threat of invasion from Napoleon, this was probably Nelson's fleet. In the light of possible invasion, one wonders whether Daniel's admiration for the French emperor was as wholehearted as previously.

William was now nearing the end of his apprenticeship with Henry Browne in Lewes. Perhaps Daniel had already suggested they might go into business together, because at the end of June William wrote to him:

> Dear Brother,
> Yours came to hand yesterday and all that I can say in reply is that I know no more than a post when 'twill suit me to go to Horley but if I can keep Mr. Browne from London next week I know of no time which will suit me better. I have spoken to Mr. Browne several times this week about it but, after reasoning a little upon the fitness of it, he flies off to another subject and leaves me just as wise as I was before. But if you write on Friday, you may, if you please, just say I rather expect to be with them on Sunday next for 'twill be quite impossible for me to go at the time you speak of, as in all probability we shall at that time be crammed full of

old clothes but I can say nothing that is certain about it, which is nearly what I said to them on Saturday last, by Brighton. I shall be very glad to meet you at Horley but don't suppose 'twill suit your convenience at this season.

I am glad to hear James has got business on his own account. I wish he may be successful. I am informed in the latter part of Fuller's time the business has been on the decline but I believe 'twas thro' the neglect of Fuller, that the diligence of James will soon regain what the other has lost by his inattention.

Your affectionate brother,

Wm. Constable

P.S. 25 minutes pass by: I have just prevailed on Mr. B. to give me a positive answer. I am to go to Horley on Sunday next if nothing unforeseen turns up.

P.P.S. The Quarterly Conference is at Ditchling on Sunday next.

I mean to go to Ditchling on Saturday night, from thence to the Friar's Oak and take the coach on Sunday morning. I suppose the coaches go on Sundays as they used to do. If they do not, please to inform me. If I do not hear from you I shall take it for granted they do.

In haste, farewell,

W.C.

Note: The Quarterly Conference referred to was the General Baptist Meeting. William's employer, Henry Browne, was a leading light in the General Baptist community in Lewes. The Friar's Oak was the stopping place at Handcross for the London/Brighton coaches.

Daniel had still not found the right business to buy by late

November when he spent a week in London on business. He travelled by coach, dining at the Greyhound in Sutton, drinking tea at Clapham Terrace with some friends and arriving at the Half Moon, Borough, about 8 o'clock. There he had a basin of gruel and went to bed: 'not very tired'. He bought a new greatcoat the next day, afterwards dining at the Half Moon on beef steak and oyster sauce. He and his great friend, Turton, met up that evening and the two young men spent some time 'lounging' about the piazzas of Covent Garden before eating 'Welsh Rabit' [sic] at the Cock Inn. Daniel was wearing his plaid cloak, but complained that he 'had no fun', which was obviously disappointing. Afterwards they made their way to the Box lobby in Drury Lane: 'the scene delighted me, being the assemblage of the most beautiful women I had ever seen'. In the morning he met Mary Whitbourn and they bought: 'a Dressing Case and Pocket Book', perhaps for Mary's impending marriage. The following day Daniel and Turton walked to Blackwall to see the new dock, afterwards they attended the opera in Covent Garden, 'in the slips at half price'. On his last day Daniel had arranged to meet Turton but they missed each other, although Daniel noted: 'had an excellent dinner at the Lock Street Temple Bar, of turtle soup and roast beef, in good company from the Temples', and sat and enjoyed himself over a glass of negus. En route home he stopped in Horley where his mother provided 'an excellent lunch of a chicken and a tongue'. There seems little doubt that the Constable family enjoyed their food and ate extremely well.

Although Daniel's good friend, Bob Wigney, had left Brighton he often came back to visit his family. One day he called on Daniel at 7.00 a.m. and they walked as far as the windmill on the Downs. This was probably Mr. Elphick's Mill, scene of many an encounter with the Customs and Excise men. This particular Mr. Elphick instructed his miller to set the sails of his windmill at a certain angle if the Excise men were sighted nearby. The sails could be seen from Brighton, and he could therefore keep an eye open, returning with all haste if necessary.

Daniel still had many friends in the town, including Thomas West, a clerk in Mr. Wigney Sr.'s bank. He and Thomas spent many an evening rambling about the town. Early in May 1801, they bathed in one of the wooden machines for the first time that year. In an eighteenth-century guide to Brighton quoted in J.G. Bishop's *A Peep into the Past* (June 1892) there is a clear description of bathing from a machine:

> By means of a hook ladder the bather ascends to the machine, which is formed of wood, and raised on high wheels; he is drawn to a proper distance from the shore, and then plunges into the sea, the guides attending on each side to assist him in recovering the machine, which, having accomplished, he is drawn back to shore.

Daniel was obviously an enthusiastic swimmer, as on another occasion he remarked: 'finding the sea as smooth as glass leaped in and had a pleasant swim'.

Like many young people Daniel and his friends sometimes overindulged themselves. He noted going with a friend to the White Horse, where they drank wine until 6.00 p.m., then on to Newingtons where they consumed brandy and water, after which they went walking on The Steine. After supper they again went to the White Horse where they got very drunk, and he noted: 'Most severely did I feel the effects of it the next day.' This is hardly surprising.

On Daniel's next trip to London, in July, he travelled by the night coach, amid heavy showers, and noted that he had most unpleasant companions. This journey would have taken some six or seven hours. The roads in Sussex were infamous for being a complete quagmire during the winter and a dust-bath in the summer. Passengers often had to alight from their vehicles during the journey to free the wheels from thick ruts of sticky clay. On this occasion Daniel went to Vauxhall Gardens, where there was a Gala night, and wrote: 'Never was I so delighted with any public place. Everything was as it should be, gaiety and good humour, the girls danced most beautifully to the tambour and cymbels [sic]. We left about 1.00 a.m. and, fatigued as I was, it was with much reluctance.'

The Prince of Wales arrived in Brighton in July. He spent a lot of time in the Pavilion, which he had extended and rebuilt from the shell of an old farmhouse. It was said that he had mirrors installed in his room so that he could watch the activities on The Steine without stirring from his quarters. Daniel attended the Military Review, where he saw the Duke of York and the Prince of Wales. He also went to the theatre to see Mrs. Jordan (mistress of the Duke of Clarence). It is apparent that he met her on several occasions and was later to be appalled at the treatment she and her children received from the royal family. Daniel recorded that the Coldstream Band performed for the first time on The Steine and, perhaps with tongue in cheek, that he stopped the Imperial Ambassador to tell him to button up his breeches.

The autumn of 1801 arrived and there was still no sign of a suitable business for Daniel, but not for lack of trying. He journeyed to London on 1 October, by the night coach, this time on a fine, pleasant night. Next morning, as he was breakfasting, news arrived that the Preliminary of Peace had been signed. Daniel noted: 'London was in an uproar'. On 12 October 1801 there was a General Illumination to celebrate the Ratification of Peace between the republics, and general rejoicing. Back in Brighton Daniel noted that after supping at the Old Ship he went to join his friends at the White Horse. They celebrated by drinking seven bottles of sherry. Daniel engaged the Hurdy Gurdy to play republican music, and afterwards he and Thomas West, the banker's clerk, went rambling over the Downs, no doubt much elated by the news. No doubt, too, they had sore heads the next morning from drinking so much sherry.

Christmas came and on Boxing Day William and Daniel both set out for Horley Mill, arriving in the early evening. They were forced to wade through water to get there, as the River Mole had flooded. It was always prone to flood, although this time it was worse than usual, as the road at Povey Cross (between Horley Mill and Lowfield Heath) was nearly three feet under water. The next day all the family, with the exception of James and Charles, celebrated Christmas together at home, and it takes little imagination to see the roaring fire in the great hearth and the table laden with the festive goose and plum pudding.

The New Year of 1802 dawned with heavy snow. Unfortunately the third Constable son, John, left no journal or letters, so what is known of him comes directly from the observations of his brothers. Aged twenty-one he was also on the lookout for his own business. He found what he thought might be suitable premises in Burwash, Sussex, but although his father and elder brother, Daniel, rode over to negotiate terms nothing came of it. Burwash was some 25 miles from Horley and Brighton, a good distance to cover on horseback although they stayed overnight to break the journey. Persisting in his quest John soon found premises – a general store – in Rusper, a small village between Horley and Horsham. Again the negotiations involved his father and Daniel, as well as his brother James. On this occasion Daniel walked to Storrington to collect James, and they made their way, through deep snow, to Rusper. While they were dining they heard that their father was already 'in treaty' for the business so they rushed out only to find the transaction signed and sealed. They all drank tea together, no doubt well pleased with the outcome. Daniel walked back to Horley Mill with his father and left the following morning with the intention of walking to Brighton (some 23 miles) but when the coach overtook him at Crawley he gave way to temptation and rode the rest of the way. The Brighton coaches at this time were drawn by two pairs of horses and were fairly uncomfortable vehicles.

Mildred had been living with James for nearly two years and the latter's business, with the additional help of Charles, was by now well established. At the beginning of March it was agreed

that Mildred should move to Rusper to help John with his new
venture. History does not relate what Mildred thought of being
moved from pillar to post at her family's whim. Daniel
accompanied James back to Storrington to fetch Mildred. They
drove back to Horley, probably in James's gig, and Daniel wrote:
'it was a fine day and we had a pleasant ride'. The young people
not only seemed to get on very well with each other but were
also prepared to offer mutual help and support when necessary.
Daniel and John set out to walk to London for the purpose of
provisioning the Rusper shop, and to arrange credit with
suppliers. The London coach overtook them, with their father
aboard, so they joined him. That evening the three of them
attended the opera in Covent Garden.

James Sr. obviously had enormous stamina as the day after their
return from London he and Daniel walked to Reigate to look at
yet another business, but: 'could not agree to terms'. The same
week John went to Storrington to paint the warehouse, window
shutters and doors on James's premises, no doubt occupying
himself until his own business started. Early in April John, with
Daniel's assistance, opened his new shop and Daniel noted that the
takings for the day were £3 (about £113 today). Daniel spent the
night at home in Horley returning the next morning with his
sisters, Mildred and twelve-year-old Susanna. The following day
Mr. and Mrs. Constable came for dinner, after which Daniel and
his father walked to Ifield, a neighbouring village, to buy a pig for
John. A pig was an essential part of most rural households as they
ate all manner of leftovers and provided fresh meat. It seems that
the Constable parents put up approximately £100 (nearly £4,000

today) for each son to start his own business. They must have been very proud of their fledgling entrepreneurs.

Towards the end of April Daniel travelled by coach to London and the next day he 'drank tea' with Mrs. Purse (Mildred's future mother-in-law) who was now living in South Molton Street with her son, John, aged fourteen. Young John Purse subsequently went to work for James in Storrington, so it seems likely that Daniel was offering an apprenticeship on James's behalf. On 28 April Peace was proclaimed in London, and after Daniel had breakfasted he set out to Temple Bar: 'the most horrid squeeze I ever got into, was afraid of broken bones, was wedged up for near two hours'. He went to the Bear to 'dine and stare at the Mansion House' (Sir John Eamer was Lord Mayor), met up with Tamplin, another friend from Brighton, and with him walked to Finsbury Square, back through the City, on to Pall Mall, St. James's Street and Bond Street: 'In Bond Street there was another horrid squeeze, reached Portman Square about 12, home by 2 o'clock completely tired.'

The peace following the Treaty of Amiens was to last only a year.

John, meanwhile, had been courting Elizabeth Eastmond, whose family came from Shere in Surrey. They married at the beginning of December 1802, by which time John was twenty-three. The marriage took place in Rusper by special licence and the witnesses were John and Mary Bridger, a local farmer and his wife, from Newdigate, a neighbouring village. There is no mention of Elizabeth in Daniel's journal. Was John quietly doing the honourable thing, or did the family disapprove of his saddling himself with a wife when he was not yet established in business? The trade at Rusper was steady, but it was a small village and it seems that Elizabeth, some seven years older than John, was already expecting their first child. This in itself was reason at that time for a hasty marriage.

James's business, in the meantime, was expanding rapidly; Storrington was a market town and drew people from a large surrounding rural area. He soon opened a branch in Findon, a small village about three miles from Storrington. James kept his own horses and a gig and no doubt enjoyed his new-found prosperity.

Daniel finally found suitable premises for himself early in 1803. This was for a linen draper's shop in Brighton, on the corner of North Street and Castle Square. William, who had now finished his apprenticeship, agreed to join him. In early May Daniel travelled to Brighton by coach, stayed with Thomas West, and in his journal on 7 May he wrote: 'Painting my shop'. The next day William arrived and the following day they were 'both painting'. A few days later they went to Storrington Fair to buy some stock for their business, staying overnight with James. The following morning they walked to Rusper, where they stayed overnight with John and his wife, walking home to Horley in the morning. Clearly, after the initial shock of the wedding, Elizabeth had been accepted by the rest of the family. She was, by now, heavily pregnant. Although Daniel and William were young and healthy, they must also have been extremely fit to walk these distances. Walking was part of the creed for these young democrats and, perhaps like other people at this time when widespread public transport was not available, or only for a price, they appeared to think nothing of it.

At the end of May Daniel and William opened their shop, which over the course of time became a large department store. Now named Hanningtons, it is still owned by the family to whom they sold it. Daniel noted in his journal that the first day was very wet and they took £14 (about £500 today); this must have seemed an enormous sum to them. They had two rooms, one for the shop and one for all their living requirements; but it was in an excellent situation and rapidly became a success, no doubt helped by the charming manner of the two tall, handsome, young men. Daniel spent his free time in long rambles over the Downs, discussing politics with his friends, while William occupied his free time sketching and painting his friends' houses and the lovely countryside. He was much taken with the new art of lithography.

It can be safely assumed that the whole family were delighted when, in June, a daughter was born to John and Elizabeth in Rusper. They named the first child of the new generation Caroline, presumably after the unfortunate Queen who had been cast out by her husband, the King, and his family. (This was Caroline of Brunswick who was betrothed, unseen, to the Prince of Wales. After their marriage he took little trouble to hide his indifference to her, to the extent that she was not invited to his coronation, when he was crowned George IV. Many of the English people felt sympathy for her.)

England and France were now at war again, after only a year of uneasy peace. At the end of July Daniel recorded that he went to sea with a party of friends, and that they boarded the new cutter from Southampton. In the middle of August he attended Brighton Races with his brother, James. James was an enthusiastic sportsman and hunted regularly with the Findon Foxhounds, so perhaps he was competing. William attended the races the following day, so they were scrupulously fair to each other over time off. Apparently it was not unusual for them to close their shop and put up a notice 'Gone for a holiday. Back next week.' William claimed that it was nothing odd to see a notice 'Gone to London for the winter', when a shopkeeper wanted a rest or a holiday.

Daniel's and William's shop was well patronised and, now aged twenty-seven and nineteen, they were becoming prosperous young men. Apparently they kept a large black Newfoundland dog, which ran about the town with a great eyeglass round its neck, in ridicule of a prevailing foppery of the time. On one occasion William, unbeknown to his brother, set up an electrical machine in the back room, and occasionally amused himself by giving an unexpected shock to their customers. (Electricity was still a novelty.)

He was also productive, however, drawing up a plan of the town of Brighton (which then extended no further than the Royal Crescent to the east, Canon Place towards the west and Marlborough Place towards the north). He paced the distances he required several times over, took the average, and to determine the angles he used a small pocket compass. He plotted his measurements on paper and when it was done Daniel asked Clio Rickman to have it engraved, so that he could use it for a card. This served as an advertisement, because people found that by becoming customers of Daniel and William they obtained a plan of the town for nothing.

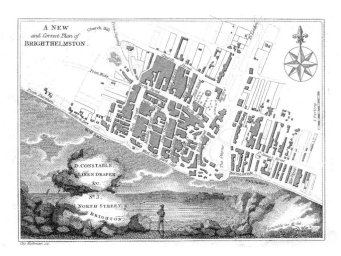

Daniel's map card drawn by William and printed by Clio Rickman.

On one occasion the two young men played a prank on the population of Brighton. They advertised that a miracle was to be seen on the seafront at a certain date. The advertisement carried a picture of a man walking on water, wearing a pair of canoe-like shoes. On the given date a large crowd gathered, including Daniel and William, who mingled with the crowd. They were apparently much amused at the gullibility of their fellow men.

On 1 August, Thomas West, together with Messrs. Browne, Hall and Lashmar, founded the Union Bank in Brighton, next door to the Constable brothers' business. Daniel arranged to become their first customer by leaving William sitting outside the door until it opened. Their father was also to become a valued customer of this bank. The Union Bank was a successful venture and even survived the monetary crash of 1825. Thomas West was obviously an entrepreneur, as apart from the bank he ran a wines and spirits business which he moved to premises adjacent to the bank. He was to become High Constable of Brighton in 1826.

In February 1803, Benjamin had turned eighteen. We know from his brothers' writing that he was delicate and musical. He had recovered his health sufficiently to return to work in London, and now became betrothed to Sophia Mansell, only daughter of a prosperous neighbouring farmer. Ambrose Mansell was a churchwarden and well respected in the neighbourhood. According to Susanna he had learnt his discipline and ethos of hard work in the army, where he had served under General Elliott, who is buried at Nutfield.

Charles, meanwhile, was by now a tall, lanky, sixteen year old. As for Susanna, a coloured drawing by William shows her as an attractive child, clad in a white, short-sleeved, empire-style, muslin gown with a blue sash; her shoulder-length hair, cut with a fringe, is drawn behind her ears and secured with clips.

At this time all looked well with the family, apart from some concern over John's lack of business in a sparsely populated area. If they had been able to see into the future they might have been more concerned. Already Daniel was planning a journey to America, perhaps encouraged by Clio Rickman's *Emigration to America Considered* (1798). Several families they knew had emigrated as well as several prominent reformers. Daniel was probably keen to see for himself how the land lay. Or was his involvement with a reform group in danger of becoming common knowledge, making his absence from England seem a good idea?

CHAPTER FOUR

An American Adventure

(of Daniel, William and Frank the Dog)

AT THE BEGINNING of 1806 Daniel and William, now aged thirty and twenty-two, decided the time had come to visit America. There is little doubt that Daniel, at any rate, was influenced by Clio Rickman, who promised an introduction to Thomas Paine, the famous radical politician. It is also probable that Daniel felt it might be a good idea to absent himself from England for a while. It was known that both these young men held unpopular political opinions, being staunch democrats. They planned to see for themselves if America lived up to its reputation as the 'land of the free'. Several people they knew had already emigrated, including Henry Browne's sister, Ann Billinghurst. (William had served his apprenticeship with Henry Browne in Lewes.) The Billinghursts had emigrated some twenty-five years before, together with a group of friends. They had initially gone to live at Sparta, New York, following in the footsteps of the scientist, Joseph Priestley, who had fled there after his house in Birmingham was burnt to the ground by an angry mob (because of his support for the French Revolution). By 1806 the Brownes had moved to Northfield, New York (later to become Pittsford).

On 10 March Daniel and William completed the sale of their shop to James Ireland. They must have been in jubilant mood when, the following day, they left Brighton and walked through deep snow to Storrington where they stayed with James for a couple of days. The three brothers probably talked long into the evening about the great adventures ahead. Although James may have felt a pang of regret that he was not to be one of the party he was absorbed in his own rapidly increasing business. Daniel and William then walked on to Shipley where they met Allen Browne, Henry's brother and a good friend, and continued through Horsham to Rusper, where they had tea with their brother John and his family (John and Elizabeth now had two children, as a son named Benjamin had been born in 1804). They reached Horley in the early evening, where they were no doubt besieged with questions as to their plans.

A few days later the pair walked to London where they spent some time carefully investing their money in the stock market. They also took the opportunity to explore several of the American sailing ships in port at the time. An average passage by sailing ship from London to New York took anything up to two months. By the time they returned to Horley they had made all necessary arrangements for their departure in May, aboard the *Walter*, owned by a Mr. Lord.

The next two months must have been full of their preparations for departure. New clothes were to be made, new shoes purchased, and so on – not to mention their provisions for the journey. Daniel noted in his journal: '28 April, Monday. Getting our baggage together, buy in our groceries etc., took them to the Custom House, Cook & Jackson our clearers. For some reason, we knew not what, our baggage did not get cleared; felt very unpleasant.' Was this because Daniel was suspected of being a member of a reform group, and a well known radical?

It must have been with great excitement that Daniel, William and their dog, a bull-mastiff terrier named Frank (named after Benjamin Franklin), took leave of their family and friends, on 1 May, and embarked on the *Walter*, bound for New York. Again, there is an odd note in Daniel's journal: 'Fine clear morn. Embarked at Gravesend about 11 o'clock, after being examined at the Alien Office and a second time called back and asked if we had any objection to swear to the account we have given of ourselves.' They were, no doubt, armed with copious supplies of their favourite biscuits, such as doughboys and johnny cakes, pies and other treats provided by the females of their acquaintance. For economic reasons they had chosen to travel steerage, which meant they had to take their own provisions. There were eighteen steerage passengers and six in the cabin, including the owner of the ship, Mr. Lord. (Daniel and William were not the first of the Constable family to sail to America; in 1662 another William Constable, also from Surrey, had set sail for Virginia.)

Both Daniel and William kept journals of their travels, and William drew and painted scenes as they went along. Many years later William was to put together an illustrated conflation of their journals, leather-bound, comprising two volumes encased in a stout, velvet-lined oak box. The book is called *Notes of a Travel in North America in the Years 1806, 7 and 8 by a Company of Three*. The book covers their travels in detail and in an amusing way.

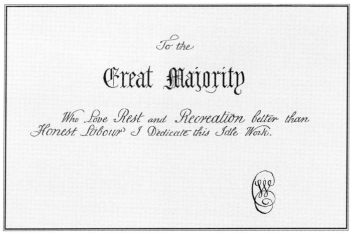

To the

Great Majority

Who Love Rest and Recreation better than
Honest Labour I Dedicate this Idle Work.

Dedication page of Notes of a Travel in North America in the Years 1806, 7 and 8 by a Company of Three *by W. Constable*

Their adventures have therefore only been lightly sketched in the following account.

They arrived in New York on 29 June, having had an unremarkable voyage, apart from seeing a total eclipse of the sun and having experienced violent seasickness. William wrote:

> We embarked this day on board the ship Walter which immediately weighed anchor and put to sea and arrived at New York on the 29th June experiencing nothing on our passage but the usual attendant circumstances of a voyage. Our approach to the shore was extremely beautiful, a hilly tract called the Highlands of Neversink was the first land to the southward, covered everywhere with trees that made their appearance. Long Island, as if springing up from the ocean stretched itself along on our right whilst right before us the lighthouse Sandy Hook directed our course, supplying

the place of the wondrous needle which had guided us across the trackless ocean. Approaching nearer, the scene became everywhere speckled with habitations and the air richly perfumed with the fragrance of vegetation. At length, passing through the straight between Long Island and Staten Island, called The Harrows, the city of New York opened upon our sight. The wind, the tide and the daylight soon after failed us altogether and when we had arrived within a quarter of a mile of the city, we were obliged to drop anchor 'til the next morning when, with the utmost satisfaction, we landed on the shores of the western world.

William makes the comment in his book that Frank had smelled land at least four days before it was sighted.

The two young men found lodgings at the bottom of Courtland Street, which had a delightful view of the shores of New Jersey. They paid $5 each per week for excellent food and comfortable lodging. Among the other lodgers was a certain James Crespin, a fellow passenger from the *Walter*, from whose company William observed that they derived much pleasure. They visited 'the old philosopher', Thomas Paine, and Thomas West's brother, who had a Counting House in the city.

In his journal William described the city of New York:

The streets of the city are not disposed with perfect regularity, particularly that part of it which borders on East River, where the greatest part of the business is transacted. Pearl and Water Strs., and all the lesser ones connected with them are much too narrow and often very crooked and seem to be rather the result of chance than the effect of

system and method. Broadway is by far the handsomest
street in the city, and is the seat of the principal retail
business, has at one end a handsome square in front of
which is a spacious building in which the governor
formerly resided, but is now devoted to the business of the
Custom House and other public offices. Its width exceeds
seventy feet and almost every house in it is a shop or as they
term it a store. The shops do not wear that showy
appearance as in English towns, a small quantity of goods
only are put into windows to denote the kind of articles
that are to be found within. It is perfectly straight through
its whole length which is two miles, though it is not
completely built much above half that distance, and has on
each side a row of Lombady Poplars, separating the foot-
paths from the carriage-way, as have all the other streets
whose widths are sufficient to allow it. The effect of this
union of nature and art, this blending of city and woodland
scenery is uncommonly fine and far more grateful to the
eye than the most superb buildings could be alone. At the
same time it is of infinite advantage in sheltering the houses
and passengers from the beams of the sun.

William also wrote that they were forcibly struck by the pale and
sallow complexions of the city's inhabitants:

...the general colour of both men and women is such an
Englishman could hardly detach from the idea of ill-health.
The colour of the skin, however, is not the criterion of
health or infirmity and the rose on the cheek of an English
milkmaid would in America be considered as an unnatural
flush; nor does she, under that glowing teint [sic], enjoy a

greater portion of health or spirits than fall to the share of the paler American.

Their ambitious plan was to travel north along the Hudson River to Albany, about 150 miles, and then to follow the path of the Mohawk River westwards towards Seneca and the Finger Lakes before reaching Niagara Falls, approximately another 350 miles. After this they would follow the southbound rivers: the Ohio for about 1,000 miles and the Mississippi for a further 1,000 miles or so, to New Orleans, before returning to New York either by sea or overland, making a journey altogether of some 5,000 miles.

Daniel and William spent about three weeks in New York, during which time they began their preparations for the journey. They intended to travel on foot, so it was necessary to be as unencumbered as possible: and their equipment consisted of one spare day shirt, a nightshirt, a cap, a spare pair of socks, a portfolio for sketches, a small journal each, a few implements for drawing, and maps and books. In the intense heat of a New York summer they found that the woollen clothes, of which they had brought a two years' supply, would be totally unsuitable to the climate; so these were returned to their trunks. Instead they purchased short jackets and loose trousers, made of thin gingham, with straw hats and a piece of black ribbon substituting for a cravat. These, together with stout shoes tied high upon the instep to protect their feet from sharp stones and gravel, completed their outfits. They did, however, have a trunk sent on to Albany from New York, and then forwarded from stage to stage as the opportunity presented itself.

The little party left New York on 25 July. They crossed the Hudson River to New Jersey where, from curiosity, they took a stagecoach and rode eight miles to Newark in less than an hour and a half, although William was less than complimentary about their mode of travel. He noted:

> In the construction of these carriages the Americans are infinitely behind the English. They have no elegance of form nor is their construction adapted to the ease and convenience of the passengers. They generally contain four seats placed before each other, each one with good crowding, is made to hold three persons. The drivers occupy one place in front while much of the baggage is stowed inside, to the great inconvenience of the passengers, whose attention is often wholly taken up in keeping it from breaking their shins and in some of the rugged roads, I think, their bones even must be in danger. They have no glass windows but the carriage is left open all round and these openings are furnished with flaps of leather which roll up and down and are fastened by brass buttons. If the passengers are desirous of shutting out a storm or bleak wind, the light must be excluded and even then the wind will find many passages through the crevices that must be left enclosed.

After rather thankfully leaving the stagecoach, they took a route along the banks of the Hudson River and while walking along they espied a sloop, which they hailed and were given a ride to Troy. At this point William wrote: 'was highly gratified by the arrival of that amiable young man, Mr. Crespin, who had left

New York this morning and intends going our round with us'. So the party of three became four.

At Albany they met some native American Indians: 'The men had bows and arrows in their hands, and they had each of them a blanket wrapped around them. They were dirty in their appearance and looked not very much unlike a gang of gypsies.' The three, plus Frank the dog, left Troy and walked along the banks of the Mohawk River to the Finger Lakes. From here they took the road to Rochester. Unfortunately Daniel and James Crespin fell out over what Daniel subsequently described as a trifle: 'In the afternoon Mr. Crespin left us, very abruptly, to pursue his journey alone, not having given us a word of notice till his departure when he wished us "Good Afternoon".' From various comments in William's journal it is apparent that James Crespin had found the pace hard going. Daniel immediately followed in hot pursuit but failed to find their friend.

They continued on their journey to Geneva, where William met Mr. John Billinghurst, brother-in-law to his erstwhile employer, Henry Browne. Mr. Billinghurst invited them to stay with his family in Northfield. During their stay William drew a picture of the Billinghurst log cabin as a present for their hosts. They also offered some practical help: 'As we had now a few hours of leisure we proposed to try our dexterity at felling trees. We accordingly took each a felling axe and went into Mr. B.'s wood and by teatime we had lain three trees of no inconsiderable size upon the ground.' After a pleasant stay they took the road for Niagara Falls. This was, according to William, a very rough road 'composed entirely of logs laid crosswise in the road without a particle of earth or any other matter thrown over them to smooth the inequalities with which a road of this kind must necessarily abound'. They stayed in all sorts of taverns along the way, some of them quite luxurious and others most primitive. On one occasion they shared a room with several other people:

> ...there not being a single candle in the house we got into our bed without any difficulty though we were surrounded almost by the people of the house among whom were three or four women. The light of day shone strongly round about us and the same three or four young women were round about near our bed. We now were in a much worse situation than poor Yorrick was at the Little Inn. We had a much greater number of ladies about us and had not the advantage of a curtain to draw between us. We wanted much to get up but could not think of turning out under such circumstances. We lay there looking out for events about three quarters of an hour when two of the females left the room, We judged it not likely that we should meet with a more favourable opportunity than this, there being but two women left, one in bed and the other, a young woman about 20, sitting at her bed foot close by ours. We judged this moment to dress ourselves, the young woman sitting quite unconcerned while we changed our shirts, drew on our trousers, etc., except that she very frequently favoured us with a full stare. How happy were we to find that we had not at all shocked female delicacy, a thing which we had at first heartily feared. (William's sense of humour was never very far from the surface.)

They usually set out early in the morning, stopping in the heat of the day for a rest and something to eat, and then continuing in the cool of the early evening. On one occasion they found an empty tavern and shinned down a ladder into a well to obtain a drink of water and

> ...for our better convenience in this business we took the liberty of breaking into the deserted tavern to borrow a basin which was easily accomplished as it had no other fastening than its latch, the string of which was drawn in and as the door was not made to shut so close as in some houses we had only to put a knife through and lift the latch. We then went into the garden and cut two or three cucumbers, with all which we made a comfortable repast. We were about to return the basin to its place when a cow, with its udder ready to burst with milk, appeared before us. We easily persuaded ourselves it would be an act of the most christian charity both to ourselves and the poor beast to ease her of a part of her load. With this consideration in our favour we soon set about milking which, considering it was our first attempt in that way, we flattered ourselves we were pretty dextrous at as in a short time we obtained two or three good basins of milk. We then put the basin in its place with a sixpence for our milk and after reversing the order of the furniture pretty much through the whole dwelling we departed in peace.

Thus replete they walked on towards Niagara Falls, spending some time in an Indian encampment on the way. At this stage they were accompanied by a local man who had taught himself the dialect spoken by this Indian tribe. William commented: 'These Indians possess a piece of land here on which they keep cattle and horses. They have likewise planted an orchard of apples and peaches; they likewise cultivate a small part of it on which they raise Indian corn. This business is executed (like all their other laborious employments) by the squaws entirely while the male Indians squat themselves contented and coverless under the shade of their cottages.'

They found Niagara quite magnificent and stayed some little time so that William could sketch many different views of the great waterfalls. William described his first impression of Niagara: 'To say anything worthy of this place is absolutely impossible and any description given in human language must fail of conveying even the feeblest idea of the sublimity of grandeur of this majestic scene.' During their stay they attended a service given for the Indians and here they had quite a different impression of them than earlier: 'The Indians were generally very clean in their persons and the squaws all wore their blanket or, in lieu of it, a square of broad woollen cloth. They appeared to be all decked out with all the finery they could muster; some of them had their faces besmeared with paint, very whimsically, which looked like dry red lead.'

From the mouth of the Niagara River Daniel and James took a boat to Presquisle (later called Erie), during which journey they were extremely seasick. They then walked overland to Franklin, Pennsylvania, where they bought a canoe and paddled themselves along the Allegheny for 140 miles to Pittsburgh. This must have been a pleasant change from walking and probably meant they had time to enjoy the passing scenery. At Franklin they had heard that James Crespin had arrived some time earlier and had also bought a canoe. Apparently, however, he had had second thoughts about the dangers of attempting the journey alone, and so had subsequently sold it. They heard no more of Mr. Crespin until their return to New York.

During their passage down the Allegheny river they bought bread at landings along the way. Daniel rediscovered his boyhood love of fishing, and sometimes they shot game for their dinners; so generally they lived very well on virtually nothing. William often drew the birds and fish they caught, in order to illustrate the difference between the North American and English wildlife. They saw many rattlesnakes and brown bears, but neither caused them any harm. Frank, their faithful companion, often ran along the riverbank, chasing squirrels and possums which afforded him both exercise and entertainment.

Upon arrival in Pittsburgh William noted:

Poled our canoe round into the Monongahela River and drew her up on the strand at the bottom of Market Street. Pittsburgh is rather smaller than I expected to find it, it contains about 3,000 inhabitants. It is regularly laid out and is very fast moving. The houses are not fine buildings – there are however some few good substantial dwellings. They are of various materials as brick, stone, wood and some log. Its situation is extremely beautiful and is calculated equally to capture the eye of him who loves the many charms of picturesque scenery and the men who delight in more solid and palpable blessings of commerce; it lies in the acute angle formed by the junction of the two navigable rivers, Allegheny and Monongahela.

They decided to remain here long enough to order new clothes as they became aware how shabby they had become. Then, as William wrote:

> Having quite made up our minds to descend the Ohio in our own canoe if by no other means we called on General O'Hara to enquire for a Mr. Comfort Tyler, a gentleman that D.C. had met with at Canandaigua and who had politely requested him to call on him when we came to Pittsburgh. Mr. O'Hara informed us that he was now at the Falls of Beaver and as we were already determined on going up Beaver Creek to the falls in case we went in our own canoe, the calling on Mr. Tyler quite came into our plan.

Daniel and William left Pittsburgh on 6 October and canoed down the Ohio as far as Beaver Creek. They found the creek very shallow and had some difficulty in making their way: 'I was obliged to wade most part of the way and drag the canoe after me.' They finally reached the Cross Keys tavern where they met Mr. Tyler whose conversation appeared most interesting: 'He informed me that he in conjunction with several other gentlemen were about forming a settlement on a tract of about 600,000 acres on the Ohio river where much of the practical part of surveying might be obtained; at the same time hinting that they might make it worth our while to accompany and assist us.' Daniel and William thought they might as well stay and see how the land lay.

After a few days, relates William, Mr. Tyler assured them:

> That if we would wait and descend the river with him he
> should be able to put us in a situation where a mutual
> reciprocity might subsist between us. That he with many
> other gentlemen were engaging in an enterprise in which
> if we chose to take an active part both pleasure and
> emolument might accrue to us – at the same time it would
> be forwarding my views as a surveyor, would be the means
> of introducing us to many persons of the first rank and
> respectability in the United States and give us an extensive
> practical acquaintance with this country.

At this point Daniel decided to ride to New York to fetch more
of their clothes and Mr. Tyler charged him with some business.
This journey was some 700 miles each way, over the mountains
and rough terrain. He was to travel on horseback.

Daniel and William had unwittingly got themselves caught up
in the infamous Burr Conspiracy. Aaron Burr was the Republican
vice-president until 1804, when he killed his political rival,
Alexander Hamilton, in a duel and fled to South Carolina. The
conspiracy's aim was to raise a force to conquer Texas and establish
a republic. Major Tyler was one of the conspirators.

As is clear from the above William had by now decided that
drawing and painting, much as he loved these occupations, would
not sustain him, and he had decided to become a surveyor. He
occupied himself, while Daniel was away, in assisting Mr. Hoops to
lay out the plan for a new town being built on the banks of the river
at Beaver Creek. He was asked to name it, and after telling them that

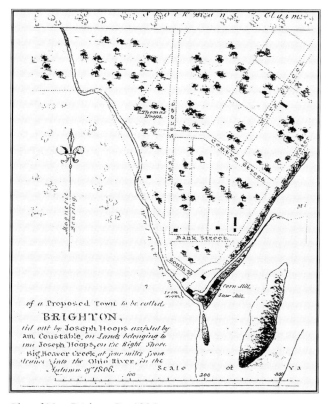

Plan of New Brighton, Pa. 1806

he came from a very nice town in England called Brighton, it was called New Brighton. He also became friendly with the Townsend family, who had built a watermill on the banks of the river opposite the new town. Many years later John Constable's daughters, Caroline and Eliza, were to open a school here.

While in Pittsburgh Daniel finished the letter to their parents that he had begun in the Genesee region, and he sent another from New York, explaining his mission. He also wrote to Thomas West. As he was en route to the East Coast he realised, from newspapers and overheard comments, that there was something dubious about the activities of Messrs. Tyler and co., but having agreed to carry out the commission he kept to his word. However, on his returning to New Brighton he and his brother sensibly extricated themselves from this group and continued on their journey, by canoe, down the Ohio River to the Mississippi River.

They had not heard the last of their former companions at Beaver Creek. On landing at Blanerhasset's Island in order to deliver a letter they found 'some of our old comrades from Sharon who had proceeded thus far on their expedition and were staying at Mr. Blanerhasset's who it seems is one of the principal men in the affair'. As they travelled further down the Ohio they became aware of increasing military activity.

As it was by now December the weather became extremely cold, with violent snowstorms. With a certain common sense, they decided to buy an ark, a flat-bottomed boat with a small wooden house – complete with chimney – built on top. Thus they were able to be totally self sufficient, using the fire both as a source of heat and to cook their meals. They lashed their canoe to the side of this raft and pushed on down the river, sometimes giving lifts to people they met and sometimes carrying a small cargo for profit. They halted at Cincinnati, which they found a handsome town with broad streets, many brick houses and a market where William bought a fowl: 'My fowl proves to be a cock. We have given him the liberty of the boat and if he behaves himself properly and crows well in the morning we think of making him a part of the family and treating him as a brother, if not he surely dies.'

A little south of Cincinnati they stopped at Big Bone Creek where they bought an enormous tooth, measuring 9" x 4" and weighing 8$^1/_2$ lbs. William negotiated with the owner of this tooth and noted: 'We offered him a dollar which he accepted and no doubt thought he had found a fine market for them for he laughed heartily with his comrade as soon as our backs were turned.'

Continuing on their journey they stopped in Louisville for a while, where William made a drawing of the town of Jeffersonville (which had been laid out by Thomas Jefferson, the American president). They also stopped in Natchez where they met up with several of the group from Beaver Creek including Mr. Hopkins, Mr. Tyler's nephew. William observed:

> We learn from these gentlemen that the object, whatever it may have been, of the mysterious expedition with which we have been in some danger of being implicated and which has excited so much suspicious interest throughout the States, is now entirely put down by the interference of the government and many of the persons engaged in it are returned to their homes. The prime mover, Colonel Burr, has absconded from legal attention. Tyler and his colleagues still keep up the farce of an intended settlement of lands in this country.

The brothers arrived in New Orleans in March 1807, from where they wrote long letters home. They had their boat broken up, and sold the timber for more than it had cost them to have it built, which greatly pleased them. William described the city:

> The general appearance of New Orleans, more than any
> other town we have seen in America, reminds us of
> London, probably from the older appearance of the houses
> for in a multitude of other respects it is widely different.
> The houses are some of brick, others of wood. The Levee
> is a very busy place, being crowded with the stalls of a
> multitude of little traders. Here too is the market, open
> today (Sunday) like all other places of business.

They debated whether to return to New York by sea or to take
the longer, more perilous overland route through what was
known as The Wilderness, comprising the Indian lands. They
eventually decided to take the overland route, mostly because of a
fear of seasickness, so they bought two mules and set off through
the uninhabited country. At this point Daniel developed what
William described as the 'Ague', similar to malaria. This delayed
them for some time, but they found the Indians very kind, and
they stayed in an Indian hut for a while as Daniel recovered. They
did find lying on the earthen floor, covered only by bearskins,
very uncomfortable and were quite relieved to be able to
continue on their way as soon as Daniel recovered his strength.

For the greater part of their journey the pair travelled alone,
although occasionally fell in with other travellers. These people
were either families moving with all their goods and chattels or
men carrying out some commission. The two young men were
regarded as oddities since they were travelling entirely for their
own pleasure. They continued at a leisurely pace, William

drawing the passing scenes and Daniel occupied in fishing or shooting for their supper. They described the lands around the Cumberland and Duck Rivers as being very popular for settlers, and recorded how they met many wagonloads of families making for that area. They found some difficulty in getting their mules to cross the rivers, until they discovered the trick was to send them over alone with a thrash on the rump, and then to cross themselves, often getting wet in the process.

They eventually reached Washington, a city which they found most impressive although it was only half built; and recorded that they saw Thomas Jefferson, the president, riding around the town unescorted. Apparently he did not stand on any ceremony and when visiting a house he simply hitched up his horse to the post provided, like everybody else. They had great trouble in selling their mules, but eventually managed to find a home for them, even if not for the price they had hoped.

Frank was obviously a most remarkable dog, as he accompanied the brothers throughout on their journeyings, sometimes getting into fights, sometimes killing opossums and squirrels, and frequently getting very sore feet. A lovely oil painting depicts him as a handsome, reddish brown bull-mastiff type, wearing a brass studded collar.

Daniel, William and Frank reached New York in the middle of July 1807, having travelled for over five thousand miles. It had taken them just a year but a year in which they had experienced events only dreamed of by their contemporaries.

CHAPTER FIVE

Letters from Home

DANIEL AND WILLIAM found several letters from home when they arrived back in New York. Not all of them were welcome, especially one from their father, dated December 1806:

My dear Sons,

A few weeks after you left England Mr. West informed me that he was writing to you by a lady of his acquaintance going to New York. I sent a letter to him to go by the same conveyance, neither of which I find you had received on writing your last letter. Since I have not wrote for which neglect I am very sorry and all I can say in excuse is that from a variety of trouble, hurry at business etc. and not apprehending you would be back at N. York for many months I did not do it and now it is with much concern that I acquaint you with a circumstance that I know will be very distressing to you.

Benjamin, a few days after you left this country, had a relapse of his old disorder. The afternoon of that day he found himself very poorly but said he did not apprehend anything of his old complaint. The next day a great deal of blood came from him and he brought away a great deal at different times for two or three days. Thus he was reduced to the weakest state imaginable, so weak that he could not turn himself in bed. Dr. Smith attended him, who had attended him in all his illness before and acted upon the prescriptions of Dr. Bavington who had been his physician in London in his last illness. After some days we thought him something better and the bleeding subsided but soon a swelling in his arms and legs took place, attended with great pain and soon symptoms of swelling took place in his body. Further medical assistance was called in but all to no effect; the swelling increased. Dr. Blair from Lewes was next applied to; his prescriptions produced no favourable symptoms. His disorder gained ground and the last resource was tapping; this was pronounced to be absolutely necessary as the last resort and this operation was performed the 12th August by Dr. Smith and Dr. Steele (from Brighton). 10 quarts of water was taken from him; by this he consequently seemed eased of a very great burthen [sic] and we had some hopes that he would get better. He laid more quiet and easy that afternoon and the forepart of the night than he had done for some time but about one o'clock he was seized with violent pains in his stomach, with sickness and vomiting. I was called up and went to him at that time. These pains continued very violent for five or six hours when they abated something but his breathing was very hard and difficult. Between 11 o'clock and 12 o'clock he desired his mother and me to lift him up, saying 'Perhaps I shall get my breath better'. The instant his mother had raised him up he went off in a kind of a fit. The Doctor had not left him ten minutes; I sent after him and he was presently back but all this, alas, was of no effect. He never came to any more; he went off in his mother's and my arms as easy as a person goes to sleep. He bore his illness with amazing spirit and fortitude. His two sisters were his nurses the whole time, night and day.

Mildred was taken ill the day you left London and was had to Mr. Rose's where she continued very ill for three weeks. As soon as she was thought able to be removed we got her home and she soon got well enough to help to look after Benjamin and in a few weeks entirely recovered and at this time I have the satisfaction to acquaint you we are all well. The mill falls into my hands next Michaelmas. I have disposed of the business at Rusper and sold the premises to a young man of the name of Turner; his father, who has been dead some years, kept an Inn at Chiddingly and he, the young man, served his time at Burwash, part with Mannering and part with his successor in the same shop. The purchase of the premises is £350 with £15 more for the fixtures in the shop. I let upon these terms, viz. to take £500 of the stock by valuation, £350 paid down, the remainder to be paid in three months from entrance. He entered the 20th October and £544 of stock was valued to him; the remainder I took which John and I have been ever since taking account of at all leisure times and just now finished: the amount £530. John and his family are now at our house. We are upon the lookout for something for him but have not yet found anything quite to our minds.

We have looked your letters over with a great deal of attention, tracing your route by the maps and have got a very clear idea of the road you pursued, finding almost every place you have named in one map or the other. This was a matter of great pleasure as you seem much to have enjoyed yourselves in your peregrinations and that the same good luck and satisfaction may attend you in your farther progress is our most ardent wish and your safe return will crown the whole. You may depend upon it that I shall very soon send another letter.

In your next let us know as much as you can of your future views and proceedings, which way, how and when you think you shall return to England. I wish in your next you would be as explicit as possible in your mention of prices of American expenses, etc. We don't clearly understand you; in your last you say at Albany that you dined with the Judge and Councillors upon the best of everything and that you paid $1¼ (5s.7½d) per day lodging, etc. included. Now you do not say whether this was so much each or whether for William and you together or whether likewise included your other companion.

As for the political state of affairs in Europe undoubtedly you get a better account than I can pretend to tell you. However, things at present wear a very gloomy appearance. Bonaparte has entirely conquered Prussia, with every German State in alliance with that country. He is himself in the Palace at Berlin and the King of Prussia has escaped to Petersburg. Hamburg is likewise in the possession of the French and all the English property there confiscated, with all the English found there or in any other of the conquered countries made Prisoners of War. He next threatens to take possession of the Sound and stop the English out of the Baltic.

Corn of all sorts is very dear; the last harvest by no means a plentiful one. Wheat is now three and four and twenty pounds per load, oats 26/- to 30/- per quarter, barley 44/- to 48/- pease 56/- to 60/-, flour is now 75/- per sack of five bushel. In all probability from present appearances corn will be a very scarce article before another harvest and flour a very dear article. Perhaps an adventure of this sort in the summer from America might be an advantageous one. I shall be perticular [sic] in my subsequent letters to tell you the state of the markets.

Pray write as often as you possibly can. We all are at present in the enjoyment of good health and join in love and best wishes for your welfare and safe return. I have not yet had the letter you mention from Mr. West but suppose I shall in a day or two.

The Brighton Union Bank opened account with me the beginning of July and I have had a regular weekly correspondence with them ever since. I get rid of about £100 of their notes per week.

Poor Ireland has had a most horrible disaster in the first part of the summer. In bathing one morning alone by some means he got out of his depth; he was observed by some people on the beach who went to his assistance. He was taken up, to all appearances quite dead. He was taken home and medical assistance called in. It was a great while before there were any signs of returning life. However, he was recovered but continued in a very poor state of health for some months. Whether he is yet perfectly recovered I do not know, having not heard of him for some time. It is said that he has plenty of business.

James was very well, about a week ago. I have not yet communicated your letter to him but shall in two or three days.

I am,

Your most affectionate father,

J. Constable

P.S. George is gone to Storrington. He went the beginning of September. He is very much approved of there and I believe he will make a very nice boy.

Note: Daniel and William were devastated by the news of their brother's death, as is shown by William's letter to his parents. William and Benjamin, next to each other in age, had been particular playmates as children. The George mentioned was a small cousin, aged eight, taken in by James and Susanna, and now sent to James Jr. in Storrington, presumably to be educated, as well as to make himself useful. Mr. Constable's couisn, Thomas, and his wife had both died recently so it seems likely that George was their child. John seemed to have bad luck in Rusper. There is no evidence that he was not a hard worker, but the area was a rural, sparsely populated one and probably the local population preferred the market towns of Crawley or Horsham. The Ireland mentioned was James Ireland to whom they had sold the Brighton business.

Daniel also received a letter from Thomas West, telling him all the local gossip, recounting how much the town of Brighton was growing and how much he was missed by all their friends. West warned his friends to beware of losing their money in any incautious venture: 'Americans are adept in commerce and not over nice about the means of obtaining riches.'

In April 1807, Mildred had also written to her brothers giving the first hint that she, too, would like to travel and experience living abroad. She was staying in Maidstone with the Ing family and she appears much more concerned over John's situation than her father:

My dear brothers,
With infinite pleasure I have read your interesting letters and

am much pleased that so far you have been well satisfied with your ramble and adventures, to the disappointment of many who expected you would be heartily tired before you had been long in the new world. If you were to settle I should feel great inclination to be with you.

Ere this reaches you, you may have sailed for England. Our ideas lead us to expect you this summer, particularly our mother who feels so conscious of seeing you in a few months and I sincerely hope her expectations may be realised.

I am on a visit to my old friend here for the amendment of my health and have the satisfaction of saying it is improving. London certainly injured my constitution and at times I have felt slight indispositions ever since. You are not to think I have laboured under a serious fit of illness, nothing of the kind, but we have endured a severe trial in the loss of our dear brother B., together with poor John being so long out of business. Being ever present in these troubles it affected my health. I sincerely wish for the sake of all parties he had a situation wherein he could live.

I have been three weeks in Maidstone, have no fixed time for returning, perhaps may stay as much longer when after a short time I intend to pay brother James a visit and if he and I should agree in our sentiments I may perhaps stay at his Findon house and look out for him there a little. He has mentioned his wish in it as his apprentices are one or two of them out of their times. At any rate I shall go and see him as I have not made him a visit since I left him. I saw him a month ago; he looks well and grows very stout. He is in expectation of being obliged to buy his house or leave it this spring. Most likely he tells you these things himself.

I feel very much at home at Miss Ing's when I get behind

the counter, which has been my station for some days past; we have been stocktaking, quite a busy time. Miss Ing is going tomorrow to London and is so obliging as to take this for me, which I hope will arrive safe to you, though it contains little to interest you. Yet I am well convinced my poor endeavours will meet a kind reception and be by you esteemed.

When I go to see James I shall spend a day or two with Mrs. Smith who has been so kind as to invite me.

The idea of Ireland occurs and induces me to tell you what a dashing fellow he is which is certainly no news. But that he has his hands full with another shop and a wife may be news. He has got that shop which was Alexander's, the grocers, and has married somebody from Woolwich.

I wish I had an interesting subject to go on upon but I trust you will take the will for the deed. I am not in the way for novelty as you are. This town is extraordinary dull, trade is quite on the decline. It appears quite an altered place, the Assises and Sessions have both been held since I have been here which produced a little bustle; an Election is expected in about ten days.

I left Mrs. Townsend hastily at last and am still sorry I staid so long. A severe and alarming illness followed; notwithstanding I had engaged and fully intended to fulfill the engagement with Mrs. Matthew, until I came to the country when finding the fellow so ill quite diverted me from my purpose which I am well satisfied was quite wisest and best and most satisfactory to my feelings. I have had no inclination to take a situation in Haberdashery or Millinery in town or country since, nor do I think I shall ever like to do it again.

I think it quite a serious thing that there are so many

difficulties in getting brother J. into business. They have sought after several but have not found any that seems quite adapted for him but their being at my father's is such an additional family beside the additional expense. I fear at Horley they will find themselves greatly encumbered when they get that crazy mill into their hands – I dread their having it.

I am greatly in hopes that there will be a letter from you at Horley by the time I arrive, that I may have the inexpressible pleasure in perusing it. Your accounts fill me with wonder and are so truly interesting that I should like to witness many of the novel things you have done. I am quite anxious to know whether you have any views of settlement and if you have, what those views are. But we expect you will not do this until you have visited us again in England. I long for the arrival of that happy time which will indeed be a joyful time with us all. Some are of the opinion if you come to England you will never return to America; only you know this. If you like the country and should get a comfortable establishment I should think America as well as anywhere else, though certainly it would be most agreeable to us to have you in this Kingdom. If you have not wrote to Horley I sincerely hope you will for the comfort of our dear father and mother. I also hope you received the last letter of my father's written in January and we were very sorry you had not received the former ones; are astonished at the meaning of it.

I hope, my dear brothers, you will not expose yourselves to dangers and I sincerely wish you health and happiness with every blessing of life.

I am, dear brothers,

Tedhams, watercolour by E. Bass-Smith, early 20th century

James Constable Jr. (1777-1844)
shooting at Storrington,
oil painting by C. Dowley, 1836

courtesy T. MacCracken

Tedhams Cottage, watercolour by E. Bass-Smith, 1919

Mildred Constable
(1781-1852)
Daguerreotype of
painting c. 1830

Courtesy Philippe Garner

Photograph of Tedhams (The Old Mill House) today, *courtesy Mr & Mrs Watts*

Charles Constable
(1786-1867)
daguerreotype c.1841

Spikemead, watercolour by E. Bass-Smith, early 20th century

Watercolour of river Mole at Horley, artist unknown

William Constable (1783-1861)

Susanna Constable (1790-1879) c. 1800

Lowfield Heath Windmill, oil painting, artist unknown

Thomas 'Clio' Rickman (1761-1834) copy of painting by W. Hazlitt, whereabouts unknown

Lowfield Heath Windmill today

Enclosure of land around Lowfield Heath Windmill by J. Constable, 1827

The Reigate Hundred from C. Smith's Surrey map, 1804

Your truly sincere and affectionate sister,
M. Constable

Mildred was fortunate in being able to be so independent, as many girls had no freedom whatsoever. Votes for women were not to be authorised for another 140 years. The lease on the mill was about to expire and James was looking forward to having it back in his hands, even though Mildred differed in her opinion.

On 19 July 1807, two days after Daniel and William had arrived back in New York, William wrote to their parents:

Dear Honoured Parents,
We arrived in this city two days since from New Orleans. We here found several letters from our friends in England which would have given us abundant pleasure had it not brought us the distressing intelligence of the death of our beloved brother.
We sympathise deeply with you all in the loss of that unfortunate and good young man whose life, had heaven been pleased to have spared it to us, I trust would have been a blessing to his friends and an honour to human nature. With you we bow with reverential submission to that Divine Providence, who orders all the affairs of the world with consummate wisdom and goodness and however distressing his dictates may sometimes be to our feelings, are doubtless the best adapted to our general welfare; and honourable as is the grief we feel in the loss of a worthy and beloved friend, it is our duty to remember it with philosophy and reason and a firm reliance on the goodness, power and wisdom of the deity. We hope that our mother

and all of you have borne up against the afflicting loss with fortitude and patience. The letter containing this distressing information is from you dated 15th December and is the only one we have received from your hand. The one which you forwarded by the lady friend of Mr. West's we have heard nothing of.

A letter from Mildred dated Maidstone, 16th April, 1807, we found here with yours. From it we learn that you had written us again in January. This letter likewise we have never received. By what means this was forwarded her letter does not reveal. By the way I would observe that a private hand is the worst and most uncertain mode of conveyance of any. The regular method by post or by putting a letter in a ship's bag is the most certain of any and letters dispatched in this way hardly ever fail of a direct passage. If a letter is put into the Post Office, its postage out of the country must be paid or it will never be forwarded. This I daresay you know, however it is not improper to mention it. Besides the two letters mentioned Daniel received two from Mr. West and myself have one from Josh. Langridge of Lewes and another from our old friend and companion, Mr. Crespin, from whom we have not heard before since our separation from last August at Geneva. He returned to London last winter and had prepared to return immediately to America when a pecuniary loss unfortunately delayed his voyage. He informs us that he has still hopes that he shall be able to accomplish it at a future period, though he does not say when. His letter is very concise, he does not even explain what his object in this country will be. I have reason to believe that the spot he intends to settle in is in the State of Connecticut, perhaps at or near New London. I shall answer his letter in a day or two and hope his next will be more explicit. As you would probably like to see him I will give you his address, which is No. 9 Little Russell Street, Bloomsbury, London. If at any time you should be in London and be disposed to call on him you will find the name of Constable a sufficient introduction and you will please to present him my respects.

We are afraid the troubles of our family since leaving England have been great indeed, though the restoration of Mildred and all the rest of you to general health is a blessing which we hope has brought you to a state of tranquil happiness, at least as perfect as the changing state of all subliminary things will allow. We look forward with an ardent hope to the moment when we shall again embrace you and the rest of our beloved friends. This, our arrangements have fixed at sometime next spring.

We suppose that you have received a letter which Daniel forwarded from New Orleans by the Ship Romulus for Liverpool. She sailed on the 23rd March and the letter was dated a few days before, though none of yours are of a date late enough to acknowledge it.

I believe that the letter alluded to informed you that we intended to return to New York by land, preferring the toils of a journey of 400 or 500 miles through a wilderness country inhabited only by Indians to a voyage by sea. On the 30th March we left New Orleans and commenced our journey in a small kind of boat called a Peroque eventually arriving in New York a few days since.

In New York we have met with or heard of all our fellow passengers in the Walter; all seem to be satisfied with exchange of country they have made.

With respect to the queries in your letter respecting expenses I reply that at Albany where one of Daniel's letters mentioned that we lived on $1^1/_4$ per day it was $1^1/_4$ each one. This at that time was considered very moderate for the style in which we lived but our more recent expenses in the western country have taught us to think it high. At Louisville on the Ohio we lived in a style equally good for $3 each per week and permanent boarders are doubtless charged considerably lower.

We lament that you should be under the necessity of paying the high prices you mention for flour while there are so many people here in this country that are glad to get $3^1/_2$ for a barrel of that article containing the net quantity of 100 lbs and who will sell you any quantity of wheat for $^1/_2$ per bushel. These are current prices on almost any part of the Ohio.

New York is still very healthy, no symptoms of the fever having appeared this summer and I hope it may again escape altogether. We are staying here only a few days to rest ourselves and to write to you and some other friends and make some little preparation for a short trip through some of the New England States which we have as yet not seen anything of, besides the approaching season would be a critical one for abiding in New York. We trust that having performed our walk through New England our curiosity will be fully gratified and we hope to return to you in spring and to lay the result of our enquiries before you.

We feel sorry that John should remain so long out of business but hope ere this he has met with something that suits him. To our sister, Mildred, we feel greatly obliged for her kind and attentive letter. We hope she will continue to write to us. To any other of our family who will bestow on us the same attentions we shall feel equally grateful. We would write to all individually that we might have a juster claim on each of our brothers and sisters for their individual replies, did we not know that very long letters from this country are always expected and that the task would be greater than our time will allow us to accomplish.

We forbear at present to give you any of our sentiments respecting settlement in this country. On our return we will have a long talk on the subject when the pro and the con shall be well considered. In the meantime we will endeavour to collect as much useful knowledge as possible; if it should ever prove useful to our friends we shall find in that circumstance our greatest gratification. We salute you all with the most affectionate regard, for my brother and self, I am, dear and honoured friends,

Your most dutiful son,

Wm. Constable

Another letter from their father, dated 29 June 1807, was received shortly thereafter. James Sr. was obviously very proud of his two adventurous sons, but concerned that they had not yet received the news of Benjamin's death. However, he was able to give good news regarding John and his family:

My dear Sons,

It is with the utmost pleasure and satisfaction we hear you are well and that you have thus far gone through your difficult and dangerous undertaking and that the same good fortune may attend you until your return to your native land is our most anxious wish. It is with no small degree of pleasure we have traced out your route by the different maps, making out most of the places you mention.

I wrote to you the 15th Dec. last, when I acquainted you of

the loss of poor Benjamin. He died the 17th August (a few days before we received your first letter from New York) after an illness of more than three months. This affected your poor mother very much but not to so great a degree as I feared it would. At present we are all in the enjoyment of good health and things with us are going on much in the old train. James is well and has plenty of business and tells me he is doing very well.

I was some time since like to be engaged in a law suit. Josh. Jordan got to his old tricks of poaching. He was suspected; a warrant was taken out to search my premises at Lofield Heath and a bird net was found in the old stable. Of this I nor anybody belonging to me had any suspicion. In consequence of this I was served with a copy of a Writ and I put in my appearance. But Sharp, by the advice of his attorney, dropped his suit as there could be no evidence against me. Upon this I turned Jordan off and Charles has managed the Mill ever since with sometimes the assistance of a boy. We have plenty of home custom to the Mill and always keep her going. I have disposed of the business and premises at Rusper quite well to my mind and have just placed John in a situation which I hope will answer. It is at Brasted in Kent. It is a very neat little town surrounded with gentlemen's houses, fine plantations of hops and corn. I do not know of a more clean and pleasant country anywhere. It is two miles beyond Westerham, three from Riverhead and four from Sevenoaks. Mildred is now with John to assist till he gets settled then she goes to Findon to look after James' business there.

In my former letter I told you that from a rather short harvest last year corn was expected to be very dear but, however, this has not been the case. Large supplies of wheat from Scotland (where their harvest was very abundant) and flour from America has kept the markets much lower than was expected. And wheat has been very steady at from £20 to £23 and £24 per load which is now called a very moderate price. We have the prospect of a very fine harvest, corn of every kind and particularly wheat was never known to look more promising.

From what you say in your letter I think we may expect to see you in England the beginning of winter. I make no doubt but you will write again the first opportunity. Your grandmother is dead and was buried on Thursday last. This circumstance eases your mother of a great deal of care and anxiety as she had been in a helpless state for a great while. I have nothing more to say to you at present but that we all join most heartily in love and best wishes for your welfare and happy return.

I am,

Your most affectionate father,

J. Constable

P.S. July 14th. This was not sent to London till this day, having sent your letter to James and not took a direction. Since this have been robbed by a servant (old Hirt's daughter). She is in prison and I am going tomorrow to appear against her at Guildford Sessions. I swear positively to a piece of print of 7 yds., valued at 12/-. She took a great deal more of different articles which we found at several places but not having marks I cannot swear to them.

Note: The grandmother referred to was Susanna's mother and James's mother-in-law, Mrs. Jordan of Charlwood.

Since she had been bedridden for some time it was probably a happy release. Mr. Sharp had inherited the Manor of Gatwick through his Jordan grandmother, so the Jordan involved in the poaching incident was related to him as well as Mrs. Constable.

CHAPTER SIX

Further American Adventures

DANIEL AND WILLIAM set off for their New England tour in late July 1807. This was to be a journey of some six or seven hundred miles, along the east coast opposite Long Island Sound, through the States of Connecticut, Rhode Island and Massachusetts to Boston. They stayed in Boston long enough to explore the city, and then walked on through Concord and Lexington, places rendered famous, as Daniel noted, 'perticularly [sic] the latter as being the spot where the first blood was shed at the commencement of the revolution'. William made a drawing of the stone monument here and copied the inscription:

> *Sacred to the Liberty of the Rights of Mankind.*
> *The freedom of Independence of America*
> *Sealed and defended with the Blood of her sons.*
> *This monument is erected*
> *By the inhabitants of Lexington*
> *Under the Patronage and at the expense of*
> *The Commonwealth of Massachusetts*
>
> *To the Memory of their fellow citizens*

Excerpt of a letter from J. Constable in Horley to his sons, Daniel and William, in New York 1808

Ensign Robert Monroe, Messrs. Jonas Parker
Samuel Hadley, Jonathan Harrington Junior,
Isaac Murray, Caleb Harrington and John Brown
of Lexington and Asabel Porter of Woburn
Who fell on this field the first victims to the
Sword of British Tyranny and Oppression
On the morning of the ever memorable
Nineteenth of April Ann. Dom. 1775.

The Die Was Cast
The blood of these
In the cause of God and their country
Was the cement of the Union of these States, then
Colonies. And gave the spring to the spirit firmness
And Resolution of their Fellow Citizens
They rose as one man to revenge their Brethren's
Blood and at the point of the sword to assert and
Defend their native Rights.
They nobly dared to be free.
The contest was long, bloody and affecting
Righteous Heaven approved the solemn appeal.
Victory crowned their Arms: And
The Peace, Liberty and Independence of the United
States of America was their Glorious Reward.
Built in the year 1799.

Daniel and William travelled on through the countryside of New
Hampshire into Vermont, over the Green Mountains to Albany
once again. From here they journeyed back along the banks of

the Hudson River to New York. Daniel observed that 'the States are generally under close cultivation besides the roads and rivers and the farms are as smooth and neat as those of England.' The two young men walked about twenty-five miles a day in spite of the intense heat, starting at sunrise and walking around ten miles before their breakfast of beef steaks or ham and eggs, with dried shad or salmon and cheese and butter, tea or coffee. They then rested for an hour or two before setting off again and generally ate no more until their dinner when they would have a similar meal, with perhaps the addition of dried fruit or a tart and custard. Daniel noted 'that lounging slip slop tea meal is unknown here.'

They arrived back in New York in early September, much disappointed at not finding any letters from England. Daniel wrote and told the family that they had decided not to return home at the moment but to undertake another journey down the Ohio and Mississippi rivers, this time for the purpose of profit. Their plan was to travel to Pittsburgh, buy another ark, load her with produce and navigate themselves down the rivers to New Orleans, where they would hopefully sell their cargo at a profit.

He also noted that 'a large boat to go by steam has been fitted up at great expense and has made one voyage to Albany'. This was Robert Fulton's paddle-wheel steamboat, which was to become so successful. It is clear that they met Robert Fulton, probably through their connection with Thomas Paine. It is perhaps not generally known that Thomas Paine himself had worked on powering boats by steam, as well as designing bridges.

Daniel and William stayed in New York City long enough to

have their clothes laundered and repaired and to make preparations for their next journey. They left New York on 8 September and walked to Philadelphia, where they wasted some time in waiting for their baggage to catch up with them. It finally arrived and they arranged for it to be sent on to Pittsburgh by wagon. They, themselves, made an uneventful three-week journey over the Blue and Allegheny mountain ranges to the city of Pittsburgh, but although uneventful it was 'certainly not without interest, particularly of the human variety'. Twice they left their hostelry of the night without taking the breakfast offered, with Daniel once making a reproving apology by begging that the hostess would trouble herself no further on their account – as, not liking such dumb, sullen people as her, they would go somewhere else for breakfast.

They commissioned an ark immediately upon arrival just outside Pittsburgh and set about looking for a suitable cargo. This proved more difficult than envisaged. However, it was getting late in the season and no doubt the local population thought they could offload goods of perhaps not the finest quality. Fortunately, Daniel and William were well versed in the ways of the world and dismissed all such offers. As they waited for their boat to be completed time lay heavy on their hands, so much so that Daniel read the complete contents of their host's library, although this was probably quite small. He also carved a chess set. William was more fortunate in having his sketches to work on.

They finally acquired a small cargo of apples, cheese and onions, expecting to pick up more freight in Pittsburgh. When they reached the city, however, they discovered that they were too late and that all the available cargo had been sold. After a few days of living on their boat, they reluctantly decided to abandon their entire project. They did so for a variety of reasons, not least because the weather was becoming so cold they were afraid the apples would freeze and would then be worth nothing. They had also become increasingly aware of the hostile feelings between Great Britain and the United States, caused, in their opinion, by England's assuming the right to search American vessels for British seamen. They realised there was an ominous threat of war, and so decided to return home as speedily as possible.

As for Frank, although he was generally welcomed in the taverns, they record on at least one occasion having an argument with the tavern keeper:

> Last evening on our going to bed a rumpus took place between us and the landlord about our dog, he positively declaring our dog should not be in the house with us. We told him if that was the case, we should not go to bed ourselves: we having travelled together thro' all the States, territories, cities of the Union together and as yet had never been so behaved to on account of our dog. He had always invariably been in the room in which we slept and that he was infinitely cleaner and more delicate in his person than the greater part of American men.

One can only imagine the landlord's reaction to Daniel's words.

They were fortunate in selling their boat, complete with cargo, for only a small loss and almost immediately started back to New York, where they arrived on Sunday 3 January 1808, having travelled in total over seven thousand miles. It was not until 27 February that they left New York. By this time they had received letters from Mildred and their father, dated January 1808. On 7 January Mildred had written:

My dear Brothers,

I am greatly hurt and ashamed at the neglect we have treated your kind and endearing epistles with, which has not altogether been wilful or careless indifference, far be it from either of those. On the contrary your happy adventures and industrious search of knowledge is an increasing agreeable and pleasing theme for us when we assemble and ungrateful as it appears in our not being more regular in our replies to your very interesting and valuable letters are not the errors of the heart (I will take on me to answer for us all) and assure you that it is at very short intervals that either of you are absent from our minds and I quite hope and trust you will put the right construction on it; that is a little thoughtlessness and uncertainty of conveyance, the latter we have been perticularly [sic] unfortunate in.

In my last I believe I told you I was at Maidstone for the reinstatement of my health (which for some time has been happily completed). I staid [sic] there for three months with my worthy friend (who has married since I left her). While there I learnt our brother, John, had engaged business at Brasted by Sevenoaks. Hither I repaired to assist him, preparatory to his opening the shop and continued with him till I saw trade in a regular way, though on a small scale. While I was with him he had another daughter born. This part of the country I greatly admired, it is so romantically beautiful. I staid at this pretty place till the commencement of the autumn when I returned to Horley.

During my stay Miss Ing wrote me of her intended marriage with a gentleman in London. This awakened my sentiments to a propensity to reside again in this pleasant, happy town. I made a proposition to Miss Ing for a share of the business but here appeared many queries about her disposing of the house, it not being her own, she was not at liberty to do, etc. and the business not being worth having without the situation I declined it altogether and turned my thoughts to keeping James's house at Findon.

In my way hither I came to Brighton early in October. My visit was to Mrs. Smith who, together with her son, made very much of me and was as proud to see me as though I had been a princess, principally on your accounts, I am sure. I staid with these kind people three days in which time I saw some of your old friends, one of which was Mr. West. He has an increasing family of a daughter. The old German I called on twice who expressed much honest heartfelt satisfaction at seeing the sister of one of the best friends he has in the world. I was at Mr. Scott's in St James Street with Mrs. Smith, who sat for her likeness. He has lately lost one of his sons of a consumption, he has one other son and a daughter who are ill of the same malady. I called also on Mr. Williams, he was well and begged kindly to be remembered to you. He has buried his sister near twelve months, after a long illness. Mrs. Panyhere and Mrs. Coningham, with their husbands and children, were in lodgings in North Street and at times were Mrs. S.'s visitors while I was there. The old lady has been for some time in a bad state of health. I think Vaughan a most forbidding, disagreeable man. I believe I have told you of all the persons I saw of your friends in B.

The generality of the people seemed much pleased to hear of you. I arrived in this village the day I left B. and have found myself very quiet, happy and comfortable in it since I have been a resident. I have not at all left it but by chance a day to Storrington which occurs seldom. James is in good health, looks well and grows lusty. He begs his affectionate love and says he does not write but hopes you will not think the worse of him on that account. He has written you two or three letters which you have never received.

With ardent hope and pleasure we wait the time of your return and the undescribable [sic] joy that will elate all here who are deeply interested at so gratifying a sight. May that happiness be ours as early in the spring as possible. I participate the pleasure of spending much time in your society and greatly hope I shall not be disappointed. We are all enjoying the blessing of good health and as my father is writing he will tell you all family circumstances.

I am, dear brothers,

Your most truly affectionate sister,

M. Constable

It seems odd that Mildred, aged twenty-six, should be so happy to be buried in this tiny country village. A second look reveals that John J. Purse, still working for her brother James, was probably the attraction, although he was some six years younger. Possibly her brother, James, knew about this but did not discourage the liaison particularly, perhaps because he also was involved in an affair of the heart.

The letter from their father contained news of the watermill that, following the expiration of the lease, had returned to him.

He told them that he had determined to wait until their return before making any decisions about it and that Charles, meantime, was working the mill with the assistance of an apprentice. James Sr. also told his sons about the business in Brasted for John. He added that Mildred had gone to help in setting everything up. Probably the most astonishing news his letter contained was that James had married Sophia Mansell, Benjamin's betrothed:

> Now I am going to give you the most interesting news. Your brother, James, has entered into the marriage state. Last Thursday only, the ceremony was performed at Horley in a very private manner. It is to Sophia Mansell, daughter of Mr. Ambrose Mansell of Horley. James came to our house on Tuesday and went to Mr. Mansell's the next day. A post chaise took them the next morning to church, their only attendants were the bride's father, Charles and Susan. As soon as the ceremony was over, they set off immediately for Horsham where they dined privately at the Anchor Inn, took tea and in the evening James, his bride and Susan set off for Storrington and Mr. Mansell and Charles returned home. James has agreed for the purchase of the premises where he lives and has begun to make some alterations and intends to take down the old part of the house (which is the shop and warehouse) and rebuild it.
>
> *Note:* Clearly, Sophia's heart was by now mended, enabling her to marry Benjamin's elder brother.

Daniel and William, meanwhile, finally left New York on the *Royal Mail* sailing ship, on 25 February. They had a fair passage, apart from two rather alarming incidents when they were pursued by unknown ships. One turned out to be a Royal Navy frigate but the other, being unidentifiable, they outran. This must have been a terrifying experience although they lived to tell the tale. They arrived in Falmouth on 21 March. They decided to walk home, sending their baggage on ahead by wagon. Their route home led them through Truro, Polperro, Plymouth, over Dartmoor to Cullompton, Wellington, Glastonbury, Bristol, Bath, Andover, Basingstoke, Guildford, Dorking and Leigh, finally arriving in Horley on 6 April, having covered some 300 miles on this last lap of their astonishing journey. In all they had travelled some 13,000 miles since their departure from London in May 1806.

There must have been a great welcome at Horley when they arrived after an absence of nearly two years. They found all well with their parents, their brothers and sisters, and they also found a growing band of nephews and nieces as John and Elizabeth had produced another daughter the preceding July, bringing their brood to two daughters and a son, and James's wife, Sophia, was expecting a baby in December.

CHAPTER SEVEN

William at Home

WILLIAM, BORN IN 1783, was the fourth son in the family. He was just twenty-five years old on his return from America in 1808. He was a handsome young man, much resembling his younger sister, Susanna. It seems he was a gentle character who revelled in the glorious countryside around him. Here he spent hours drawing and painting his favourite scenes. He was also fascinated by the concept of lithography which gave an extra dimension to his drawing.

It is likely that the whole family, fired with the tales that Daniel and William had to relate, must have discussed long and hard whether they should consider settling in the New World. However, relations between Great Britain and America remained strained, so any thought of travel was postponed for the time being.

A pressing problem was the question of the watermill, which was in an almost derelict state. There was probably much discussion before the decision was made to demolish the big, old mill in order to start afresh. The various family members made a good team, since James Sr. had many years' experience, Daniel was an excellent negotiator for the labour and materials needed, William had the expertise to make all the necessary drawings and plans, and Charles was young, strong and, no doubt, enthusiastic. It is probable the preparatory work to demolish the old structure began in the spring of 1809. The project was an ambitious one, including demolition of the existing brick and timber building and the construction of a three-storey wooden building. They also took apart the existing double waterwheels before reconstructing a massive, 18-foot, wooden one, in addition to all the other machinery required. When completed the mill was capable of grinding up to thirty loads a day, with storage available for a thousand sacks.

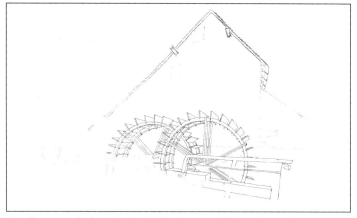

Double water wheels at Horley Mills drawn by William Constable before demolition c. 1810

By this time relations between Napoleon and Russia were becoming more and more strained and in 1810 William was enlisted into the local militia. Stationed in Kingston, Surrey, he wrote to Daniel on 18 May:

Dear Dan'l.,

I write today rather in compliance with your request than from having anything of importance to say, for a soldier's life in quarters is as monotonous and devoid of adventure as that of the most plodding mechanic.

The only thing which any way diversifies the lives of the local militia men here is the idle grace with which they brook restraint and the positive resistance which they make against receiving the shackles of a common soldier. The spirit of discontent which you witnessed in our company on Tuesday night has procured considerable mitigation in the severity of our drilling for we have never since been ordered out before breakfast, we have considerable time allowed us in the field and we commonly leave it something earlier. A more serious riot had like to have happened last night in which rank and file again came off victorious, by having their demand instantly complied with. It seems that a private of a battalion company was charged in the ranks, by a corporal, with being intoxicated and was immediately ordered by the commanding officer to the guard house. Two other men, knowing the accusation to be false, ventured to stand up in his defence and were likewise put in confinement with him for disrespectful behaviour to their officers. Immediately on dismissal from parade the battalion companies crowded round the guard house demanding the release of their comrades in a very clamorous manner, threatening to open it by violence if their demand was not instantly acceded to. A long and loud parley took place between men and officers in the course of which an officer drew his sword upon the soldiers who unanimously returned his compliment by charging on him all their bayonets. In the tumult which lasted about an hour no serious mischief happened. It was at length ended by the colonel.

Besides these occurrences, our lives remain unchequered by any variety in the drill lines which you saw us go through. We are to be reviewed on Tuesday next by some general officer. We have this morning been drawn out to hear a discourse in which much eloquence was expended to show the propriety and justice of bloodshed and war and in which we were called upon to be ready to practice its horrible rites by a professed disciple and humble follower of the peaceful, 'the meek and lowly Jesus'. I hope and trust it was heard with the contempt which it deserved.

I am just now going to Richmond to dine with Mr. Crespin and his mother. We have a rumour that we shall be discharged on Saturday next. I cannot answer for its truth.

Yours affectionately,

Wm. Constable

P.S. I wish you would get my clothes from Blacketts and leave them at the Queens Head in Southwark in case I should return by London with Crespin. I may want them on Sunday.

Note: Daniel, William and James Crespin had obviously sorted out any lingering ill-feeling since their precipitous parting while travelling together in 1806. Blacketts were linen drapers in Borough High Street.

William was back in the militia by May 1812, for the third year running. The Napoleonic wars were now raging across the

Channel; the British had occupied Madrid and the French were retreating. He wrote to Susanna from Kingston, where he was again stationed:

> My dear Susan,
>
> As I know it will give you pleasure to hear of my wellbeing I take the liberty of informing you that I am again equipped in all my finery and feel all the fine and sublime sensations which such beautiful trappings are calculated to inspire. I arrived on Tuesday at noon. I walked from London and have taken possession of my old quarters and I feel myself very snug in them.
>
> We have no new occurrences in the assembling of the local Militia, further than that we are led to hope this will be the last time of our meeting but there is a sad blot in the history of the regiment since last year. It is that one of our officers has made his entrance into the land of spirits, led by the ruthless hand of the common executioner, a degraded victim to the offended laws of his country; his crime was forgery.
>
> Richard Blundell has coaxed the Colonel to give him leave of absence; by his means I favoured this, he will return on Sunday. If you can spare me George for a day or two and he can travel with Richard, pray send him along. I shall be glad to show him all the fine things hereabouts and I doubt not he would be pleased.
>
> I find here all my old military acquaintance, among them Beal and Wilton. I enclose the cards that Wilton had for you when at Horley Mill last Sunday. They prove to be cards of business instead of compliments and one from Betsy to you with her love.

Mr. Crespin met me here on Tuesday on my arrival. Perhaps I shall see him again today. I shall dine with him on Sunday at Richmond.

I am intruding on the hour of drill and have only time to add that I feel myself very comfortable. I beg you to present my love to Mildred and all the rest and particularly to my dear little friend, Louise.

Believe me, dear Susan, thine very affectionately,

Wm. Constable

P.S. Half past one, afternoon. Just returned from a very easy drill. Ordered out at six tomorrow morning, am now clear for the remainder of the day.

Note: William's finery would have included a red coat with much gold braid, white breeches and a plumed hat. Richard Blundell, whom he mentions, was the son of George Blundell who had leased Horley Mill. The Blundells were neighbours and friends who lived in Ley Street; there would be a family connection through marriage before long. George Constable, the orphaned cousin, now aged fourteen, had returned from Storrington, being considered old enough to be useful in the Horley shop. He appears to have been treated as a poor relation, which was probably his position in the family. (This was not unusual for those days and certainly a better alternative than the workhouse.)

The mill had been completely reconstructed and was now a weather-boarded wooden building, three storeys high. The machinery had been overhauled and rebuilt where necessary. William made several paintings of the mill when it was finished, and these paintings were transferred on to several objects, such as small wooden boxes for trinkets, tin trays and so on, and the mill was obviously a source of much pride. In one of the paintings he shows a couple dressed in fashionable clothes, probably his parents, standing on the path beside the Mill House. Once the building was completed Daniel and William, with the help of Charles, ran the watermill between them. Millers had to be conversant with wood, engineering, grain and the mood of the river, so it was considered a superior trade. William worked as a grinder in the mill, as well as maintaining the machinery, which suited his engineering talents. He was responsible for dressing the stones (keeping the furrows well cut), using a special tool called a millbill. These had removable handles, came in different sizes, and were sharpened at both ends. They require sharpening every fifteen minutes. He was also responsible for altering the gap between the stones depending on the grade of flour required.

By the spring of 1813 William was able to leave the mill for some weeks while he took a journey through Derbyshire and the Peak District and on through Wales to Snowdon, accompanied by the ever-faithful Frank. The purpose of his trip was to make drawings of machinery for the Turton family, whose son was Daniel's great friend from Brighton days. He kept a journal of his trip and painted scenes that particularly struck him. He wrote to Daniel from Derby:

> Dear Dan'l.,
> A circumstance, with the unpleasant nature of which you are acquainted, keeps me this day a prisoner in Derby. It is that my box of clothes which was promised to be in Derby

last night arrives not 'till this afternoon and is inaccessible to me 'till tomorrow morning but the day has been so miserably bad that I hardly regret the event which confines me within doors.

I reached this town yesterday afternoon and have upon the whole (save this day's stoppage) made much about the headway I had calculated on. I made the first day 26 m., the second 32 m., the third 28 m., the fourth 28 m., and yesterday 16 m. I do not yet find myself a great deal wiser than when I started nor have the people or the things I have seen as yet sufficiently interested my feeling to repay the toils I have sustained but I now feel a happy exultation in the prospect before me and tomorrow I begin to reap the harvest of my labour.

I have hitherto kept to the Mail road, save in one instance when I left it to traverse the dreary waste of Chorley Forest. I was so unlucky as to have rain every step of my crossing it, otherwise I must have been delighted with its wild and rugged beauty. It is the twin brother of Dartmoor and having seen one you have a correct idea of the other. The beauty of the other parts of my walk has been of the calm and tranquil kind, smooth, soft scenery that one looks on with pleasure but which captivates not the soul.

30th May, Sunday, Matlock:

I had not the most distant idea at the time I began this letter that it would be so long ere I concluded it but I have seen a world of novelties and had a great deal to do. The calls of my attention have been so increasing that I have delayed from hour to hour and day to day, expecting a less occupied moment, 'till so much time has elapsed that I am now almost ashamed to write at all. Besides this not writing to you I have had my journalising ever since my arrival at Crich such a dead weight on my hands that I have seized every moment which has put a pen into my hands to bring up that business. I have worked at that all this day and find upon turning over the leaves that I have scribbled 21 pages today but I must compress my matter.

I have spent twelve days with the Turtons at Crich and Fritchley in the most agreeable manner, for though I have had a great many things pressing on me, they have all of them afforded me pleasure. I was known some distance as I descended the hill to the house at Fritchley where I found the whole family of the Turtons assembled at the tea table and where I experienced a most friendly reception. I worked very assiduously the first eight days, drawing machinery for Mr. Turton. I have since that been with him to Derby and many other places in the neighbourhood. All convenient opportunities I have considered it my duty to seize, to comfort and raise the depressed spirits of poor Mrs. Turton, whose great misfortunes lay very heavy on her heart. I have the satisfaction of being assured by her that my admonitions have been not altogether unavailing. I took my leave of the whole family yesterday; we had grown strangely into each other's good graces and our farewell was of that painful kind which is always experienced at the separations of those who love each other. Mrs. Turton and family will go to America very speedily, if possible, so will the whole family if Mr. T. consents.

I am staying here today principally on account of an accident which you will be sorry for. Poor Frank has been in a sad scrape; he has been in the jaws of a large dog twice as large as himself and came out again sadly lacerated in one of his legs, so as to make him very lame. Indeed, he travelled very dull the whole way to Derbyshire; his rest at Crich had greatly renovated him when two days before his time of renewing his journey came, he fell into the clutches of the ferocious beast who has almost disabled him from travelling at all. I think his wound is better today; I must try his strength again tomorrow.

Those who have visited this valley of the Derwent attempt to describe its beauties but they have been forced on me in a manner so unexpected that I have been astonished and enraptured at every step. The cliffs that bound the stream yield to none I have ever seen in beauty of sublimity. They would eclipse the majestic beauties of the Passaic were it not for its stupendous cataract. I shall start tomorrow for Castleton, thence thro' Dove Dale to the potteries and then hold on for Snowdon with all convenient speed, which place I hope to reach in a few days.

I have been thus far a true gangarid in practice tho' not in principle. I think it probable I shall now hold sound 'till I reach home. I long to know what is doing at Horley. Be so good as to write to me at the Post Office, Birmingham, which place I shall certainly pass as I return and I hope shall be there in a little more than a week. I shall write again shortly; you must excuse my slovenliness.

Your affectionate brother,

Wm. Constable

Mrs. Turton's misfortunes were indeed great. In October 1799 her eldest son, James, had died in New York from yellow fever. Her second son, Henry, had died just over a year later, also of a fever. As if this were not enough the cotton-spinning factory known as Fritchley Mill, in Crich, owned jointly by her husband and their third son, Thomas, had gone bankrupt and was auctioned, along with their house, on 3 March 1813, just before William arrived. The house was described in the Derby Mercury as follows:

> All that capital freehold stone built messuage, tenement or dwelling house, with stable and other outbuildings, yard, and extensive walled garden, well stocked with choice fruit trees in full bearing, and 10 acres of excellent arable, meadow and pasture land, comprised in four small fields lying in a ring fence, around the house.
> The above premises are in a compleat [sic] state of repair, fit for the occupation of a genteel family, and delightfully situated so as to command most extensive and picturesque views, and in the centre of a sporting country, only 12 miles from Derby and 3 from Matlock Bath.

No wonder Mrs. Turton was so upset. Sadly, she never went to America as she died less than a year later, in May 1814.

A week later, William wrote to Daniel again, this time from Caernarvon. Using his artist's eye and imagination he described the majestic countryside in which he found himself:

> Dear Dan'l.,
> I reached this town this afternoon full of hope of news from Horley but find not a syllable. I shall, as I have before said, expect to be favoured with a letter at Birmingham where I hope shortly to be, on my returning course.

Since I wrote you from Matlock I have seen a world of beautiful and romantic scenery. The north of Derbyshire affords an endless variety of the bold and beautiful; my route has been through Matlock to Castleton, thence through the high and absolutely naked part of the country, where the season is at least a month behind that of Surrey, to Dove Dale, through the potteries of Staffordshire, taking your route into Wales thro' the Vale of Llangollen, Corwen, Cerrigydruidion, Capel Curig and Snowdon to this place. I was equally delighted with the romantic beauties of the High Peaks, of the river Wye and of Dove Dale but I have not seen a spectacle more gratifying to me than that noble piece of aquatic architecture, the Aqueduct across the Vale of Llangollen. Bold and happy must have been the genius which gave birth to this noble design, equally striking for its simplicity, beauty, matchless grandeur and extensive usefulness. The work seems as happily executed as designed and its stability must enable it to withstand the tooth of time for many ages.

I was for a long time disappointed in my expectations of Wales. It was not 'till after I had passed the village of Cerrigydruidion a considerable distance that expectations were at all realised but on reaching the river Conway I found myself in the middle of scenery equalling my highest wrought conceptions. The great hills here rise in such profusion and so intimately, with a wretched sterility, as at once to gratify the sight. I travelled on thro' these desolate scenes where each mountain seems to view the other's improbable grandeur and yesterday afternoon, half past four, found myself at the footstool of the Prince of them all, the towering and far famed Snowdon.

I got a boy to start me on the right road and immediately

began to ascend the mountain. He led me about a tenth of the way up and gave me an excellent and clear direction by which I easily found the way to the top. I toiled with unremitting industry for three hours nearly, a steep ascent on loose stones, along craggy and terrific precipices, upon the margins of several beautiful lakes in basins in the mountain side. The labour and difficulties of ascending far exceeded my expectations; by increasing perseverance for nearly three hours I was enabled to surmount every rising difficulty and I beheld the proud honour of Snowdon whose aspiring head claims a place in the heavens, beneath my feet. I exulted in my victory and in the matchless scene which my victory had given to my view. I saw mountains piled on mountains in long perspective, lakes glittering in their bosoms and streams and rivulets winding their devious ways in every direction. A broad expanse of this high scene was for a while bewildering to the sight and I was some time before I could distinguish the ocean from the sky. I staid on the mountain 'till near sunset and then descending on the western side, coming to the road at a little turn saw the Snowdon Rangers House, a house of which I think I have heard you speak.

Poor Frank has mended beyond my hopes. He has lost his lameness and his wound will soon be well. The poor fellow seems to enjoy himself pretty well; he trots along generally close to me but has sometimes a little flow of spirits which displays itself in more lively and active motions. He is still weak in his loins but I think in that respect he is something better. For my own part I have much the same strength of body with which I started, though the flesh of animals has in no instance made a part of my food. I have a longing for dumpling and cabbage, which I reckon among one of the

blessings Horley Mill is to give me. I hope my absence has not occasioned any inconvenience at home. I feel that I have been a long while out and shall speed home as fast as I can. Your affectionate brother,
Wm. Constable

Note: At some stage Daniel had become totally vegetarian but William, although he went through periods of abstaining from eating flesh, was essentially a meat eater. Frank, the terrier, must have been getting on in years by this time, at least nine or ten years old but still a faithful traveller.

Once the watermill at Horley was running smoothly it was decided that Charles would manage the day-to-day operation, leaving Daniel and William free to pursue other careers.

William decided to pursue his surveying career, while still retaining his share of the watermill. John McAdam, surveyor to the Bristol Turnpike Trust, had recently patented his invention of crushed stone bound with gravel for surfacing the highways, and this had led to a spate of road improvements. William had also fallen in love with a beautiful red-headed girl, Jemima Mott, the niece of Daniel's old friend, William Radley Mott.

Jemima, born in 1786, was the eldest daughter of William and Martha Mott of Birmingham. She had had a traumatic childhood. Her father was a strong supporter of Dr. Joseph Priestley, the famous chemist, Unitarian Minister and social reformer. Dr. Priestley had his house and personal effects, including all his books, burned by a mob because of his support of the French Revolution, and his speeches against the Tory privileges, arrogance and greed all around him. By 1794 he found life in England untenable and he had emigrated to America to join his son. William Mott, together with his wife and young family, emigrated as well, but tragically within a year both he and his young wife contracted yellow fever and died. Robert Mott made the long and dangerous journey across the Atlantic to bring his brother's children home to England (with the exception of the eldest son who, at the age of thirteen, was considered old enough to make his own decisions, and remained in America). Jemima, aged eight, returned to Birmingham with her elder brother, Samuel, where they lived with the Sherwood family. As soon as she and her younger sister, Martha, were old enough, they moved to London to housekeep for their brother, Julius. Julius, however, became betrothed to Eliza Thompson, whose father felt that Jemima had too much of a worldly influence on her brother, so poor Jemima was forced to leave his house during the winter of 1813/14. In later years Eliza said that her father had been unjust to treat Jemima so harshly and the two became fast friends.

Daniel and William had met Jemima's eldest brother, William, in New York in January 1808, prior to their departure for England. They brought letters from him to his siblings. It was probably at this point that William met the young Jemima, then aged twenty.

Jemima wrote to her brother, Julius, on 9 January, 1815:

To my beloved brother,
According to my promise made to you sometime before I

left London, I have, my dear brother, to acquaint you that the ceremony in which our friend Wm. Constable and myself are to be made the principal characters is settled to take place at Brighton on Thursday next, the 11th inst. I should, my dear brother, feel peculiar pleasure in having you to present me to my future husband did not Uncle Rob't. object to my expecting you to pay us a visit for that purpose. He says it will be impossible for you to leave your business just at this time and that it is much too far for you to come on so trifling an occasion.

I received a letter from William the other day wherein he says he has rec'd. some of the things I left in London but that you had not sent the bed with them – but as you did not know, perhaps, that we should want it at Horley so soon, you thought some future opportunity of sending it might do as well; as we think of living at Horley in the course of a week after our union we will thank you to send it to the Half Moon at Borough, directed to Horley, where the waggoner will be told to inquire for it. I would not trouble you to send it on so short notice but as there is not any feather bed in the house I cannot go to Horley until that arrives.

We are all very well in health here.

With my best wishes for your health and happiness, believe me, my dear brother,

Your affectionate sister,

Jemima

There must have been feather beds at The Old Mill House, but perhaps not a spare one for William and Jemima. It may be imagined what Jemima's feelings were to read that her wedding was considered a trifle!

The wedding took place as planned, and the young couple set up home at Doversgreen, a hamlet between Horley and Reigate, in a house belonging to their friend, Richard Blundell.

CHAPTER EIGHT

Clio Rickman

BECAUSE OF HIS IMPORTANCE to the Constable family, and his influence in the thinking of the younger generation, the following background and information about Thomas Rickman, known as Clio, may be of interest.

Thomas Rickman was born into a Sussex Quaker family in 1761 and brought up in Lewes, Sussex. He was an old-fashioned radical, assuming the name of Clio, the Muse of History, and styling himself 'Citizen of the World'. As a young man he was a member of the Headstrong Club which met at the White Hart in Lewes. A fellow member of this organisation was Thomas Paine, at that time an exciseman in the town. The two became firm friends, although this landed Clio in tremendous trouble from time to time. For many years Clio was a bookseller and publisher in Marylebone High Street, and Thomas Paine lodged with him while writing his famous *Rights of Man*. Apart from sharing political beliefs Paine and Rickman both had a mechanical turn of mind and worked together on designs for iron bridges. Clio also patented a signal trumpet.

A description of Clio by Charles Fleet in his *Glimpses of our Sussex Ancestors*, 1882, reads:

How well do I recollect the feeling of awe and wonderment with which I first encountered the heavy brow and severe looking eyes beneath a low crowned, broad brimmed hat; with what astonishment I looked at his quaintly cut blue coat, with enormous brass buttons and square lappets, and from the pocket of one of which peeped the corner of a silk handkerchief, at which many generations of London thieves had pulled and tugged, and which was securely sewn with stout packing thread into the inner lining. That handkerchief was for show, the fellow one was for use, a huge coloured cotton one and it lay safely within the low crowned straw hat that covered that capacious brow.

The hat itself was a prodigy in the hat-way. It was a feat for us youngsters to lift it, or to try to lift it; for its weight was enormous, and was yearly increased by a pound of solid paint bestowed upon it. It was the whim of its wearer so to freshen it up. But he had another reason: namely to strengthen its powers of resistance to the blows of highwaymen (there were highwaymen in those days) or collision with mother earth. Men in those days, when they travelled, rode on horseback like men or in gigs like travellers. Stage coaches had not yet commenced their career and removed the responsibility of travelling singly in your own vehicle. Clio Rickman was a great traveller and he owed his life more than once to the strength of that straw hat, which had been shattered to pieces by a fall instead of his skull.

Clio was faithful all his life to the dress he had adopted as a young man: blue coat, yellow leather breeches and black top boots, together with a yellow straw hat. He must have cut a fantastical figure on the streets of Brighton and London. An educated man, with excellent command of French and the classics, he was a republican in politics and a kindly man by nature. On one occasion when Mr. Fleet, editor of the *Brighton Herald*, was gaoled for publishing comments on a certain class of man (officers) who, in his opinion offended the public, Clio took over the editorship of the paper, with the help of Mrs. Fleet. He also contributed a weekly column for this newspaper, which often included his poems.

Clio's first wife, Maria, died in 1784, less than two years after they were married. He and his second wife, Jane, had seven children, all their sons being named after Clio's heroes: Paine, Washington, Franklin, Rousseau, Petrarch and Volney. He kept a notebook full of anecdotes and quotations from letters he had received, ideas for poems, and so on. Under the title of 'mottoes' he jotted down the following: 'Love God and know nobody. Reason and no coercion. Truth and it only. Be just and leave consequences. Integrity is the best riches. Reason and independence. Elect to serve. Nothing is beautiful but truth. Truth alone is lovely. Be explicit. I don't like the motto "Fear God and honour the King". It is long since I did either. I could alter it to "Love God and honour no man".

Clio was under suspicion as an associate of Thomas Paine. In 1792 while in hiding for this reason he was protected for a night by Maria Fitzherbert (Maria Fitzherbert had secretly married the Prince of Wales). He was again in trouble in 1794 for publishing and selling Paine's *Rights of Man* and in 1802 underwent persecution for publishing the second part of Paine's book. This time he again fled to France, where, in Le Havre, he bade a sad farewell to Paine, who left Europe for America, never to return. In 1804 Clio was arrested yet again, although he was allowed bail; this time, however, all his books and papers were seized. His wife appealed for his possessions to be returned but was told: 'Serve you right, Mrs. Rickman, 'tis your own fault'. Clio wrote in his notebook:

> I write this at the moment of most severe suffering incurred by a Government prosecutor, brought on me by a vile perjured forgery committed informer and followed up by open cruelty and base treatment. It is on this account and with feelings like them that I cannot degrade God by any belief in hell or future punishment. Indeed to suppose this of a being who could prevent the crime instead of punishing it is with me impossible. Hell and the gallows have never done any good nor the threat of punishment here or hereafter.

In 1805 he wrote:

> It is often said and well said that virtue has its own reward for it seems to have no other. I fostered Paine in this country and lodged him and fed him at my board. The boasted principles of liberty I have day and night laboured alone to promote; the emancipation of my fellow men from

their oppression and miseries I have day and night, at all hazards, sacrificed everything to accomplish. At the end of this I am embarrassed and my family reduced to poverty because I have no support from those who affect the Cause I labour in.

Clio knew many of the influential people of his day, among them Horne Tooke and John Thelwall, eminent liberal politicians and founders of major reform groups, the Constitutional Society and the Corresponding Society; Mary Wollstonecraft, the writer and feminist; Benjamin West, well known artist and founder of the Royal Academy. Clio visited Benjamin West's house, where he saw 'the originals of *The Death of Wolfe*', and noted '*Nelson* just done'. He also saw '*The Landing of King William, Cromwell's Dissolving the Long Parliament, The Battle of the Boyne* and *La Hague*'. He found Mr. West simple and lively and they debated the progress of the abolition of slavery. One of Mr. West's grandfathers had been among the first emancipators of a slave, in the county of Westchester, New York. 'He shook me repeatedly by the hand, congratulating me on my 'Satire of Corruption', just out, appraising it highly for matter and manner. He said he would send a copy to Jefferson, the President of America. He gave me also, as usual for years, strong assurances of his regard for my principles and respect for my talents.'

Clio must have grieved sadly for his friend, Thomas Paine, when news of his death reached England in 1809. Thomas Paine had not forgotten Clio, however, as he bequeathed him part of his farm in New Rochelle.

By November 1810, Jane, Clio's wife, was seriously ill. Clio and his son, Volney, paid a visit to the Constable family in Horley. Volney, aged thirteen, wrote a note to Susanna, in beautiful copperplate writing:

> Dear Susan,
> My little effusion on Horley Mill I inscribe to you, with my kindest love and I am, dear Susan, with respects to the family,
> Your obliged,
> Volney Rickman

> *Far from the din of London's noise*
> *From scenes of wickedness and transient joys*
> *I hail sweet Horley Mill.*
>
> *There dwells warm hearts benign, and free*
> *There's wisdom, happiness and glee*
> *At quiet Horley Mill.*
>
> *Nature's rare beauties all around*
> *And love and friendship there abound*
> *At peaceful Horley Mill.*
>
> *Three charming brothers there you'll see,*
> *With minds expanded, noble, free,*
> *Such dwell at Horley Mill.*
>
> *Apart from all that's bad and vile*
> *From fashion's noise, commercials guile*
> *Is lovely Horley Mill.*

> *Oh may its inmates long be blest,*
> *With love, with labour, liberty and rest*
> *And happiness reside at Horley Mill.*

Tragically Volney was drowned just a year later. He and William had been sailing together when the boat capsized. In spite of William's efforts to keep Volney's head above water, he was unable to save him. Volney's body was swept away in the current. This must have been the last straw for Clio's wife, and she lost her fragile hold on life soon after.

Clio was desolate at her loss. He spent months every year travelling around the country and in 1812 he visited more than sixteen counties of England.

In 1813 Napoleon had been forced into exile and Louis XVIII was reinstated as king. However, encouraged by rumours of Louis's unpopularity Napoleon escaped from Elba and landed in France with 1500 men. Gathering up more supporters en route he entered Paris in triumph, forcing the king to take refuge in Holland. In April 1814 Clio wrote:

> That the harlequin General should leap from Elba to Paris as he did certainly could not be anticipated but that a revolution in France would happen in less than a year after Bonaparte was solo and the Bourbon nag bought, I have always said. From the commencement of the war I always asserted it could last 50 years. A republican Government in France would have circulated all Europe and made her happy but the Bonaparte is not what he ought to be. He is giving useful lessons to kings and their influence, and

Church craft, is upon the whole throughout the world diminishing. He has done France great service; the capital he has made healthy and tasty, twenty five times more the water than it used to have, he has conveyed there. Extensive granaries for corn, roads, canals, sciences, taste, a code of law excellent, the brilliant and useful arts, etc. and great things France is indebted to Bonaparte.

Impromptu for the Combined Kings.
The next time you get Bonaparte in your clutches
Do not put him, as boys do rabbits in hutches
To Nell, and not Elba has he dispatch
Lest again he should laughingly break thro' the hatch
But while this your doing, ye great Kingly crew
Take care that to hell, he does not send you.

By 1815, after long years of war, Clio claimed that half the population of Europe did not know what peace was and that war 'impoverishes, paralyses, poisons'. He felt that 'peace was far more likely to revolutionise and reform nations than war'.

As a consequence of the government's concern over the influence of Paine and his followers, they were now hounded by the press and public alike. In April 1817 Clio wrote in his notebook:

Mrs. Jukes of Newgate St. had my prints of Mr. Paine to sell and for months kept them in her window. In this month the silly stir of sedition etc., see the newspapers some months past and the history of the day. The Parson of the parish and other ruling persons in it obliged her to take the prints out of her window on pain of their displeasure and taking away their custom, etc. She, a widow, complied but told me had her husband been alive, he would have dammed them and sent them about their business.

Clio continued to experience personal misfortunate. Another of his sons, Clio Rousseau, died in 1817 and a year later another, Petrarch, was banished to Jamaica because of bad conduct. By Christmas time 1819, Clio was alone and rather maudlin:

> With my adored Jane passed many years of happy, blissful Christmases and some of these with a large family of children. It is nearly eight years since heaven called to itself its most deserving object and since Christmas Days have passed as I could get rid of them but never in any way approximating to happiness. Here I sit fallen off in circumstances, without a single companion. To weep bitterly in remembrance of the happy past, to spend the house in tearful retrospection of blissful days never to return. I have by this time four grown up boys and a girl, the latter, good and amiable as she is, untoward circumstances have driven from under my roof, and my boys are gone, tho' not all badly estranged from me while they seek not my company from me.

In 1822 Clio was yet again arrested on a charge of selling subversive literature, and spent a week in the Fleet Prison. After his release he stayed at Pillar Cottage as a guest of the Constable family. During the dry autumn of 1822 the river was unusually low, which was naturally disastrous for a watermill. In October he penned the following verses:

Chronicle of the House of Horley
And it came to pass in those days of great dryness
That William & Charles, of the House of Horley, waxed exceedingly
Wrath, inasmuch as their Mill could not grind.

And they would have money, even ten shillings an
hour, for torrents of rain to descend; but interest sways not the
Lord of torrents, and he bade the sun to shine, instead of bidding
the rain descend, as his wisdom saw meet.

And lo! the wandering Bard Clio from the great city, was
sojourning at the House of Horley, and he was poetizing, and
indulging in vain imaginations, heeding not whether it was
foul or fair.

And while he was in the midst of the idle delusions of his brain
He marvelled much, to hear the tempest without, and the
showers beat heavily against his casement.

Then did Charles and William, of the House of Horley, repent
them of their wrath, and became very humble, and thankful
before the Lord.

For the rain descended, and the floods, and flowed
into their river, the Mole and Lo! the Mill again made a great
noise, and much corn was ground.

Now did rejoicing take place at the House of Horley,
And its Millers were exceedingly glad, and even the profane
Bard Clio, exalted his voice in gratitude.

And it came to pass when he had ended his scribblings,
And as the Mill wheels went merrily round, the people were in
high spirits.

And the House of Horley assembled and slayed the Hogs
And Geese, and the Ducks, and the Chickens, and gathered
The fruit from the trees and partook largely thereof;
And songs of rejoicing were heard and much sweet sound.

And Lo! the profane bard joining in praising the Lord
With the House of Horley, and great joy was with them, and
much fiddling and dancing among the people.

In 1823 Clio again spent Christmas at Horley Mill, together with James Sr., Charles, George, and Susanna Jordan, this latter being a cousin from Charlwood: 'kept it up, sung, drank, smoked, spouted and played Christmas games and pranks'. Susanna Constable embroidered a purse for him and he wrote to thank her:

How sweet, when absent from those eyes whose ray
Beams on the soul, the heart makes right and gay,
Shedding a sunshine o'er the mind;
How sweet, when Susan's voice no more I hear,
That voice, ordain'd to fascinate and cheer,
Ever endearing, interesting, kind.

How sweet, when her dear form no more I see
When absence steals those eyes, that voice from me,
To view uncaptured, this memento bright;
A sacred talisman, its touch shall prove,
Its sight each feeling give, of truth and love,
Each sentiment of virtue and delight.

When woman, Susan! lovely girl! shall be
In mind as rich, in manners sweet as thee,
Then vice and folly blushing shall receive,

Her blast in such society as thine
In talents, manners, rectitude, shall shine
Shall worthy be thy name, be men indeed.

He added a postscript to the verses:

To your father revered, with thanks for his cheer,
To the Lass of the Mill, our Jordan so dear,
Present my best love, and my wishes sincere
To honest, fat Charles, my heartiest regard
For the Cousin of Horley! no dear of the Bard.

Heaven send me again to your coverts so snug
With my chair in the corner, my pipe and brown jug
And the next time I visit your lovely retreat
May no horrid bitters be mixt with my sweets;
No snake in your paradise suffer'd to be,
To hurl fell destruction on mine or on me.

Heaven prosper you all★, sincere in my prayers
And send me your smiles, hope our friendship to share
And in your blest haunts give the go-by to care.
★Including Pillar Cottage, of course.

The following year Clio yet again spent Christmas and New Year at Horley Mill, together with a large party including William and Jemima, Charles, Susanna and her beau, Henry Grece. In January 1825, before leaving for a long tour through the country, he wrote a note to Susanna, thanking her for his Christmas gift:

My dear Susan,
I return you many thanks for your kind present of the

socks. I will wear them in grateful remembrance of your many, many kindnesses and indulgences to me.

Mary Browne went away without my knowledge of her going, so that shake her by the hand I could not, nor say to her God bless you!, as I should have said it. 'Warm from the heart and faithful to its fires.' She has my best respects and sincerest regard. May we all meet again.

To your father, my particular esteem. To yourself, more than I can anyway express. You have long been sealed among my heart's best beloveds – a share is no happiness.

I do not pray for you.

Clio

P.S. I don't know that you will perceive any blue devilism about this, but yesterday and today I have been destroyed by it.

God bless you all! Shall I not see you, or some or you before I quit your country forever?

Clio

Note: Mary Browne was Henry Browne's niece (Henry Browne had been William's employer in Lewes) and Susanna's great friend. Mary's father, William, had failed in his business and his wife and children were taken in by members of the family. Some years later, his son, William, together with his mother and sisters, Eliza and Lucy, emigrated to Baltimore, Maryland. Mary was intending to join them.

In April 1826, however, Clio replied to a letter from Susanna in which he complained bitterly of her addressing him as 'Dear Sir', rather than 'Dear Clio'.

Dear Madam,

Now I suppose I must use this in reply to your Dear Sir! What the hell is the matter now? What is become of Clio, indeed Dear Clio and My Dear Clio I have seen for many years written by fair hands and pronounced by sweet lips.

Is this to be discontinued now when I most want cheering up, am I to lose things long delightful to my heart and soothing to my soul? No, no, my dear Susan meant not any annoyance to my feelings.

I have, indeed, Susan, traversed very widely by sea and land this long tour and I have seen sublime and more beautiful nature than ever I did, with few exceptions, at home or abroad. You shall hear about all this, and see my poetry about it, which heaven send may be soon.

Thanks for ever to Daniel! But for him I had never got any money from America. As to Carver, I was told long since he meant me foul play. What I did to him and to many, was to say, 'Get me the whole of my American legacy in a lump and I give you £100' but Carver never got me my legacy, and as to Webster and Radcliffe I have never known them in any way, or concerned with them. I see they have it in contemplation to rob me – damned agony – but my sheet anchor is Daniel Constable! Countless thanks to him!

I came to town in a very impoverished state so that the news of this money is most welcome but for reasons pure, good and political, that I get or have got any money from America, had better not be known. I hope Monday, when I shall be in, will bring me the money; and I beg, your bill may be sent receipted, and accounted in the payment.

And now, my old benediction

'God bless you all! best love to Charles, William and Jemima, to your father and kind remembrance to the

consorts about you who care for me, the Greces, kind and grateful respect. To yourself, my dear, dear Susan, my most affectionate regards and ardent prayers for every good, every happiness. Semper idem.
Clio

Note: The Grece family were fuller's earth merchants and farmers, who lived on the top of Redstone Hill, some four miles north of Horley Mill. Bearing in mind that Thomas Paine had died in 1809, it certainly took a long time for Clio's legacy to reach him. The wheels of the law did, indeed, grind exceeding slow, even in those days.

On the occasion of the centenary of the *Brighton Herald* (1906) W. Bartlett described Clio with affection:

men such as Clio Rickman, men whose names should be regarded with affection by every lover of liberty and progress. They were men, indeed, of hearts, talents and enthusiasm. Clio Rickman, in a way that was characteristic of him, came to the assistance of the Brighton Herald when it most needed assistance. That is what one would expect of the friend of Thomas Paine, the genial poet and the equally genial bookseller of Marylebone.

From the tone of his letters there is no doubt that Clio had fallen on rather hard times. The Constable family, among others, supplied Clio with tobacco and other small luxuries. Apparently he retained one room in Marylebone, to which he retreated, like an old lion to its den, when he was too infirm to travel. He had kept, too, his treasured possession, the table on which Thomas Paine had written *The Rights of Man*.

Clio Rickman died in his sleep on 15 February 1834 and was buried in the Quaker burial grounds at Bunhill Fields.

CHAPTER NINE

James The Country Gentleman

JAMES, BORN IN 1777, was the second Constable son. James was a sportsman, excelling in games while young, and growing up to be a passionate huntsman, fisherman and shot. While his brothers were in America his business in Storrington and the branch store in Findon, three miles away, had become very successful. He began to acquire other property in the town of Storrington. After his marriage, in 1807, to Sophia Mansell, he virtually rebuilt the house attached to the shop.

During the next six years James and Sophia had four children: Matilda was born in December 1808, Charles in August 1810, James (who became known as Jemmy) in August 1812 and Clara in October 1814. When each child was born Susanna, James's younger sister, moved to Storrington for several months in order to help. About this time James bought a farm just outside Storrington, a small estate, and spent all his spare time hunting and shooting snipe, and other game.

In May 1815 Susanna was still in Storrington when tragedy struck the family, as we learn from this letter written by William:

Dear Dan'l.,

A most shocking circumstance communicated within this hour from Storrington occasions me to write. The unfortunate Sophia is no more.

Painful as is the task of relating circumstances which will impress you with the most acute sorrow, truth compels me to add that she has been her own destroyer. She found an opportunity of perpetrating the dreadful act this morning, between six and seven, by suspending herself by the neck. Susan writes the intelligence but is unable to give any reason for so rash a deed. It does not appear that any circumstance had led to the least apprehension of such an event. You will, of course, return home as speedily as possible. Mother is made acquainted with it. I hope she will bear the event with tolerable fortitude but I am full of fears for poor Mr. and Mrs. Mansell who I am just going to.

Yours affectionately,

Wm. Constable.

P.S. Will you be good enough to inform Mildred of the circumstance. You will, of course, do it through the medium of Purse.

Reigate, 8 o'clock. I am come here in hopes of finding Mr. Mansell here, it being Fair Day, but find he is gone home. Mr. Thomas Mansell will go to the house with me. I shudder at the scene I must appear in.

William was not exaggerating the appalling scene he would provoke in telling the Mansell parents that their only child had died by her own hand.

Because Sophia was unable to be buried in consecrated ground, her parents bought a small piece of land just outside the graveyard at Horley, beyond the old yew tree, and there they buried their only child. However, her name and dates are defiantly engraved on the Constable family vault in the churchyard.

A family story, handed down in identical form through the family on both sides of the Atlantic, has it that James Constable Jr. fathered an illegitimate son at this time, and that Sophia had come to learn of it. The story tells of a baby being left under a tree in their garden. Even if there is some truth in this story it should also be remembered that Sophia had quite recently given birth to her own child, so that she was in a vulnerable frame of mind. It is obvious that some sort of extreme mental anguish led her to commit this desperate act. Susanna remained in Storrington and became surrogate mother to the young family, thus sacrificing much of her youth. Nobody knows Susanna's feelings on the subject, but it seems that she was sympathetic to Sophia. Since Susanna's son was later to name his only daughter after Sophia, it is probable that she and Susanna had become firm friends.

Many years later Jemmy wrote a memoir of his life, which was included in a privately printed book about the American side of the family:

> My mother died when I was under three years old, consequently I never knew a mother's care. My father had a branch store at Findon, about four miles from Storrington, that was conducted by two ladies and I resided a great part of my time with them. It was here that I was first breeched and I remember well the first suit of boy's

clothes I had, the letters on the buttons had FF on them for Findon Foxhounds, a pack of which were kept in the neighbourhood. I was sometimes at Storrington but more frequently at Findon. I was not very fond of study and I recollect more than once being pinned by my pinafore to one of the lady's dresses because I would not stay still whilst saying my lessons. My grandfather and grandmother Mansell had retired from Horley, where he was a farmer, to Reigate; one or the other of us children were usually with them.

Susanna was now twenty-five years old and it must have been an enormous responsibility to be a surrogate mother to her brother's four young children, ranging in age from seven years to under a year old, even with all the help that Mr. and Mrs. Mansell were able to give. Clara, 'Tinney', seemed to be a great favourite of the whole family; she was less than a year old when her mother died. There is still in the family a small, painted, round box on which is written 'Clara Constable 10 Oct'r 1814'. This was Clara's christening date. Was it Daniel who carved the box and perhaps Matilda who added the decoration and the words, written in a childish hand?

During the next few years Charles and Jemmy moved to live with their grandparents in Reigate, where they attended school. Susanna stayed in Storrington until she was needed at home, by which time little Clara was old enough to be sent to school herself.

By 1823 James's two sons, Charles, aged thirteen, and Jemmy, aged eleven, had left Mr. Barker's school in Reigate and moved to Mr. Gannell's School in Pulborough, about five miles from Storrington. They were day pupils in the summer half and boarders during the winter.

Byne House, Storrington, home of James Jr.

Mercy Mansell, James's mother-in-law, died in April 1825, probably worn out with the care she had given her grandchildren after her daughter's premature death. Matilda was now a young lady of eighteen, the two boys, Charles and Jemmy, sixteen and fourteen, were fast growing up, and little Clara was twelve.

James never remarried, appearing quite content with his growing brood and his love of field sports. A boy called John Maple was apprenticed to James Sr. at the Horley shop and when his apprenticeship finished it was James Sr. and James of Storrington who put up the capital he needed to start his own business. This business was destined to become a household name: the furniture store, Maples. John's father, William Maple, died when John was a year old, leaving his mother, Hannah, with two small children. It is quite possible that James, a kindly man, gave Hannah employment, either at home or at the shop, thus enabling her to keep her children.

CHAPTER TEN

Daniel at Home

IT IS LIKELY THAT DANIEL attended Mildred's wedding in the summer of 1809 before he left for a walking tour around England, Scotland and Wales. Was this to find out how the provincial reform groups were progressing? En route he no doubt visited the Turton family in Crich, Derbyshire. Of his visit to Scotland Clio Rickman noted:

> My friend, Daniel Constable, met the Reverend Joey Paisley of Springfield, near Gretna Green, on the 15th Sept., drank five half pints of brandy by himself. He was 76 years old, had officiated at Springfield 50 years and often drank 3 bottles of brandy in a day. He was a hearty old man with a face free from pimples and clean complexion and exclaimed, 'Sir, this head of mine never aches'. He admired the works of Mr. Paine and desired if ever Mr. Constable saw him again he would tell him the old Scottish priest could beat him in drinking Brandy.
>
> *Note:* Was Daniel revisiting the place to where his parents had tried to elope?

In the spring of 1810 it is likely that the watermill renovations began. Daniel was still in touch with his erstwhile travel companion, James Crespin, at that time lodging in Brighton and keen to return to America. He wrote to Daniel in April 1811, feeling rather restless and unhappy with life:

> Dear Sir,
>
> Brighton at first did not agree with me and I was quite unwell for two or three days, tho' I am now very well and pass my time agreeably in Mr. Mott's company. Yet with respect to this town I never was in one I so disliked. What could make it so resorted to as it is every summer I was unable to conceive until I considered that those who come from London to loiter their time here do it in dancing, drinking and gambling and sporting their figures on the Parades, which may amuse them independent of any beauty in the place. But to I who am not in that line and can do none of those things the sea is the only object that is pleasing and I have been in many places in which it was much more so. On the other side, the hills without a single tree are so devilish dreary that I should not have had courage to go on the top but to go down the other side, but Mr. Mott with whom I walk before breakfast in the morning, has led me over them and we converse on the subject of politics, on which he has a great deal to say and on the comparison between this country and America. But for this entertainment, our walks would be much shorter. He has engaged me a very good apartment which I like the better for being out of the town. It is near a Crescent at the east end but principally I like it on the same principle that Dr. Johnson did the prospect in Scotland, because he could

see the road to London.

About going to America, Mr. Mott says that, after a full consideration, he thinks the balance of advantage is on the side of staying here, that unless you come down and can turn his opinion he is a lost man from the gang. He is at present too much occupied to come for you and thinks it a very hard case that he can't get you down without travelling so many miles to fetch you and I think so, too. We desire to know when you will come, so say. We want you here, to take into consideration a plan of going over to Jersey, that is the place he and I have concluded it best to go and settle in.

Jas. Crespin.

Note: Although James Crespin declared himself so interested in politics, he does not seem to take into account the uneasy relationship between Great Britain and America at this time, not to mention the wars raging across the channel.

His reference to the South Downs is interesting in that these hills inspire much affection from those familiar with their gentle rounded outlines, their wooded lower slopes and their myriad ancient pathways. To strangers, however, they can sometimes appear treeless and inhospitable.

The Mr. Mott referred to was undoubtedly William Radley Mott, Jemima's uncle, recently qualified as a surgeon. William Mott, Daniel and William Constable were great friends. William Mott became a leading citizen of Brighton and in 1809 the *Brighton Herald* reported that he addressed the citizens of the town regarding street lighting, etc., with great eloquence and that his proposals were carried unanimously. He also designed a way of heating sea water in the public baths, most innovative for the times.

A few days after this James Crespin wrote again, obviously disappointed that Daniel had not been to Brighton as planned, but still hoping to see him and to persuade him to be one of their party, even if their destination was Jersey rather than America:

> I have seen Mr. Whilms and his Spring Cupboard and other curiosities. I think he would be likely to make one of the transatlantic company if it was gone on with but it seems at present to go on but slowly. When you come you must bring your best persuading tackle for you will find a good deal of opposition and you must prepare yourself with better objections and more logical reasoning against our intended expedition to Jersey than that it is neither French nor English. This we conceive to be the best circumstance belonging to it: as being between the two neither dares show the cloven foot there. That to which it is said to belong cannot tyrannise there yet it is still of sufficient consequence to be worth their while to protect. It is surprising that men in your situation being placed so remote from the seat of prejudice should think of attaching so much importance to names, as to despise a land which for many years has been free from the invasions of the taxing man merely because it has not a name among nations.
>
> We thought a chimney corner at Horley Mill more favourable to correct thinking but begin to fear its inhabitants have twists in their heads like other people. Instead of my getting any nearer towards persuading anyone here to go to America they are trying to persuade me not to go but in that they cannot succeed but have actually frightened Mrs. C. out of it. Pray come and help us out of this hobble.

Although Daniel was also very keen to return to America, he no doubt saw the foolhardiness of venturing on the high seas during the current political situation. Perhaps he was able to dissuade James Crespin from any impetuous enterprise.

The watermill project was probably finished during the summer of 1812. As mentioned earlier William and Daniel worked in the mill until everything was running smoothly. Daniel's role was that of mealman (a broker colloquially known as a 'badger'), buyer and seller of corn and wheat on behalf of the farmers on the one hand and the market on the other. A business card belonging to Daniel survives, obviously drawn by William and probably printed by Clio Rickman, which shows the newly restored mill building.

Horley Mill after reconstruction c.1812 by W. Constable

It was probably in 1813 that Daniel decided to go into partnership with William Butler, a chemist and druggist with a property in Southwark High Street. William Butler had begun his business in 1805 and Daniel was to join him as a tea broker. He therefore moved to Charterhouse Gardens in London, where he probably lodged with the Butler family, and in 1814 the firm of Butler and Constable opened its doors. Butler and Constable were described in the various trade directories as being 'chymists, druggists and tea brokers'. It was not far removed from Daniel's job at the mill, except that the commodities were obviously tea and drugs, rather than corn and wheat. He could satisfy his wanderlust by travelling over the country to buy, no doubt taking the opportunity to call in on the various radical groups that survived in most of the larger towns and cities.

Daniel always felt the responsibility of being the eldest of the children. He kept a close eye on his younger siblings and offered help and advice when needed. There is little doubt that Daniel still yearned to return to America, a country seen to have a much more liberal attitude than their own. Daniel and his friends were true republicans in their outlook and believed that many of the evils in their own country were caused by the corruption of the monarchy, the church and the government.

CHAPTER ELEVEN

Mildred The Pioneer

MILDRED WAS THE ELDER DAUGHTER in the family, born in 1781, and probably a welcome addition after three boys. She was a striking looking, dark-haired girl with a strong resemblance to her father.

Mildred had spent her youth helping out with her brothers' families. She had returned to Findon in the summer of 1808, where she ran her brother James's branch store. In her letters she appears oddly content to be living in this tiny hamlet buried at the foot of the South Downs. However, it seems that romance was in the air. The tall, rugged looking John Purse, whom she had met in Storrington, was the attraction.

It seems likely that John and Mildred married in the summer of 1809. It was probably around this time that John started his own business in Havant, Hampshire. Havant was situated on the main coaching route and was also near the teeming docks of Portsmouth. William designed a map card for John and Mildred similar to the one that had advertised the business in North Street, Brighton. The card advertises John Purse as a Linen Draper, Hosier and Haberdasher. However, times were hard as always in times of war and John stated firmly on the card that his terms were 'For Ready Money Only'.

John Purse's map card of Havant, Hants, by William Constable c. 1812

In the spring of 1810 Mildred returned to Horley. Here, on 4 April, she gave birth to their daughter, Emma Rowena. Although John Purse is recorded as owning a cottage in Horley this was probably a wedding gift to Mildred from her father. It should be remembered that at this time women were not allowed by law to own property after marriage.

When peace was finally declared in 1815 (after the Battle of Waterloo on 18 June), poverty was widespread and no doubt the Purse family, like many others, struggled to survive. Daniel's enthusiasm for the New World had undoubtedly fired Mildred's imagination. John probably agreed that they would have a better life in America. Perhaps the appalling events at Peterloo on 16

August 1819 were the final straw (when innocent men, women and children were mown down after a peaceable demonstration). It is also possible that their business in Havant failed altogether as it is evident that they had to borrow money from William and Charles in order to emigrate.

In the late summer of 1819 John, Mildred and Emma Purse set sail for America, full of enthusiasm. Emma was now nine years old. They were to settle in the south-western corner of Indiana, still known as The Wilderness, on the banks of the Ohio. A small community of English people was already established in the area. Among her possessions Mildred took with her a small wooden box, made by Daniel and decorated by William with a painting of Horley Mill. She also took a painting of Horley Mill, showing the property before the recent alterations. No doubt Daniel promised he would follow as soon as he could wind up his affairs in England, which, inevitably, took rather longer than planned.

It is clear from their letters that, after their long, dangerous sea voyage and subsequent equally long, tiring journey to the banks of the Ohio, John and Mildred found Indiana, in its native state, much wilder than they had imagined. John was essentially a Londoner, and he found the work of clearing the land backbreaking, and was plagued by the insects that feasted on the new blood. Mildred also found the heat excessive and herself prone to lassitude. According to W. M. Cockrum's *Pioneer History of Indiana* this lassitude or 'tire' as it was called was a common complaint of the settlers, not many of them realising it was a medical condition. It seems likely that it was transmitted through milk. Unfortunately the Purse family arrived just as three consecutive years of fever started. Apparently many of the country towns were depopulated. John and Mildred also both found the other people on the settlement quite unfriendly, coming as they did from the big circle of extended family and friends.

Mildred clearly had an exceedingly nasty shock when she arrived in Indiana, after having left on a wave of euphoria. The country was wild and untamed. They had to make a clearing on which to build a log cabin, then laboriously cut down the trees and finally pull out all the stumps before they could sow their crops. They had no fences, so any livestock they purchased soon vanished into the virgin forest around them. John, although obviously a hard-working man, lacked the essential knowledge needed to wrest a living from the soil. Emma was old enough to help with the chores, but no other babies arrived to swell the ranks, and the little family must often have regretted the decision they had made to leave England. Mildred, particularly, must have often thought longingly of the Great Parlour at Tedhams, and the comforts she had been used to. She had not grown up accustomed to doing the heavy work in a house, let alone settling land, and it is evident that she suffered enormously, although she never gave up.

Mrs. Constable had been very concerned about Mildred's venture to America, not just because she would lose her elder daughter but also because she had grave doubts that Mildred's physical and mental health would stand up to the difficulties ahead. In this she was probably right to have her doubts, but sadly by the winter of 1819 her own health was deteriorating. She died in May 1820, much mourned by her husband and children.

Mildred must have been devastated when news of her mother's death finally reached the wilds of Indiana.

By the end of 1819 the English reform movement was in a state of collapse, which is perhaps why life in America beckoned. Daniel finally arrived in New York in the late summer of 1820. There he spent the winter, leading a pleasant life, catching up with his friends, lounging in the coffee houses of the city and, no doubt, spending long hours discussing politics with like-minded friends. As is evident from his letters and journal entries of this time Daniel was beginning to get slightly disenchanted with America; his first flush of enthusiasm for the New World was wearing thin. He was beginning to realise how much he and his sister missed the rest of the big, closely knit family and that it was not that easy to simply change countries leaving behind everything dear and familiar. Perhaps he was even a little lonely.

In January 1821, he left New York and started his journey to Indiana to see John, Mildred and Emma. Armed with seeds and various other articles brought from England, he walked via Philadelphia to Baltimore, a distance of nearly 200 miles. From here he wrote to his father and complained, as all travellers complain, of the lack of news from home. He told of his return visit to the Falls of Passaic and how much they had changed, of the large brick buildings of the town of Patterson. He also told of spending the day with Joseph Bonaparte (this was Napoleon's elder brother, the ex-King of Spain), saying he was a fine, large, lively man, much liked in Bordentown. Daniel mentioned in this letter that he had heard that Mildred was getting better reconciled to life in Indiana, which was not strictly true.

Having travelled along the new turnpike to Pittsburgh, a big improvement on the old rough road, and along the Ohio River, Daniel finally arrived in Evansville. Here he spent the autumn and winter with the struggling little family, no doubt working alongside John Purse on the land, and spending time giving his sister help and encouragement. He built an outdoor oven for her and no doubt made many improvements about the place. She must have been delighted to have her favourite elder brother staying for so long. Perhaps it was during this time that Daniel realised that Evansville was as yet too primitive for the Purse family.

In the spring Daniel took his leave of John and Mildred and journeyed on down the Ohio and Mississippi rivers to New Orleans. From here he travelled by sea back to New York. Upon his return to New York Daniel wrote home to Horley, enclosing John and Mildred's letters, from which it can be seen that they were already hoping to leave Indiana:

Dr. Sr.,

Our affairs jog on about as usual, much hard work and but little recompense, many things to worry and some few to gratify. The ticks are biting as spiteful as ever and the wetness of the season promises a plenty crop of mosquitoes. Vegetation is full three weeks earlier than at this time last year; many of the peach trees we planted have bloom on them, the apple scions from Black River are most of them alive, the currant slips from Harmonie are generally in leaf. I planted them in a nursery as soon as the frost broke. Of the grape vines there are but thirteen living and of all the fruit stones you brought for me from Horley but one (a Black Heart) has yet made its appearance. A cherry tree you brought from Pittsburgh is very flourishing; it is evidently different from any cherry in this neighbourhood. The old cow, Matt, died in the cane but all the rest came out safe and fat. We milk but one cow yet, a young one with her first calf but expect another to calve daily. I am likely to have all my ploughing, hoeing, etc., to do, except a little piece Barker has put in Flax, all we could get seed for.

Jas. Maidlow intends moving to Baltimore in a few weeks. He intended going sooner but has been detained in consequence of his wife's confinement; they have got another son. His object there is to be a manager or overseer. I understand these places are often to be had with from $200 to $600 per year and does not require first rate farming knowledge. J. M. will write me from Baltimore more perticularly [sic] about it. Something I must do; money will slip away in spite of everything and you well know here are no means of bringing any in. The money I owe William and Charles troubles me; I know they must want it in use. If I do not get a favourable account from Jas. Maidlow I shall make a trip to N. Orleans in the fall. When at Harmonie I visited all the work shops and factories, everybody seemed pleased to hear of you and wished to know if it was likely you would ever come again to see them.

I met with Mr. Rapp just out of the town, he was perticularly [sic] pleased to hear of you and with your favourite, Rachel, for an interpreter, we had a long talk. I thanked him for all the currant trees he gave you and told him they were all growing at which he expressed satisfaction and said they would make good wine. Their wheat is so strong, they have mowed and carried to the town about 100 waggon loads to feed the calves. They have laid the foundations and made some farther progress with a new stone church in the rear of the old one. For ornamental pillars they are turning Sassafrass and Cherry trees, which are of so large a growth they will square eighteen inches, 28 feet from the butt end.

John Purse

Mildred added a few lines to her husband's letter:

Dear Daniel,

I work out some little on the land. From inability I can't do the things I wish to do and suffer from tire much as I used to do last summer when I am fretful and peevish but you need not this be told. Purse can give me a character for things of this sort, if required. I think if we were where there was less to do I should be more calm.

As regards leaving this spot of land, my sentiments are no way changed. When we can change to advantage, with a prospect of being more comfortable, I shall escape from this with pleasure. If it is a fault to wish to be nearer my own people, I acknowledge this fault. Here is nobody in this settlement that will do us a neighbourly turn or that we need to care about. Disputes run higher and quarrels more frequent and violent than when you left. To the best of my knowledge we have so far escaped them.

I hope you will find at New York letters from our dear English friends. It gives me pleasure to find by Charles's and Susan's letter which we forwarded to you a few days since that they are all well.

Mildred

Note: James Maidlow, the friend of Mildred and James in whom they rested their hopes, started a market garden near Baltimore which became a successful business. He and his family remained there, although for some reason the Purses decided not to join him. George Rapp had founded a Protestant sect in his native Germany, but had moved to America to escape religious persecution. In 1815 the group had moved to Indiana and established the town of New Harmony. However, many of the members found both the climate and frontier life too hard, and left the society. The Rapp religious philosophy was essentially that no property should be independently owned, new members should be on a three month probation period, there should be no marriage since they did not believe in carnal increase, errors committed would be pointed out by a brother or sister, etc. Their main studies were 'to find out the fall of Adam fundamentally within us which will cause us to hold Jesus Christ for ever indispensably necessary as the mediator, in whom are lying profusely all treasures of wisdom and knowledge'.

How the Rapp society thought they would survive is not clear since they did not allow marriage or carnal increase.

Mildred had obviously not heard from Daniel when she wrote her previous letter as she wrote again barely a month later, a letter which he also forwarded to the family at Horley:

Dr. Daniel,
Welcome, most welcome was your letter which brought us the desired intelligence of your safe arrival at New York. We had great anxiety for your well doing on your voyage but

little thought the misery you were enveloped in. Your Captain's cruelty was beyond endurance; when the thought comes across me I have not patience to think with calmness. I have often thought the independence which is so much this country's boast and pride is greatly abused and under some circumstances a serious evil. Ourselves have suffered from it by the insolence of those whose savage ignorance has misled them to mistake the former for independence.

Your troubles and mortifications made me, for a time, forget my own of which I have this spring a pretty large share. The wetness of the season has thrown us into the background with our planting. We have now partly planted, with our fields yet in weeds and the mosquitoes so great an annoyance that we can scarce work more than half the day. The heat has set in and I have, to use an American phrase, backed out of field work. Poor Em follows it daily with sore feet and often without shoes or stockings. I have put her into trowsers [sic] to save her from mosquitoes, myself wearing the same and this a poor defense against such terrible rapacious invaders. They drive us sometimes almost to madness; we wear more clothes than we know how to carry about and keep constant smokes within and outside the house. Poor Purse is more molested by them than anybody else that we hear of. What this venomous insect is directed to torment us for is what I can't think how to account for.

We have been living all the winter until the present time upon corn, saving our little wheat for summer use. We have had one outdoors baking (thanks to you and your oven) which we shall continue as long as the wheat lasts.

You say I am to write you things as they are. What can have changed your sentiments as regards some things respecting this country is not for me to judge but that such change has taken place in your mind, from a train of thinking and perhaps some experience, I cannot dispute. It is a subject whenever I go into I shall always be honest enough to express what I feel and say what I think. No fear of ridicule can intimidate me. I acknowledge my expressions have been strongly marked by dislike, contempt and disgust and have felt, perhaps, what others could not feel. I have indeed a great deal of torture in mind and body and am out of spirits this spring. As to succeeding on this farm, then I have been before and am, heartsick of this turmoiling life, with the rigours of the season calculated to injure comfort to feeble body.

Purse says he shall go to New Orleans in the autumn. I could not object to this if I could see how he will dispose of me. I cannot stay here alone; I shall be in fear of the Hooker gang, who are indeed great rogues. With the folks I am on terms as usual; I continue to think well of Mrs. Barker.

Our colts have deserted us. We got them home once from a distance of eight or nine miles but they did not stop with us more than three or four days. Pegg has a beautiful foal of nine days old; this may appear an odd expression but I esteem our domestic animals more than any of the humans about and see but little to admire in animated nature but the humming bird. Early in March we did considerable gardening but eight weeks of rain have thrown it into weeds and ruin.

I am indeed interested in whatever may please and delight you in the east or northeast part of this continent and hope one day I may see some of these good things myself. Our grateful thanks at all times to you for past kindness and future offers. I should have been glad indeed if good news from home had accompanied your letter. I am always in dread I shall hear something unwelcome of our dear father. He is much in years now and so many of his neighbours are gone before him. We hope you have letters from England. We are very sorry to hear of the distress of our countrymen. We have not written home since the letter you took to N. Orleans; you can transcribe any part of this if you think it proper. We cannot write there. Purse says if fortune changes about he will write for the present and the past.

Mildred

John Purse attached a few lines of his own to Mildred's letter:

Dr. Sir,

Since the annexed was written a relation of the Ungets is come to this country from Washington on the representations or rather misrepresentations of old Henson, who had him to understand he might do so much better here than there. To this man I have let off about 4 acres of land on shares and have been sometime assisting him to get it planted which is now completed. Owing to this, my own crop has been much neglected. I hope a few days will make a considerable appearance in it. This person whose name is Earl, seems something above the cut of an English labourer, steady and sober and I hope, honest and pretty conversant in farming business. We have been talking on the subject of his taking the farm but this requires some further consideration. If this should be the case I think we must try our fortune near some of the eastern cities. Jas. Maidlow is not yet gone. I should have been glad to have heard from him previous to coming to any conclusion with Earl. Perhaps you may meet with something more eligible in your travels, that may suit us better than the pursuit that

J.M. is upon?

Of all the cherry stones one only is growing, the rest having rotted in the ground. A few goose berries and currants from the seed are growing, several have died off. I have often thought of the observation you made; the want of benevolence in the system around us where one thing gives pleasure, fifty conspire to torment. I have planted and replanted corn four and five times in the same place and after all a fifth part is taken up by the partridges and this work has been done in the greatest misery from mosquitoes. The air has been literally full of these tormenting insects. Another torment has been in the neighbourhood that I have escaped, called the army worm. They are a kind of caterpillar that eat up everything in their way; they have destroyed a considerable quantity of grass and wheat and rye for Maidlow, who has been the greatest sufferer. The wheat is blighted worse than last year.

J. Purse

P.S. If I agree with Earl as the probability I shall, a part of the livestock will be left with him on Peck's security. I think I like the man. Should this prove the case he will have a three year lease and we shall be turning our thoughts eastward. Of this I will write you again as soon as settled. Violet is now working by the side of Fran and makes a good plow [sic] beast.

In the summer of 1822 Daniel left New York for Boston, Providence and Rhode Island. By this time he fully agreed that John and Mildred were right in their decision to leave Indiana. Whether it was his idea in the first place, or theirs, to settle in Indiana, is not documented. He now had thoughts that perhaps they would like Providence or Rhode Island and that maybe John Purse could find a congenial pursuit among the manufactories of the area.

In December Daniel again wrote to Susanna, saying that he had forwarded William's letter to James and Mildred Purse. From William's letter he had learnt that George Constable had gone into business with a Mr. Postlethwaite from Storrington but the affair had foundered, leaving some bad feeling. Daniel now had the idea that perhaps John Purse could take over this business, thus solving two family problems.

Yet another rather sad letter from the Purse family was sent on to England from Daniel. Things were indeed in a bad way if Mildred felt unable to write directly to her family at home.

> Dear Sir,
>
> We have been sometime anxiously expecting a letter from you, the more perticularly [sic] as we hear such distressing accounts of Yellow Fever from N. York and other places, yet we hope you have not ventured near the places where the disease prevailed. I have often enquired for newspapers at the Post Office but have got none since your letter. A paper occasionally would have enabled us to ascertain where you were. We have had no letter or intelligence from England since those you transcribed for us except the letter per Mr. Wheeler.
>
> When I last wrote I told you I was in treaty with a man for the lease of the farm and that I would write you again as soon as settled. It has been settled a very short time only

and is come to nothing. In the first place Peck refused to go security, according to his promise so we then made other arrangements and altered the conditions. The contracts were made and ready for signing when he [Earl] altered his mind and backed out entirely. He has been living in the stable and working on the plantation all summer, yet the crop is by far the worst I ever had. If he had never been here I should have done better.

The affairs of the settlement go on about as usual, both with ourselves and our neighbours. The summer has been sickly, the weather generally wet and unpleasant. Hornbrook has taken another venture to N. Orleans; he started the 9th inst. Maidlow, Potts and Ingle have loaded a boat jointly with which Potts and Edmund M. go down; they start at the end of this week, some of their loading is bought on credit. I, at one time, had made up my mind to go with this cargo but altho' the wage was not entirely my object I did not choose to go for the small sum they thought it right to give. Grace goes down with them for $25; he is on his way to Cuba, he has a brother there.

Jas. Maidlow started 6 July for Baltimore with his wife and family in a waggon. He writes from thence he had not got any employ but was in treaty with a gentleman for $30 per month and found; says there are many things I could do there to advantage and would write me perticularly [sic] soon. They had a narrow escape in crossing Licking River, in Kentucky, getting below the ford into deep water; the body of the waggon floated off the wheels, down the river, with the whole party in it. They were at length stopped by a planter, where they remained 'till assistance came from the shore.

We have a sort of Debating Society established for the discussion of questions and taking of newspapers styled

'The Society for Promoting Useful Knowledge'. The members are but 11 in number and not very regular in attendance. At the Saturday meeting at Mansell's Mill, the only newspapers we yet got are Niles' 'Weekly Register' and a N. York printed English Ministerial paper, called 'The Albion'. Our neighbour, Barker, is made a Squire; he is one of the members.

A new State road has been laid out from Evansville to within a few miles of Fort Harrison. From Evansville to Princetown it deviates but little from where the old road now runs, going some nearer but on much worse ground. The funds are much less than was at one time expected so that, at present, all timber over 18" in diameter will remain standing. I have engaged to clear two miles, commencing a little on this side of Carlile's and extending some distance beyond Scott's, all timber not exceeding 1 ft. in diameter to be cut level with the ground, all over a ft. and not exceeding 18" to be cut 12" in from the ground and the brush to be cut and cleared off. This I have taken to do at $23 per mile of which I pay Barker $5 for hauling off the timber. 'Tis rather a hard bargain but is now nearly completed. C. Dunk has been helping me and part of this money, when I get it, I shall have to lay out upon corn. We have now got a Post Office at Scott's, therefore for the future please to direct: Saundersville, Vanderburgh County, instead of Evansville.

Yours affectionately,

J. Purse

Mildred added a note:

Dr. Daniel,

Purse is desirous that I should fill up the paper but requests me to be moderate in complaining. In this respect I shall be actuated by my feelings and beg not to let my expressions of discontent in the smallest degree affect you.

In the first place, let us hear from you. These long silences give great uneasiness. Perhaps you have the same request to make to us and may think with as good reason. We could not well write to you sooner as we were off and on all the summer letting our farm to a whimsical fellow and were at last disappointed. I don't despair of escaping from the wilderness; something will turn up to release me from banishment. I am not so warm to return to England as I was two years ago. I do not wish to leave this country with all my prejudices hanging about me. I want to live where providence has scattered the good things of this world with a more bounteous and liberal hand and to prove the difference of living like savages, without comfort or convenience, with a life of civilisation.

I found as much difficulty in getting through this summer as any of the preceding ones in America. The last two months has been all Nov., as murky, dark and smoky as any weather that ever visited our foggy island. The summer sickness of the surrounding country dispirited me. Poor Mrs. Maidlow was impressed with the notion that she should live to experience poverty and want and poor Mrs. Carlile's illness was brought on by hard labour, grief and trouble. I think I may say she died of a broken heart; her family had been ill all summer. Poor soul, in her illness and death she had not a bit of linen or calico to wrap her body in. This was a hard case after a life spent in spinning, weaving and domestic toil.

Purse tells you a few individuals have formed a society for discussing questions and promoting useful knowledge but it has not yet taught them to act with justice and honour towards each other, as he has in a small way experienced. I fear it will take a considerable time to teach some of them this.

I can only add our best wishes and affectionate remembrance to you and all our dear friends in England.

Yours truly and sincerely,

M. Purse

P.S. You asked if C. Dunk put in the piece of wheat which he partly promised to do. He never did put it in. We got nine bushels off the piece put in last fall are now upon corn bread for five or six months. Violet and Dido do grow fine beasts, the first of these was put to work last summer, was as steady and diligent as an old horse. Hately has brought us a calf within the last month, which gives us a winter cow. All our other cattle must go to the cane. We found our black steer [Mott's calf] dead at the end of the summer, half eat up by the buzzards which is all the cattle we have lost since last winter. A great many of our hogs have died, as have most of our neighbours'. We have done no building, not even laid a foundation; it rains always, day and night. I don't think we have had three settled days fine together for more than three months. I can't think of any family but ourselves that has escaped the diseases incidental to the country anywhere near us. In this perticular [sic] we have been fortunate. I have had sick headache and a disordered stomach for half a year; am getting over it now. We all had bad legs through the summer, mine were alarmingly so. It was not the effect of high living as I consider myself abstemious. I hope you have escaped altogether the illness and disease so prevalent throughout the country.

It appears that, after all, John Purse took the opportunity to visit New Orleans, so he must have found someone to look after Mildred and Emma. However, in the summer of 1823 Daniel received a letter from Mildred saying the trip had not been successful:

Dr. Daniel,

Your much esteemed favour of newspapers we got safe last Sunday. At the arrival of these our pleasure was great; to hear you were well and all our dear friends in England. Yesterday our joy was doubled and trebled in getting those interesting and more than welcome letters sooner than expected. The receipt of such gratifying information, all the wellbeing of you all, together with all other interesting matters is almost the only remaining comfort I have. You desired we would write often and I think you are punctually obeyed. It is not in my power to express how much these letters interest me.

We are all doing bad enough on the settlement. Corn is a scarce and dear article; many of us are without it and don't know where to go for a grain. The tables are turned; wheat and grain now comes from England to America. I have often thought they might raise corn to eat green in England, what we here call 'roasting ears'. We have a better prospect for a corn crop than we have ever had before; fourteen acres is our quantity on shares. We finished our first planting 28th of last month and hoped we had done but were replanting the day before yesterday a piece between three and four acres. We have had less to do of this work than most of our neighbours, altho' the severity of the winter so thinned the number of partridges that we did not see one for many weeks and after those severe nights that killed our cattle, our boy found numbers of these birds dead in the fields. Yet there are enough left to torment us in pulling up our corn. Red birds were so tame in the winter that we frequently caught them in our traps, kept them in a cage made by Mr. Dunk, but with all our tenderness and attention could not get these beautiful creatures to live more than three weeks; blundered, no doubt, in selecting their food. Their note is the prettiest I know which I was never acquainted with 'till this season but in a little hickory just above the yard gate is a nest and the male bird frequently entertains us with his cheering note. Our wheat upon the ground is a very light crop. The Maidlows think this a more unpropitious season than last year but we don't know any difference. We have had a bountiful share of mosquitoes the last seven weeks, their numbers are now abating but we are still teased with them a great deal of an evening. Ticks and all other annoying insects as teasing as ever. We are continually forming schemes for getting away but can't bring any of them to bear. We think Barker would rent the farm, though we don't feel quite certain of it. Here appears as much difficulty of disposing of our multiplicity of wares as of parting with our farm. The only way that presents itself is to trade them for cattle for the Orleans market, which is a roundabout, improfitable [sic] and dangerous mode and one that we dislike. In two or three years this has a chance of being a handsome farm. More of Ingle's family are coming out but there is little chance of our selling to them; the Maidlows are laying by to catch them. They want to sell off their land and clear off entirely; even the old gentleman is desirous to dispose of his farm and remove.

Both his boys are about to leave him in the fall and, from what I can gather from his conversation and their family disputes, he is very uncomfortable. He was here yesterday, offers to take his waggon and go off with us. Edward [Maidlow] is in unsound health; he thinks to go down the river in the fall and across to England, never to return to Indiana and perhaps not America. Sometimes we think we will take our things up to Wheeling, being the most likely place to catch the Flatts to sell our farm to but we don't know at all what we could do there. We hear it is the most flourishing place between Pittsburgh and New Orleans. My heart sickens at the prospect of continuing to farm in the wilderness. Purse certainly misses his milk and butter very much, tho' perhaps not the comfort of it more than I do; a less portion satisfies as well. Within the three years that we have owned cattle, our loss has been twelve head and most of them milch cows. Mr. Maidlow says it is not policy to speak against the Western Country; it will prevent us from disposing of our land. The cut and army worm have been partially about; we have not suffered much, the latter has not injured us at all.

The English are flitting about us, renewing professions of friendship. We think Cawsons are the most sincere and we have been to see them and they have been two or three times with us and, upon better acquaintance, we think them in understanding and candour preferable to most others on the settlement. I said I should not work out but I am about something almost daily in the garden. I find it the best antidote for melancholy when my active body is set at rest by heat; my spirits are constantly depressed from the lassitude I suffer. This is what I endure from the long summers here and what I should dread from going farther south. The season has been wet and cool to within two or three days; the latter suited me and now we have a material alteration. For myself individually I was in no way inconvenienced by the severity of the winter, wore neither sock or stocking from Oct. 'till sometime in April when I was compelled to put them on to defend me from the bites of insects.

From the fine package of seeds and stones you brought us we have only one small tree, a few inches from the ground, of the plum kind, one currant, a foot and a half high, one bunch of currants on one of the Harmonie trees, six gooseberries on one of the two trees we have, twenty three English apples from seed, looking well. The Black River nursery, which you assisted us to plant, has been for two winters so badly barked by the rabbits they have had to be cut even with the ground. We have nine vines alive, am sorry to say they are not doing as well as they ought from want of attention. We shall be rather late with melons, our first planted out were cut off by the worms and bugs. Your books from Phillips we received a considerable time ago. What will be the duty on goods conveying them from Orleans to any of the Eastern ports?

I do not know how to object to conducting a dry goods store in Baltimore, connected with Mrs. Browne or any other way. Earl spoke of city lots in Washington selling cheap, two, three or more acres a short distance from the city. Can you speak to this?

Purse seems hardly as warm to garden at Natchez as he did. A Yankee of our neighbourhood told Mr. Maidlow he had been there and would not have land there on any account. It was never knowing when winter was gone, worse than 'tis here. We hear Ingle has applied to be appointed to the

Post Office; if he should become Post Master, our letters must come to Evansville. The Albion paper was recommended by a friend of Potts at Cincinnati. The Society are about to dissolve, being too poor and perhaps too quarrelsome to hold together any longer.

We are aware that money can be sent to this country from England. Our motive for mentioning it refers to the cottage in Mill Lane; we think perhaps the title should be transferred to some part of our family.

We don't know if you will like us to invite you again to The Wilderness. It was a poor place to come to two years ago and it certainly is not improved; must leave it discretionary with you. If you were to come, we should endeavour to do the best we can for your comfort. We are always glad to know all goes on so fine with you.

Thank you for the copy of the verses addressed to Susan. Clio is pleased to compliment our sister, Susan, most gallantly. Yesterday, prior to our getting your letter, Em and myself were both writing to you on the same sheet but I have found more to say and she is pushed out for the present. I intend she shall write you a few lines, perhaps in the next. I am glad to hear of the good behaviour, improvement, progress, etc. of all our cousins. I wish our Emma had the opportunities, advantages, perseverance, emulation and industry of Matilda. She is not only in the background but most disadvantageously so. She has many good qualities and no vice but being almost excluded society, particularly that of her own age, her habits are contracted, her manners awkward and she has false notions of independence. To make her what I would wish to have her, she requires to be under strict discipline. When her father was away so much last fall she was worth more to me than a boy much older. I could put more confidence in her and have things better managed. She will put such logs on the fire as I cannot raise from the ground and draws from the well buckets of water though we have no pulley. She says Matilda would as soon think she could fly as do these things; she is quite a compound. I am anxious to have her schooled and think the labour of a persevering person would not be thrown away upon her. She knows more things from books than I did at her age and has a tolerably retentive memory. Em is right sorry she can't write to you in this letter.

The Orleans merchants say they did not lose over $5. We have six ripe cherries on the tree by the house. Shall gather pease in a day or two. We write in affection to yourself, our relatives and friends. Praying for the welfare of you all.

M. Purse

Note: Matilda was James's eldest child, now aged fourteen, only a little more than a year older than Emma. Mildred was all too aware of the difference in upbringing between her daughter and her brother's daughters. The thought of verses written to Susanna must have seemed quite frivolous to someone isolated in the wilderness of Indiana. John Purse returned from his New Orleans trip, ill with dysentery, and not only had he made no money from the venture he actually lost $5.

Daniel, still in New York, wrote home to his family that the orange trees were so cut up by the frost that there would be no fruit for six years. He also told them that John Purse was planning another trip to New Orleans in the fall and that 'there will never be any happiness for women 'till ticks, bugs, mosquitoes and cornbread in June are only known by hearsay'.

Daniel immediately after this set about making his preparations to leave for Indiana. He spent the winter of 1823 with John and Mildred, during which time they managed to let Volney Farm. They had finally decided to move to Pittsford, New York, where, apart from the Billinghurst family, there was a growing colony of English people. The climate was more favourable and New York State more accessible than the depths of Indiana. The plan was to leave Evansville around the end of May 1824, but the early summer was unusually hot and they decided to wait until the cooler days of autumn. Finally in September the wagon was loaded and the party was able to set off on its 800 mile journey.

Unfortunately soon after starting the leading horse broke the traces and galloped off into the woods. No sooner had they recaptured her when the skid chain (a form of elementary brake) tore away the side of the wagon. Nothing daunted they camped for the night only to find a huge rattlesnake under the wagon. On the second day the horses refused to attempt a stone bank and eventually the trek was abandoned.

The Purse family continued on their way overland but Daniel remained with their luggage, planning to take it to New York by boat. During their journey of several weeks John Purse fell ill with the ague (a fever similar to malaria), so they stayed with friends on the shores of Lake Erie, while he recovered. They eventually reached Pittsford where they lodged with the Billinghurst family for some months whilst looking around for a property to buy.

Daniel meantime had taken the Purse luggage by river to Pittsburgh where he organised a wagon to carry it overland to Philadelphia. From Philadelphia it was shipped to New York where he waited for the spring thaw. In March 1825, Daniel received a letter from Mildred telling of their plans in Pittsford:

Dear Dan'l,

Mr. Beech, the bearer of this letter, is the gentleman who has advanced Mr. Billinghurst the $400. He is a store keeper of Pittsford. We have not yet transacted the business respecting the mortgage but it will be done in a day or two. Purse has taken two fields to work on shares which is all the farming he has engaged in yet but think we have almost made up our minds to purchase the small farm beforementioned; the proprietors will not let it to us on any terms. The fall-down log house is levelled almost with the earth – this one of the owners did to eject a tenant. We have had an opportunity of sending to Mr. Goodrich by a neighbour who went a few days ago into that neighbourhood to remove and settle his son and calculated to be gone two or three weeks. At his return we surely shall have Mr. Goodrich's determination about the purchase of our farm in Indiana. We should have been pleased to have had your opinion and approbation respecting the purchase of this little farm, but as it is got to be the outside since we should be doing something and you feel interested in remaining sometime longer in New York we at present think it may be advisable to agree for this.

Mr. Billinghurst thinks well of this piece of land. We think we may be glad to avail ourselves of your kind offer of an

advance of about $200. It is probable in a few days we will
have a farm offered to us to rent, about 43 acres good land
equal to Mr. Billinghurst's, not quite half a mile off, our
agreeing to take it will depend on the terms it is offered, no
buildings but a tumble down log house. It is really time we
were got to a place where I can be more in the open air –
my health is not as good as when I arrived here. I cannot say
much for the health of the females; if it were the same with
the men I should pronounce the place unhealthy but the
women and girls are so stewed up in their houses, always
cooking, which I think is the reason they get so often sick.
I forgot to observe Mr. Beech has got a Note drawn by Mr.
Billinghurst on you for the amount stated. I have no wish
to deceive you and hope that will not be the case but think
you may be perfectly easy and satisfied as regards your
money being in the hands of Mr. B. Much reservedness has
been thrown off and candour substituted in its stead in both
Mr. and Mrs. B., since our last writing to you. A few
circumstances falling out awkwardly made me perhaps too
ready to be a little misled in judging of their pecuniary
affairs and to think as I did and I always write what I think
is my belief, they are both very honest people.

The sooner you arrive with our chattels the greater will be
the accommodation but we don't wish to hurry you from
a place in which you have so much interest and pleasure
until you are quite ready to come. Don't as yet know where
our packages can be stowed but on your arrival Purse will
fetch them from Pittsford and if it so happens that the
expense of storage can be saved we shall be glad to do it.

Are very glad you find yourself in your old quarters and
find yourself surrounded again by your old friends and

acquaintances. It don't seem right that you should tear up and away again directly.

I am now come to nearly the last and best subject of my epistle. The welfare of all our dear friends in England; to hear of their health and prosperity is the greatest happiness that can be imparted to me. I was greatly pleased with James' letter – it is impossible to express how much and laughed the most I have done since I have been at Pittsford. James' prosperity I am happy to hear of but John's good luck and success comforts me more than all the rest. Surely there should yet be some change of luck for me. I am in hopes I shall rise from my ashes again and write to someone of these dear folks across the water myself. I always said I would if I prospered in my removal.

Mr. Billinghurst received a letter from Wm. Browne of Baltimore one day last week which conveyed the welcome intelligence to us that all our good friends at Horley Mill were well. We have also lately got a letter from Mr. Knight, Nelsonsville, Ohio. He is making pretty good headway as storekeeper, tavernkeeper and apothecary. We hear nothing yet from our old country, Indiana. I certainly cannot relinquish the idea of returning to the paradisical society at Harmonie at some future time if I see reason for it but this depends on the success we have here and the encouragement we get from that country to join them. People are fast moving from these parts to Michigan. Numbers are going there this spring which gives good choice of land to such as want to purchase here. We think the price of land as high now as it will be. All sorts of produce at this time, a dead sale wheat only 75 cents. If it is convenient you probably will return us a few lines by Mr.

Beech. As you have been writing to England I trust we were remembered in your letters to our dear friends. It is seldom we are forgotten by them in their letters to you.

We have now a cold spell of weather. We have had it all along warm and moderate, 'til Friday when it changed cold, a great deal of rain, some snow and hail. Purse began with his new plow [sic] in Miss Parrott's field, got a good soaking and was drove home by the storm. Mr. and Mrs. B. send their respects. Will be glad to see you at Pittsford. Our best regards to yourself.

Affectionately,

Mildred

Note: Mr. Goodrich was Mrs. Barker's father. The Barkers were the family to whom Volney Farm in Evansville was let. He lived on the shores of Lake Erie and the Purse family stayed with him during their journey to Pittsford, at which time he talked of trading with Purse for his farm, for his son-in-law Barker; no money but horses, cows etc. Mr. Billinghurst had rather over-extended himself and had borrowed $400 from Daniel. The slight coolness arose as the sum first asked for was $700 and Daniel had had no wish to have so much money tied up. Mr. Knight from Nelsonville was an old friend of James Purse from Storrington days. George Rapp's society in Indiana had moved to a new site in Pennsylvania. The land had been sold to Robert Owen, who planned to found a township based on his theory that 'the advancement of humankind could be furthered by the improvement of every individual's personal environment'. It is interesting that Mildred was tempted to return to Harmony Village, now situated just outside New Brighton,

Pennsylvania, the town William had designed in 1806. John, Mildred's brother, had now moved to Cobham, Surrey, where his business prospered.

Mildred apparently found the life in Pittsford rather formal, even among the young people, after their Wilderness years, but her husband thought there was 'a tolerable good living to be got without the plague of insects that tormented them in Indiana'. It was doubtless easier for John Purse to acclimatise to their new life. As is usual his wife and daughter organised the social life of the family and it was obviously very different to Evansville. The farm they had in mind, just under thirty acres with an old log house, a barn, a spring of water, a good orchard and garden with plenty of currants, was all within a mile of the Billinghurst home at a price of $360.

Daniel arrived in Pittsford in April 1825, with about a ton of luggage belonging to Mildred and her family. They were

Mount Volney, Purse family home in Pittsford, 1824–1844

overjoyed, both to see him and finally to receive their belongings. They had bought two adjoining farms, altogether 78 acres, and Daniel immediately set to with John Purse to help re-roof part of the house, as it was not storm-proof. 'We have had to look out for squalls, both internal and external as some of the inmates complained of our being clumsy workmen.'

Daniel described the farm as inclining gently to the south, overlooking a rich woodland scene and no more than a quarter of a mile at any place from the bank of the canal, which could be glimpsed in places. He noted that the masons had finished a snug and comfortable stone house, 18 feet by 25 feet, two-and-a-half storeys high, with brick chimneys, corners and windows. Daniel described Mr. Billinghurst as a remarkable, tough and good old patriarch and reported that Mildred was much pleased with Mrs. Billinghurst. All in all it can be assumed that the Purse family had finally found their feet. According to Daniel, Mildred was as well as she had been any time in the last fifteen years, but John's health had been shattered considerably by the ague and fevers he had endured whilst in Indiana.

During the summer Daniel and John Purse made a trip to Lake Erie to see Mr. Goodrich, and had succeeded in making a trade with Volney Farm for three colts, a mare, and $70 in money and notes, making altogether about $375. This was considered a tolerable price. Mr. Goodrich also spoke of trading for the Town Lot. Daniel had planned to travel on to Canada but, having given all the help he could to the little family in Pittsford, and having seen them well established, the weather prevented his travelling north and so he returned to New York for the winter.

Mildred was much happier with her new life and now felt the desire to communicate with her family. She received a welcome letter from her brother, John, and requested one from Susanna. At last, in the autumn of 1827 she wrote to her family in Horley. It was the first letter she had written home for several years:

> My dear friends,
> A very few lines I address to you to acknowledge the gratitude due from us to you for your generous liberality and kind consideration of our need of present means to render our habitation as comfortable as we wish to make it. I yet hope the day will arrive that we may be enabled to return your bounty and discharge our debt with interest. This hangs pretty heavy on my mind and sometimes gives me considerable uneasiness. If we do not have more than a common run of luck we shall be able to clear our way quite comfortably to Daniel. We are particularly thankful as it was through his friendly inference you conferred on us this benefit which we appreciate very much, knowing it will so greatly contribute to our comfort.
> Wheat crops have turned out extraordinarily light this year in the surrounding country, much not worth the trouble of taking in and threshing. In this respect we have fared quite well as our neighbours, having enough for seed to use and a few bushel sold. Corn, oats and potatoes, about the usual average.
> Our health is now about the common standard. Purse had this autumn a pretty hard ague fit, not of very long duration

Frank, one of the party of three

Allegheny River, Pa. as seen today

In the Moose Country – Lake Superior by W. Constable, date unknown

Parker's Tavern on the Allegheny River, Pa. as it is today.

Townshend's Port, Mass. by W. Constable, 1807

*Bilinghurst Log Cabin, Northfield, N.Y. (later Pittsford)
artist's impression by Steven Pearse, 2000*

Townsend's Mill, New Brighton, Pa. by W. Constable c. 1806

Mastodon's tooth purchased by Daniel and William in 1806 near Bigtown, Mississippi

*Ohio River, by
W. Constable, 1806*

as above

Fishing, a water colour by W. Constable c. 1806

Daniel and William's ark named Gargantua, courtesy T. MacCracken

Notes of a Travel made in

North America,

in the Years 1806, 7 and 8; by a Company of Three.

In Two Volumes. Volume the first.

Hamlet .... Good Even, Sir,
        But what, in faith, make you from Wittenberg ?
Horatio. A truant disposition, good my Lord.

Title Page from William Constable's book *Notes of a Travel made in North America in the Years 1806, 7 and 8 by a Company of Three*

courtesy T. MacCracken

River scene in Massachussets by W. Constable

Niagara Falls from the Canadian side c. 1806, drawing by W. Constable

courtesy T. MacCracken

but sufficiently so to be a considerable check to his Fall business. I continue about the same as when I wrote last. I am almost persuaded my complaint is more weakness of the stomach and indigestion than internal decay (as I used to think it was), which I correct in some measure by not eating after 4.00 p.m. in the summer and 2.00 p.m. at this season of the year, going to bed early and rising in reasonably good time in the morning. A little exercise suits me better than sitting much; but fires, hearty movements or lifting make my stomach sick. I regret to tell you my eyesight has gone off greatly within these three or four years. I have declined reading (which was at first a hardship) unless it is quite large printed as I do not yet like to take to glasses. I am sorry you, William, are in the same situation. Emma is not very tough, so frequently has colds and headache. She is unfortunate in being unlike most of these hale American girls. We have some thoughts of getting her situated in Rochester for three or four months this winter with a dressmaker, to give her a taste and aspire to make her an expert needlewoman.

We have just made our apple preserves or applesauce. The way we do this is to take new cider from the press, fill a brass kettle and boil it half dry, fill it up with cider again and continue to fill it up and boil it away four or five times 'till it is considered strong enough to keep the fruit, which we are enabled to do the whole year. Previous to boiling the cider we dry our apples which is done in the following manner: peel, core and quarter our apples and, if it is too late in the season to dry them on boards outdoors, we thread them through the middle with a small twine and hitch the thread on nails drove in the joists of our room, that part nearest the fire. In about fourteen days they are dry enough for use or to hang by in bags for keeping. Many families make a barrel of 32 gallons of applesauce but about four gallons contents us. I had but little to say when I began this letter and as Emma has a line or two to write I conclude in the usual way, with respectful remembrance to all old friends and neighbours, affectionate love and best wishes to you all, in which Purse and Emma join, soliciting your friendly answer as early as convenient after receiving this.

I am, my dear friends,

Yours affectionately,

M. Purse

P.S. I sincerely hope Jemima has long been restored to perfect health.

It seems as though the family had lent the Purses a sum of money to help establish themselves in Pittsford. Emma, now seventeen, adds a note of her own:

Dear Aunt Susan,

The flower seeds you were so kind as to send us were carefully committed to the earth. The Tiger Lily never made its appearance at all, the Sweet Peas and the Coreopsis we have succeeded in raising. The latter was greatly admired for the brilliancy of its colours, the length of time it continued in bloom and the number of its blossoms. The Sweet Peas grew very strong and luxuriant.

I wish to be affectionately remembered to all my kind friends, as also to Mrs. Blundell and Ann, Mrs. Tichenor, if she is yet living.

I remain, dear Aunt,

Yours affectionately,

Emma Purse

Note: Mildred was at this time forty-six years old and William, at forty-four, two years younger. Mildred presumably thought that taking to glasses would damage her eyes further and so was putting off the evil day as long as possible. Ann Tichenor was a long time friend and neighbour at Horley; she acted as the local midwife and was probably present at Emma's birth. The Blundells were also old family friends, soon to be connected by marriage.

In a letter home Daniel described the situation of the Purses, saying that all was well with Mildred and her family, that Emma was a strapping young woman, John pretty hale and Mildred much the same, pretty weak and feeble. It is interesting that Daniel thought Mildred weak and feeble as, by most standards, she had endured a rigorous life in the wilderness. Daniel never married and perhaps he was unable to see, from a woman's point of view, how hard his sister's life had been. She could well have given in and returned home, as many settlers did, but she found the strength to carry on.

CHAPTER TWELVE

William The Surveyor

WILLIAM WAS APPOINTED SURVEYOR to the Turnpike Trust in Reigate in 1815, working directly for Ambrose Glover, a local solicitor and Clerk to the Turnpike Trust. A turnpike trust was a local board of guardians responsible for the upkeep of the roads in their care, so named after the first barriers, known as turnpikes. At this time John McAdam had patented the crushed stone and gravel road surface which improved the condition of the roads so much it led to a spate of road building. Before this many of the local roads were impassable in winter due to the heavy clay subsoil. William had the section from Sutton to Lowfield Heath under his management. He designed various improvements including a cut from Sidlow to Hookwood Common avoiding the hill at Horse Hills; lowering Cockshott Hill, on the south side of Reigate, using the excess earth to raise Reigate High Street; bridging the Lesbourne by a culvert (this stream previously ran across Bell Street on the surface); finally, proposing a tunnel under the Castle to cut off the detour by the Red Cross Inn. All these improvements would serve to increase the coaching trade through the town, much to Lord Somers's satisfaction. (Lord Somers was the local landlord.) No doubt, too, he was highly satisfied with the work of his surveyor, William.

At this time there were several roads leading from London to the south coast, all vying for the coach trade. In 1816 a parliamentary act was passed to construct a turnpike from Gatton (near Reigate) to Povey Cross (near Horley), which would avoid Reigate. Lord Somers took alarm, fearing the road might divert trade from his town, and secured William's services in order to oppose the bill. William proposed another route, but ingeniously avoided making a section so that its hilliness was not apparent to the parliamentary committee. Eventually, a compromise was effected between the two proposals. When the committee's decision was announced Lord Somers was delighted and remarked to William: 'Well, Mr. Constable, you have spoiled their road.' We don't know whether this act of loyalty was rewarded financially, but know that it was sufficiently important for William to record it with satisfaction.

Between his surveying activities and his new bride (he married Jemima Mott in November 1815) William still managed to find time to follow his other interests. Clio Rickman noted that in 1817 William visited the British Museum where he copied the hieroglyphics on the tomb of Alexander, and made out the date to be 3759 BC. During 1818 he made a plan of the estate belonging to the Thorns, a coaching inn in Horley, and was employed by the Robinson family of Lowfield Heath for another local project. The Robinson family were great family friends who lived at Lowfield Heath.

During the summer months of 1821 William had surveyed

and measured a new road to run from Ditchling to the foot of Clayton Hill, just north of Brighton. This was called the New Road. As his reputation as a surveyor grew, William was called to work further afield. A road planned between Brighton and Shoreham was proposed, the committee including their old friend, Thomas West, the banker, and John Hall; William was asked to survey the line and then attend the House of Lords on their behalf, for which he charged them 3 gns.

Eliza Mott, Jemima's sister-in-law, had been very ill since giving birth to a baby son in October 1821. Unfortunately, the wet nurse procured for the baby passed on whooping cough to both the baby and his elder sister. William and Jemima offered to have the children to stay at Doversgreen during their convalescence, and, accompanied by Martha, Julius's and Jemima's sister, they stayed for several months. On 22 May 1822 Jemima wrote to her brother, Julius, and sister-in-law, Eliza, giving them news of the children:

> My dear brother and sister,
> I beg your acceptance of a carp taken from the pond in Reigate Park this morning, it is all alive-o just now at the minute of packing and I hope you will receive it fresh.
> We beg to remind you that we shall fully depend on the pleasure of seeing you both down here the beginning of next week without fail. I think at present that perhaps I may return with you, if you, Mrs. Mott, will be guided by me about the time of returning to town. I think our little Eliza will hardly be sufficiently recovered from the effects of her cough to think it advisable for her to return quite so soon.

The baby has just been here and looks quite charming. He now laughs when he comes to see us and seems to enjoy his little visits to us very much. Eliza is very anxious to see Mama and looked out to one of the Stages yesterday to see if she was come, and she asks how many days it will be before Papa and Mama come to see her. She is quite well and would send her love to you but is just now taking a comfortable nap after her dinner, the effect of being abroad in open, fresh, country air.

In the hope of seeing you both, believe me,

Yours very sincerely,

Jem'a Constable

The following week Julius and Eliza arrived on the London/Brighton coach and were set down at the door of the house in Doversgreen. This Eliza described, in her journal:

It was a sort of cottage with windows down to the ground, opening upon a very pretty lawn. At the open window stood my sweet girl, her light hair in ringlets down her back; dressed in white with blue sash and ribbons to tie up the sleeves, a coral necklace on her pretty neck, all excitement in her little sensitive face. And on the lawn lay the babe, a bonny, fair, blue-eyed boy, with the sweetest expression of face, and dressed in white and blue: the two handsome Aunts standing proudly by to display their treasures.

Eliza also stayed with William and Jemima for some months, during which time she visited Horley Mill, where James Sr. accompanied her to church. This was astonishing, because he had not set foot inside a church for fifty years. It is not clear why he had not been to church for so long but the rumour that he and his wife-to-be eloped to Gretna Green just fifty years earlier should be remembered. Perhaps the young couple were brought back and hauled over the coals before their marriage was solemnised in London.

Eliza describes the path that ran alongside the river from the mill to the church: 'the bank full of nuts and other trees, hanging into the water. It was a great enjoyment to me.' She tells of sitting in the garden with her work and listening to Jane (Charles's wife), Jemima and her little girl singing together.

William was still working on the tunnel through the Castle grounds in Reigate and also an improvement to the road over the summit of Reigate Hill, together with a bridge to carry the footpath. This footpath was part of the famous Pilgrims' Way which stretched from Canterbury to Winchester. Apart from his drawings William often made scale models of proposed buildings, presumably so that his clients could see exactly how they would look.

He also designed two proposed houses at the entrance to the Tunnel Road in Reigate, one of which was Mr. Budgen's new shop (the first of the Budgens chain). He noted that he had to 'shew the drawings on the ground to point out the errors of the architect'. He was also busy designing the tunnel itself, which led from Reigate High Street underneath the Castle grounds to join up with the London Road, thus cutting out a quarter of a mile from the London to Brighton route. This was an engineering challenge of some magnitude but provoked an outburst from the writer William Cobbett, who condemned it as wasteful.

Another commission was a design for a toll house for Castle

Road which was requested to be in an antique style, externally at least. These usually were hexagonal in shape so that the windows commanded a view in all directions.

During the spring of 1825 the iron suspension bridge William had designed opened at the top of Reigate Hill. William's nephew, Clair Grece, claimed that this was only the second suspension bridge built in England. (Isambard Kingdom Brunel's famous Clifton Suspension Bridge, designed 1829-31, was not completed until 1864.) The bridge was drawn by chains and kept open the footpath known as the Pilgrims' Way. It spanned a cutting through the chalk, which shortened the turnpike road, also designed by William. The ceremony of the opening of the bridge was marked by twenty-four young ladies, dressed in white muslin and wearing white kid gloves which had been presented to them by William, drawing across the first chains. Among the young ladies were his wife, Jemima, his sister, Susanna, and his nieces Caroline, Eliza and Matilda. Clio Rickman wrote the following verse to mark the opening of the suspension bridge:

> *Behold the strength, the power and will*
> *Which, on this spot, where Freedom reigns*
> *Have pierced the bowels of the hill*
> *And hung a noble pier in chains.*
> *Thus may each iron hearted Lord*
> *His country's enemy and bane*
> *Receive from freeman his reward*
> *Suspended by as strong a chain.*

William was soon employed taking the measurements for a proposed new road from Holborn to Brighton by way of Cuckfield and Hickstead. He was also surveying a new road up Redstone Hill and on through Nutfield to the windmill. He probably dropped in for a chat with Henry Grece (later to become his brother-in-law), or one of Henry's sisters while he was working here as the new road passed their door. Another project was to oversee the enclosure of Wray Common, on the slopes of the North Downs, just north of Reigate.

Unfortunately Jemima was taken seriously ill in the winter of 1827. On 18 January 1828 William wrote news of her health to her brother Julius, now living in Loughborough:

> My dear sir,
> It is very distressing to me to have the task of informing you that Jemima is very ill – she is keeping her bed and has been doing so for five weeks. Up to last Tuesday I had no apprehension that her case was one of any danger but now it has assumed a very formidable appearance and I am distressed with the most gloomy foreboding as to what may be the issue.
> The illness was at first a pain in the back, in a few days it appeared to be decidedly inflammation of the spine; moderate bleeding and medicine relieved this and we then supposed that recovery would soon follow, and tonic medicines were resorted to for bringing back the strength. These did not entirely fail in their effect but the recovery was exceedingly slow and at the end of a month the progress was but little. On Sunday night last she was seized with a

violent fit of flatulent cholic [sic] which, although it lasted but a few hours, threw her back into a state of great debility. On Tuesday morning, our medical friend, Mr. Martin, informed me that there was a tumour upon the abdomen, which he had sometime been watching with suspicion and which, it appears, is of some considerable standing, 6 or 8 months at least, perhaps much more, although no inconvenience had heretofore been felt from it. But which now he considered was operating with a very malign influence upon the constitution and was the source of all the present extreme irritability. I should have stated that from the first she has been subject to very frequent attacks of spasm in the stomach and recently to constant pain in the bowels upon taking the smallest quantity of food.

Under these unfortunate circumstances Mr. Martin has advised that the counsel and assistance of some surgeon of known skill and experience should be resorted to and we have accordingly applied to one of the most eminent of the profession, Mr. Wondrop, who is to come down tomorrow when we must summon our courage and do whatever must be done. The unfortunate soul knows as yet nothing of this arrangement, nor has she, I think, any suspicion of danger. When not in pain she is in good spirits but extremely debilitated. I am sure I need not tell you what is the misery of my feelings, you who have a happy fireside can estimate the dreadful deprivation with which I am threatened.

I do not suffer hope to abandon me but know full well the dreadfully uncertain tenure upon which I now hold my happiness.

May heaven bless you both, I am, my good friend,

Sincerely yours,

William Constable

Note: William did indeed know full well what Jemima faced should she need an operation. This was some fifteen years before the introduction of anaesthesia and operations of any kind must have been horrendous. It was about this time that Eliza, John Constable's younger daughter, moved to Doversgreen to help nurse her aunt. Eliza was now twenty years old.

Fortunately, it seems that other measures were taken and an operation averted, as William wrote to Julius again on 23 February:

My dear brother,

I have great satisfaction in having it in my power to inform you that Jemima's situation is considerably improved since I wrote to you last – her appetite is much improved, her strength increased and she is generally much more free from pain. Her spirits have always been good and now, when she is at ease, she is as gay and conversible as in her best health. The great improvement has mainly taken place within the last 6 or 7 days; previous to that time the advance was exceedingly slow but the very slight changes upon the whole were for the better. 36 hours ago the improvement was greater than it is now – within that time there has been some relapse but I flatter myself it is going off again this morning.

We are pursuing a very uniform system of medical treatment, a draught three times a day of unknown properties, certainly not tonic, and which I suppose is addressed specifically to the local disease, and each other day two leeches, one applied to the tumour. She quits her bed usually once or twice in the 24 hours and sits up half an hour or an hour. She is too weak even now to walk a step without support. Her chief article of food is boiled rice, drink cocoa, a slice of fowl or bird of some kind for dinner which she now generally enjoys with good relish. Upon the whole our situation is much more comfortable and our hopes of conquering the disease much strengthened.

Jemima joins me in affectionate remembrance to yourself and the excellent lady, your partner.

Dear sir, I remain,

Yours very sincerely,

William Constable

Jemima's recovery continued, although slowly. By July 1828 William replied on her behalf to a letter from her sister-in-law, Eliza:

You will think it looks not well that I should answer the kind words you sent Jemima 2 or 3 weeks ago. You will conjecture the cause to be her inability and such is really the case, notwithstanding this she is very greatly recovered. I will attempt a brief history of how much has been achieved and what is her present situation. The formidable tumour of which I have before spoken is gone, no discoverable vestige of it, I believe, remains. It yielded to a long and steady application of medicine and leeches, both of which, that is the peculiar medicine, have been discontinued 3 or 4 weeks. The treatment of the tumour has greatly reduced the patient's strength but she is now under a course of tonics and is manifestly improving in strength, but she has yet only acquired so much as enables her to walk, once a day or so, into the adjoining chamber. But she feels pretty confident that the first warm, still day that comes she shall venture downstairs and perhaps into the garden. Her appetite is good, she makes many good meals, I don't know the exact number, every day beginning for several days past with a stout breakfast of fat-pork! What a shocking term to stand in the account of our invalid lady's diet, however truth requires it to be there.

She dresses and sits up nearly all day and chats, sometimes by the hour, with a friend that occasionally drops in; she can laugh too now a good deal like other people. Laughter has been, during the greater part of her illness, an affection that she durst not indulge in from the pain that has always attended it. Her recovery since the first severe attack may be considered as unremitting. There has been no retrograding of any consequence in any respect, and you may judge from this what was the severity of her illness when at the worst, when even now she cannot muster strength and application sufficient to answer your letter.

William must have been so relieved that Jemima appeared to have conquered her illness; they were obviously a devoted couple.

His reputation as a surveyor was growing and he travelled about the countryside far and wide. He employed an assistant in the summer of 1828. This was young Daniel, now aged twenty, the younger son of his brother, John. William observed in his notebook that he wasted a lot of time waiting for people who never turned up; on one occasion he mentions waiting for three-and-a-half hours in Charlwood Park and finally having to return the next day. This must have been frustrating as well as time-consuming. There was no method of communication available to let people know if you were unable to keep an appointment.

In February 1829 came the tragic news of the death of both his brother, John, and his wife, Elizabeth, within a few days of each other. Although the cause of their death is unknown it seems likely to have been either cholera or typhoid, both prevalent at the time. This was just before the cholera epidemic of 1830.

During August and September of 1829 William spent three weeks in Dorset, where he was surveying a road from Bridport to Whitley Cross. This included a tunnel through Hornhill similar to the one he had designed through the castle grounds in Reigate. Bearing in mind that it took two days journey on horseback from Doversgreen to Bridport his daily fee of 3 gns seems very reasonable, although no doubt this was a normal professional daily fee at the time.

Sadly Jemima died in early November, aged forty-nine. She must have had a recurrence of her illness. Since they had no children this left William alone in the world. It was certainly not a good year for the Constable family. William spent some time, after Jemima's death, with the Browne family in Lewes, who knew him so well. Hopefully they were able to give him some consolation. Whilst there he drew Henry Browne's elegant house and garden. This was to be made into a lithograph.

The borough of Reigate was growing fast and William had been asked to produce a calculation showing the quantities of land covered and uncovered with buildings. This must have occupied a great deal of his time, although his brother John's son, young Daniel, was still working as his assistant which must have helped with the workload.

After Jemima's death in 1829 Eliza had stayed with William to keep house for him in Doversgreen. Although William did not have children of his own, he was evidently much taken with his nieces and nephews. Eliza shared his talent and passion for drawing and painting, and in this he was her tutor. Matilda was also a keen artist and was fascinated by the world of fossils. In November 1832 William wrote to her in Storrington:

My dear Matilda,

Thrice this autumn have Eliza and I appointed a day for journeying forth on a visit to you and as many times has some perverse accident crossed our purpose. Our plan has always been to go to Storrington via Lewes and Brighton and the Lewes and Brighton part of it we have actually achieved at last. How it has happened that Storrington has been left out I shall now tell you.

Our last appointment was to start on Friday the 2nd instant, first for Lewes and then onwards to you. The circumstances that disjointed our first two schemes need not be told but three or four days before our final day, the 2nd inst., Eliza received a letter from Caroline, informing her that you intended going up to Cobham with Charles on the preceding Tuesday. To make our visit to Storrington in your absence could not be thought of for a moment and we felt at once that that part of the journey was lopped off and, as we knew that your promise to Cobham had been of very long standing and would of necessity extend through several weeks, we were sure the favourable season could not hold out 'till your return and we therefore determined that we would take the Lewes and Brighton part of our journey and leave the other 'till your return. If all had gone on as we anticipated we should not have had great reason to complain; you would at least have redeemed your long-given pledge and we should have made a fair attempt at the recovery of ours. Alas, how are our wisest schemes frustrated by the demon accident. Who could have foreseen that by a side communication your journey should be frustrated and ours not secured? So, however, it has happened and we had the mortification to learn by a letter from your brother, Charles, addressed to me at Brighton, that you had deferred your visit to Cobham in order that you might be at home to receive us. Even then all would have been right but I had, unluckily, 12 hours before written to Mr. Glover at Reigate and had appointed to be at home on Wednesday night to attend a meeting of the Road Trustees, which was awaiting my return to be called. I was now irretrievably committed and was bound to return home on the appointed day which was exceedingly mortifying as, but for my letter to Mr. Glover, I might very well have been out at least three days more which would have satisfied my conscience and, in some measure, my desires. Some heathen people, who believe in the fates, would ascribe all this to their agency. I, however, who have been better taught, suspect it to be only a contrivance of the devil's and if ever I catch him in the fire when I happen to be head stoker, he may be assured I will have a proper revenge. In the meantime I shall plan again and again 'till I have had the pleasure of seeing you and the rest of our dear cousins at Storrington but, before that can happen, now we hope to receive your promised visit to our hearthstone which we shall keep comfortably warm for your reception at such time this winter as may suit you.

We had a very delightful journey. All went right but the Storrington part of it. I had not seen Lewes for 18 years or more and in that town where formerly I knew everybody I walked 12 hours without exchanging a word with anyone I had ever before known. Even this had its advantages; it gave us the perfect freedom of strangers, caring for nobody and having full command of time, which we were enabled to spend in reviving my acquaintance with the almost forgotten chinks and crannies of this, to me, interesting old town. We took with us a few broken shells, found in the rocks of this country and from out of which the inhabiting animals had crept some few millions of years before the creation of the world (according to the best authorities) and with these we introduced ourselves to the eminent geological gentleman, Gideon Mantell, by whom we had a very good reception. He is the possessor of the finest collection of organic fossils I have ever seen or dreamed about, chiefly from the chalk and wealden. If you ever go to Lewes you must, if possible, see them. I hope I may soon be on terms sufficiently good to introduce you.

At Brighton we did very well. There were the sea and the shore, as interesting a twain as ever met together and seem as fitted for each other as tea and buttered toast. We spent one entire day at Lewes, one at Falmer and one at Brighton and arrived at home on Wednesday night last.

Pray accept our very affectionate remembrances, present some of it to Tit, Papa and Jem and believe in our sincere regret for the frustrations and dislocations that have happened to our plans.

Dear Matilda, thine indeed and in truth.

William C

William did, indeed, soon become on intimate terms with Mr. Gideon Mantell. In Mantell's book *The Geology of the South-East of England* (1833) William's name was mentioned: 'Mr. Constable of Dovers Green mentions having observed white chalk in the wilderness in Alabama. Mr. Constable's account is so interesting that I have transmitted it to America.' William has corrected this passage in ink at the bottom of the page: 'Not Alabama, but Mississippi, being at two or three miles from the old Indian village of Bigtown.'

William spent most of September making a plan of the land taken from the Gatton estate near Reigate for the proposed diversion of the turnpike road. He sent the plan together with his account to Mr. Thompson, as he had been requested to do. Mr. Thompson promised the account would be paid on delivery but although he sent his compliments he did not pay the account. He said he was planning to come to Reigate the next day and would call on William. William noted: 'he did not keep his word'. During October William prepared plans for the improvement of two roads over the North Downs, one up Reigate Hill and one up nearby Pebble Hill. In early November he was busy drawing the Kinnersley Estate, near Sidlow Bridge, for a lithograph, of which 300 copies were to be made.

By September 1833, William was occupied with drawing a

plan of the water pipes to and from Mr. Relf's land in Reigate; Mr. Relf was the tavern keeper at the White Hart. He was also concerned with improving the road through Folly Bottom as well as drawing plans for a new road from Reigate through Gatton Park to Hooley Lane. This was to be his last project for Ambrose Glover.

William was contemplating a career change and a return to American soil. He had been mulling over the idea of exhibiting his early American paintings, particularly those of Niagara Falls, which he thought to produce as a panorama. He anticipated that this might do very well in New York. He had also invented a microscope which he hoped to sell in the new world. As if this was not enough he had also been working on a design for a steam engine to run the watermill in times of water shortage. He had obviously thrown himself into work as an antidote to his grief over Jemima's death.

CHAPTER THIRTEEN

Daniel Returns to America

WHATEVER REALLY HAPPENED on 19 August 1819 at Peterloo will never be known. However it is known that by the end of the year many of Daniel's friends and associates were either imprisoned or awaiting trial for their republican associations. These included the printer Richard Carlile, the politician Francis Burdett, the reformers Major Cartright and Henry Hunt. The whole reform movement appeared in disarray. Perhaps it was a combination of these factors that precipitated Daniel's departure from England.

In the spring of 1820 he helped his brother, James, with some building work in one of his houses in Storrington. Behind the smart new marble fireplace he put a long, tightly sealed, bottle. Inside was a piece of paper bearing the following:

This chimney piece, bought of Mr. Warren, Mason, at Wareham, Dorsetshire, April 1820, by Daniel Constable, cost twelve pounds, five shillings, the marble and stalactite the production of the Isle of Purbeck. Forty four years of American freedom and first year of the reign of fourth

George.
Kings in heaven
Soldiers at the plough.

Nearly a hundred years later the local newspaper declared that during some renovation in a house in Storrington, the builders found this bottle and note. However the editor was perplexed as to the meaning of Daniel's cryptic words!

In August Daniel, now forty-five years old, again left for America. This time he had no plans to return. He was unmarried and able to live off his investments, so long as he continued his simple way of life. The business in Southwark he left in the care of his partner, retaining a financial interest. He sailed aboard a ship named *The Thames* in which they had a very rough start, as he wrote to Susanna:

> My dear Susan,
> I have not as yet been truly sick but queerish. I have great hopes that I am not going to be torn about as many of the poor wretches here have been. From Saturday night 'till this morn we have been riding at anchor off Deal, one and three quarter miles from the shore; the ship parted her cable soon after anchoring on Saturday night, very queer in my berth but heard the gigantic noise of that stentorian Pilot and the gang of sailors. The boats from Deal have attended us daily with fruit, bread, etc. and we got our anchor up about 5.00 a.m. today, the morn clear with the wind upon our fore quarter. We rounded the south foreland in fine style about 8.00 a.m. and at 9.00 a.m.

passed Dover and now at 10.00 a.m. are coasting along gaily, very near shore.

I scratch this early fearing I may not have the ability to do so as we get on farther. We have now a Deal Pilot on board who takes us to Portsmouth where three more passengers are expected. You, I know, will be glad to be told that I am as well fixed as I wish to be on board a ship and I think you would almost envy me, could you see me upon deck with my little Tea or Coffee Set out, the same identical little tray which has crossed the Atlantic twice with us. My repast, I assure you, in this way is very attractive and even the Cabin passengers know that I have got hold of the right end of the story. Thus far all is quite good.

Everything presages all the comfort that a reasonable being can expect who has to be buffeted between clouds and waves. Oh, the distilled! What a solid luxury, with what delight I use a gill to clean my teeth of a morning. Dr. Lamb, for this alone, deserves my best thanks and during my absence I do request that you will go and see him whenever you go to London. He will be glad to see you and hear about me.

When I began this I thought of sending it to Horley 'twas out of my mind about Storrington. To all the folks around you give my love and to that little rascal, Tinney, a double share.

19th August.

Nearly a calm. I wish now you could see how trim we are. We amuse ourselves very well. Our passengers are destined to various parts of the union. I, having been so old a soldier, they all seek my society as a sort of oracle. We expect to reach the Isle of Wight some time between this and tomorrow morning.

2nd September.

11.00 p.m. our ship struck on rocks or shingles, many passengers asleep, me for one. It had lightened in the evening and I, at first, thought the bursting thunder, the shouting for all hands soon undeceived me. A general panic succeeded, minute guns were fired, lights hoisted at the masthead, anchors carried out astern, windlass manned to endeavour to haul her back. A King's Cutter had heard and seen our signals of distress, a fine, daring, manly, young Lieutenant came on board who was very familiar with this part of the coast. The ship would probably have been lost but for the favourable coincidence of nearly a smooth sea and rising tide. In about two hours, that is about half past one, we found her begin to heave and float and half an hour more brought us off from our perilous situation. Some of our most timid passengers were taken aboard the Cutter. Our old Deal Pilot was in a woeful situation, he had been a successful Pilot for 46 years and this business, if presented, is to him utter ruin. The Captain is disposed to be quiet and the passengers wish it.

The Pilot's error was in getting too near the floating light not far from Selsey Bill, about ten miles from Chichester.

Thus so far all is well and I yet hope you will hear a good account of us.

Affectionately to you all,

D. Constable.

Note: The passage took thirty-four days, arriving in early October. Daniel noted that two children died on the voyage. He was obviously thrilled to be back in New York and at the top of several of his letters home he gave his address as: 'Region of Delight, the Granary of Abundance, the Land of

the Free and the Home of the Brave' and 'know of no
drawback to this land save for a few mosquitoes'. He also
said that he had written to Mildred, in Indiana, informing
her of his arrival and that he had been told it would be
thirty-five to forty days before he could get an answer. He
planned to wait in New York until he heard from them as
he had requested the latest time they would need the seeds,
etc. that he had brought from England. Daniel, at this stage,
obviously hoped Charles would join him in America, as he
wrote to him saying: 'from the vibration in which I left your
brain, you are the most likely one of our gang to stretch over
here'. He did, however, go on to say that he did not want to
be the cause of breaking up or dividing friends and also that
he spoke from the position of one with some money in his
pocket. The 'Tinney' he referred to was Clara Constable,
James's youngest child, now aged six (this is presumably a
corruption of Tiny).

Daniel was full of enthusiasm, as his next letter to Susanna shows.
Susanna had probably told Daniel that she could not possibly
emigrate to America because of the responsibility of their ageing
father. Daniel obviously thought the whole family should join
Mildred and himself in the New World:

> My dear Susan,
> You have not been absent from my mind, tho' this is the first
> time I have addressed you direct. What I have before said I
> know you will hear. I have today seen an apple that weighed
> $28^1/_2$ oz. Seventy nine of the same kind weighed 84 lbs.
> Now, my dear Susan, this gossip is of my hands. I want to
> be very grave and serious with you. I console myself that

our father and you will come to this delightful abundant and happy region. I can see no earthly objection. I hope never to retrace the Atlantic again. I had rather live here upon $500 a year than have $2,000 in your ugly climate. Our good father thinks there is nothing like his old England; he must feel otherwise when we get him here. My heart and senses all join me in gladness I have not felt one single drawback because I think you will be coming along, one after the other. The hasty review of our family affairs makes me feel quite easy and certain that you all can sit down here in independence and peace. Why should not our father realise his property as fast as he conveniently can, sell the shop and stock off hand and if William and Charles wish to continue in the Mill, sell it to them and remain upon the old sod. There is no reason why they should not as long as they like it. All that I have said yet as to this country applies to those who have got the White Dirt. How easy it is to get this self same dirt here I do not know but I quite believe this an easier matter to get a sufficiency for all the purposes of health and comfort, than on your own land. You would stare to see what a quantity of rich pythagorean fare a half dollar puts into my basket from the ever bountiful fly market. Each morning my table is an absolute banquet of what with you would be a rare and costly repast. I have ate more peaches since I have been here than I have done in the past ten years in Europe. All the whole tribe of roots, fruits and vegetables are surpassingly fine and many luxurious things unknown in England. A delicious pine (such as the proudest of your blasted, hated and detested aristocracy, with all the care of fire and glass, never can command) graces and perfumes my board for $12^1/_2$ cents.

In the ship 'Washington' is Jackson, a black cook who was

our man in the 'Thames', body servant to Colonel Burr in the famed expedition. William will like to talk with him upon the events of those days.

I am so beset with glad sensations which I have begun to detail in some sheets which I hope will reach you soon. The weather now chains me here – you have none like it.

I want William or Charles to send me two copies of the Black Book and any other spirited publication against your cruel institutions, two sets of Mr. Paine's works, three sets of Deists, three Palmers (Carlile's edition), two Apocryphal Testaments. Get all at trade price, except Mrs. Carlile she must have full price, all in boards as the duty is upon the Invoice price, upon books 15% bound books, of course, pay more.

To send you a sheet of paper half written when my mind is so charged is too bad but I shall make most ample amends in a few days. My white dirt is all safe in the U.S. Bank. My watch kept time with the ship's chronometer and is a nice piece of mechanism. Tell me how you like yours and how are its actions?

Should Charles come here, perhaps it may be next autumn. I wish it may as I should be very glad to take him by the hand on his arrival. This would be good for us both as I could aid him. I saw yesterday the ship was reported in the Downs on the 20th September and I am now looking for her arrival when I hope to have a good account of you all. The books are to be directed to Col. Fellows of the Military Store, Greenwich St., N.Y., who will forward any letters you may enclose for me. He is a very respectable man, a true republican, very low in faith but generally known and respected through N. York. I am proud of his acquaintance, he comes and takes his tea with me.

I am prettily fixed in a good room in a French house whose

manners and ways you know I like. I am in my element to a peg and have my tea and coffee served up in fine French china, by a fine, clean, yellow girl, who is interpreter to the house. I wish you could peep in upon me.

I have a gay, half royal, dame who sometime pays me a visit and with whom I often have a lounge over this city, its shops and public places, Mrs. Alsop, the daughter of Mrs. Jordan by that cold hearted Duke of Clarence, who suffered her to die in obscurity in Paris. He came to see her on board. She tells me many anecdotes of aristocracy, most hateful. I knew her mother when I lived at Kingston. She then lived in Bushey Park, in royal splendour and was much beloved by all the neighbourhood. Her husband is now in India. She will probably stay here and means to make a citizen of her son, a little boy, who is here.

I am anxious to hear of any folks of my acquaintance and coming, who and when. Let me hear what you all think of the accounts I send you. This is a queer, idle, disorderly letter. I hardly know what you can make of it. When I talked of filling only a half sheet I was fearful the page would be taken away before I could get it done.

Affectionately to you all,

D. Constable.

Note: 'White dirt' was slang for money.

Richard Carlile was the printer and publisher of several of Thomas Paine's works, as well as other reformist literature. In 1819 he and his wife were fined and sent to prison for publishing Paine's works. Mrs. Carlile sent a petition to the House of Commons, which provoked an uproar through the country. Upon their release from gaol they found that their supporters had provided them with an establishment in Fleet Street, from where they were able to sell the same books with no further problems. Mrs. Carlile was released from prison earlier than her husband and found herself in dire financial straits, thus the reference to giving her the full retail price for Palmer's books. Daniel's friend, Col. Fellows, was described by the poet Walt Whitman: 'a gentleman of the old school, a man of perfect truth and exactness, who thought that Thos. Paine had a much larger following than was generally supposed'.

In a letter to his father around the same time Daniel wrote:

There are several ferries at different stations to Long Island and the Jersey shore, both team and steam boats; the horses work in a circle under cover, from eight to ten. Upon the decks of these boats, waggons, coaches, gigs, etc., all drive as if on a bridge. The Long Island boats are only ten minutes in crossing, they have a tavern on board that no time may be lost in consuming this world's goods. Here are steam boats, or rather ships, that coast round to N. Orleans and touch at some of the large towns that are immediately on the coast. One sailed, or rather worked away, a few days since that had 37 passengers from the City Hotel only. They are most surprising and magnificent vessels and one feels proud to live in such an age of science where mind may be said to be omnipotent over matter. The people have done great honour to their scientific citizen, Fulton, by naming after him one of the fine, new streets. It would have been much to their credit had they done the same thing by our immortal countryman, Thomas Paine. His 'Crises and Common Sense' ranked among the most sterling and useful books of the world.

Daniel was so pleased to be back on American soil that the fact that the weather now prevented him travelling to Indiana until the following spring did not seem to bother him at all. He probably could not understand Mildred's reactions to her surroundings, apart from the troublesome mosquitoes. He found the wild, untamed countryside exhilarating – but then he was not trying to wrest a living from the soil.

As already mentioned, in the spring of 1821 Daniel travelled to Volney Farm, Evansville, Indiana, where the Purses had settled. He spent the spring, summer and autumn with them, working alongside John Purse in his endeavours to improve his farm.

A year later Daniel took his leave of the little immigrant family and travelled south via the Ohio and Mississippi rivers. In New Orleans he bought various necessary articles for the Purse family which he forwarded before returning, by sea, to New York. In April, he wrote to his family in Horley. By this time his unparalleled delight with America was fading somewhat:

> Dear Folks,
> Landed here, twenty three days from N. Orleans and eighteen from the Baliere, we ran down in 22° lat., light head winds. For six or seven days we were in these warm tropical seas, sleeping constantly on deck, our ship miserably crowded with passengers. I roughed it in the steerage, fare $15. Near the midnight watch in the Mississippi our ship was discovered to be on fire and we had a horrible confusion for a short time but it was soon got under, the

cargo principally cotton.

I was sadly disappointed at not finding any letters from any of you on my arrival here. I am quite in anxious darkness about all of you and your affairs, since William's letter of July last. How can this be? Some of you must have written since that time certainly. I am full of doubt and perplexity about all these matters. A letter from Purse and me was put into a Liverpool ship's bag at N. Orleans. I have no letter from Indiana since I left in Dec. but am daily expecting one. I think of walking on to Boston in a week or two.

I board at a private house at a very good table, orderly folks, for $3 a week. There are eight inmates, foremen and journeymen printers, clean and well dressed and well behaved citizens. I have a snug little cabin to myself and my hostess provides me plenty of such fare as I want. The society of this house very much before that of Mr. Crane's. The novelties of this place are rather gone by with me and I don't known what to write about that you care for. I have some different notions about many things from what I had when I first arrived here. All then was enthusiasm and delight.

The disappointment of the poor folks in the western regions is a considerable drawback upon my pleasurable sensations. There is a great deal of true and useful caution in what Cobbett says about these remote countries as regards a certain class of English emigrants but as regards this fine city I do not see much but what I can still stand by in my former sayings. There is a little more dirt and misery than I once thought there was but it is a surpassingly fine place and is increasing fast. The fly market is taken down and a very complete one erected at the bottom of Fulton St., called Fulton Market. The park has had a new light iron fence round it, several new churches and meeting houses with new streets and squares and things are going on gaily as far as I know.

The want of some personal intercourse with some of you and some of my old cronies is what I feel the want of a good deal but now that I am here I feel it is but a little affair to put my matters on board a Liverpool packet and make one among you again. This thought often hovers about me. I wish Volney Farm was within a reasonable distance of the seaboard as I should like to put on my brown tow shirt and trowsers [sic] and help those folks frequently and now have often regrets that I left them so soon, as these poor wretches have ever so much work pressing upon them and I so frequently want jobs. And then again the reflection that it tends to so little profit is another hard case, for never during their lives will they ever have a chance of obtaining the things they have been used to have. They would be much better off if they had a long train of hardy girls and boys growing up, as their labour and companionship would be worth so much more than their consumption.

May 4th.

I fear things are going from bad to worse with a great portion of the best and most useful on your land, so I judge from the public print, the meetings of the agricultural men and these evils, I fear too, will press hard upon millers and shopkeepers, members of our own family. I want always to know how things progress with you all in your trading affairs.

May 6th.

I have never been at N. York before at this season and here has been some coarser weather than I expected. The contrast between this climate and N. Orleans was great indeed, though it was a month later on my arrival here. The middle and early part of April here was cold, raw and often damp. Two or three days almost as bad as an English November. It seemed a struggle between winter and summer but at the last end and beginnings of May, the latter completely triumphed and summer opened upon us at once. Bright sun and rapid vegetation burst open and things now are most delightful. I yesterday took a walk, about three or four miles, up the shores of the North River and never in my life saw more of the fine and beautiful, the villas and gardens fresh from a fine, warm shower, lilacs and peach, cherry and apple trees in full bloom, the bold bluff, rock and wood scenery on the opposite shores with the shootings in all directions of sloops, boats, steam boats and my heart wished for a host of you around me. But still we have not that pretty, placid and lingering spring season. Take an American gardener and set him to work in England and I think he would be very impatient at the tardiness of his crops.

As for any of you coming to this land, under present circumstances I could not advise you to do so. I am often very sorry that our poor mother was made uneasy about Mildred's coming. About that business she judged better than any of us. I believe you all feel pretty well fixed, save Charles. Perhaps he is better anchored than he was. Among all the blunders I have committed how glad I often feel at not having encouraged Charles to come out with me. That indeed would have been a bad business and I wonder now how it ever could have been thought of. William's good nature in offering to take all the weight of business would have led to much evil and misery and I trust you all to feel that all was for the best upon that score. If any of you feel to be overdone with care, or work, I want it to be understood that if I can render any of your concerns a service that I shall stand ready to return. The long time since I have heard from any of you may have made considerable alterations among your general affairs.

If it is possible that you have not wrote to me, I pray you write directly on the receipt of this. If you would have a sheet of paper laying ready and any of you write on it events, as they occur, such as who breaks, marries, dies, how goes times, prizes, health of people, crops, etc. etc. Susan, how is that little Tinney? Tell me about her and poor little Mo or Wiz. I know you will be very good to him. I am sometimes sorry for having teased that poor, little, unoffending wretch and yet I liked him and he always capered about my person if I had been a little absent. How devoted the poor creature was to our good and kind mother. Give him some caresses for me and her and do you, Susan, get a sheet of paper and scratch about it when ever you find yourself in the humour to make a short say. If written at twenty different times it will be just as well and better.

May 9th.

Susan and Charles's letter of Nov. has just reached me. It had travelled to Indiana; they opened it, resealed it and sent it back to me here. Purse says he will write to me in a week or two, has only room on your sheet to say they are all well as usual and have received all the things safe which I sent up by a steam boat from N. Orleans.

That you continue to be all well in health is the first good thing and your letter, upon the whole, is pretty good. That part of it in which Charles talks of coming here is the worse part of it. I have many doubts if he will be more likely to find a better home here. This separating families is not a good plan; it leads to uneasy feelings. If he has not started, my opinion would lead me to say be easy as you are for a time; see the events of things a little farther. Time, money and many inconveniences would attend an expedition of that sort just now. Keep him easy for a time. Susan and Charles's letter of Feb. I received in Indiana, May 12th, and there seems to have been no letter missing.

I presume, by your letter, that you drew an inference from what I wrote, that affairs at Volney Farm were looking better. I thought perhaps my account was calculated to make such an impression. What I stated were all facts, about the increase of hogs, etc. but then these things bring next to nothing at all and all they want to buy is so very dear. The hot suns, biters, blood suckers, drillers and borers of the house timbers, filling every place with powder of post, so far from home and all home folks, the want of domestic aid and help and a nameless and undescribable catalogue of etc. etc. etc. etc., all combine to make life uncomfortable, particularly to an invalid. You must write to them and tell Mildred what I tell you about their situation. She has got some notion, I think, that I want to reconcile her to her present situation; if I could help her into a better one I am sure I would. The mortality among John's neighbours is great.

If Charles does come and I miss him I shall be much vexed but I hope he will stick to his home stall for some time longer.

I am sorry that folks pay more than ever. I feared it must be the case. I think 'tis best to keep in shore with your trading matters, be as safe and easy as you can. Peace, prosperity, harmony, health and all earthly goods be with you all. I am sorry I have no individual to join me in affectionate remembrance to you all.

D. Constable.

Dr. Susan.

Excuse me for reminding you to stand by our good father and don't put him out of any of his old beaten path ways that he has trotted in so long and so good naturedly. His ways and his apple pies, he must have; I wish you had some of these delicious cranberries to sharpen them a little.

Note: Mo or Wiz was the little dog that belonged to Daniel's mother.

Daniel did not go to Boston for various reasons, one of which was sorting out Clio's legacy from Thomas Paine. He found the trustees incompetent, if not dishonest, and had legal wrangles for some time, but eventually managed to obtain some money for Clio. He sailed to Poughkeepsie in a sloop, and then on to Albany, where he met Major Smith, their old friend from the Beaver Falls days. Major Smith, by now a successful businessman, took Daniel for a 20-mile trot to Troy (an enormous distance for any horse to trot) in his family wagon with his wife and some other friends. Daniel noted that this part of Massachusetts and Connecticut were quite equal in beauty to the finest part of Surrey, round Dorking and Leatherhead, and that an Englishman would not feel like a banished man in this part of the country. High praise, indeed, and no doubt he was thinking of John and Mildred and that perhaps this might be a good part of the country for them. By this stage he was most concerned about his sister and her plight and fully agreed that they should move to another part of the country.

Daniel finally left for Boston, Providence and Rhode Island.

He had thoughts that perhaps John and Mildred would like this area and that maybe John could find a congenial pursuit among the manufactories of the area. No doubt he wrote to John and Mildred giving his opinion as to whether these areas might be suitable or not.

On his journey to Boston Daniel visited many of the places he and William had been to during their first trip to America. He found that some of them had declined while others prospered. He went to New Rochelle to visit the tomb of Thomas Paine, and tidied up the grave, replacing the curbstones apparently disturbed by Cobbett's men three years earlier. William Cobbett, visiting Paris in 1792, had become disgusted with the French Revolution and the French revolutionary leaders, among whom he included Paine. After Cobbett's arrival in America he became convinced Paine was a drunkard and not worthy of his fame. However, when Paine's *The Decline and Fall of the English System of Finance* was published Cobbett changed his mind and became eloquent in Paine's praise. In 1819 Cobbett apparently dug up Paine's bones and took them with him to England although the mystery of their whereabouts is still unsolved. (Some of the curbstones around the grave were displaced, probably at the time of the removal of the coffin, and it was these stones Daniel replaced with his own hands.) Daniel seems to have been quite happy in his wandering life; there is no mention of his looking for any employment, in fact he noted: 'while I am a professed wanderer, as my expenses are not at all increased by travelling I may as well keep moving'.

In October 1822 Daniel had reached Middletown in Connecticut. Here he stayed for a while and wrote home to his sister, Susanna:

> Susan, should you ever come unmarried to this land and seek a husband you must make up your mind to have a tobacco eater, for the habit is almost universal. Priests, lawyers, Generals, nearly all do it but with the nicer men it is managed with considerable delicacy. This Judge Bristol, for instance, whose manners and person might captivate the most fastidious lady, put into his very handsome mouth little tiny bits of this delicious weed and changed or rather renewed them pretty often. He spit the least I ever saw a chewer and to do this dirty trick in they have a broad shallow box, with a piece of green turf fitted into it; this I call a pretty nice notion as the eye is not offended but here also are a nasty, nauseous gang of two legged animals who will lay in bed and spit against the walls of chambers. The walls of tavern sleeping rooms often bear ocular demonstration of this habit of the nasty wretches.

Daniel was amused by the tavern keepers who felt at a loss how to classify him; a lone walker was unusual in America at the time. He always asked for: 'a pair of sheets that have not been slept in and a single bedded room'. He returned to New York in November and was again disappointed at finding no news from home. He was still battling with Clio's legacy from Thomas Paine but instructed Susan to pay Clio $80 out of his English bank account. He also asked Susan to give 20 shillings to the Jordans, their mother's relatives, who had fallen on hard times. Perhaps Daniel felt guilty at the way he had treated his mother's family while she was alive and urged Susan, if his letter arrived before Christmas, to be kind to them as their mother had always made such an effort to make this day happy for them. (It seems to have been Mrs. Constable's brother, Richard Jordan, and his family, who were in financial difficulty.)

Daniel also told William, in his covering letter, of a French naturalist of the name of Neel coming to England who had succeeded in taming several poisonous snakes, among them a rattlesnake about 5 feet long. Daniel gave this man an extract from Wilson's *Poetical Journal about Rattlesnakes*:

> *A large, grim rattlesnake of monstrous size*
> *Full twice three feet in length enormous, lies*
> *Fix'd to the path we momently stood.*
> *He, slowly moving, sought the adjoining wood*
> *And said, or seemed to say*
> *Move on in peace, let each pursue his way*
> *But when the uplifted musket met his view*
> *Sudden, in folding coils his form he threw.*
> *Dunkin, pleading, stop'd the barbrous deed*
> *Oh! Spare the brave, our general pilot cried*
> *Let justice, Sir, let mercy now decide*
> *That noble foe, so terrible to sight*
> *Tho' armed with death, yet ne'er provokes the fight*
> *But dare his life, behold he rises brave*
> *To guard that being bounteous nature gave.*

Daniel tells William that he has a very fine rattlesnake skin, bred and brought up on Volney Farm, 5 ft. 9" long and that it was the smallest of three killed soon after he got there. It is not recorded what Mildred thought of the huge and dangerous snakes that obviously abounded on the farm. He also tells William that Cap. Candler is coming to London again shortly, but he feels the Constables have remunerated him well enough with hares, geese, etc. and not on any account to think of entertaining him.

Daniel was still in New York early in 1823 and described the New York scene in one of his letters home:

> The hackney coaches have all left their stands and in their places are sleighs of various fanciful shapes, from one to four horses, gaily painted and furnished with white and black bear, buffalo and other robes and wrappers, lined, trimmed, vandycked with warm woolens [sic]. Each horse often wears sixty bells, on straps of leather round the body, the collar, etc; they are of glass, round and of various sizes. All the various works of carting, pleasuring, etc., all done upon sleighs, the whole forming a fine, active, showy, pompous pageant. Sleigh riding is an almost universal amusement and whole families crowd together in these darting vehicles; night is the most general time, a snow covered ground, clear sky, broad moon is just the arrangement that suits this fun, the tinkling sleigh bells are heard the greater part of the night.
>
> Have today heard the Examination of several female helps (for none acknowledge the degrading term, servant). It would surprise you to witness with what ease and confidence this class of people give their testimony in a

Court of Justice. All the female witnesses of every grade and colour have a chair handed and these helps sit and tell their tale at ease and unembarrassed. A reticule or bag is the universal appendage of every female and many clad in Canton crepe and leghorn bonnets, etc. Here are no Bettys, Molls, Nans, etc.; they are all Misses. Nor do these saucy, grinning lawmen dare to behave to any person with impertinence in consequence of humble station.

Experience has convinced me that this city is not so free from poverty, filth, vice, crime and dissipation as my imagination once pictured it. Probably here is quite as great a portion of these evils in proportion to the population, as in any city in the old world.

The person gone down the river with Purse is Squire Barker. He is a nice, orderly man of this State and his wife Mildred seems to like. He, you will see, is going to be partner in their farm next year. The Town Lot being sold is a good thing.

Daniel planned to take a sloop to the Delaware River as he had not visited Philadelphia for two years and he particularly wanted to see the bridge over the Schuylkill, designed by Thomas Paine. After that he intended to return to Indiana to be on hand to help John and Mildred move. He had thoughts he might buy a wagon in Pittsburgh or Cincinnati and float it down the Ohio to Volney Farm; planning that the wagon, pulled by the Purse horses, might carry all their possessions.

Daniel also asked Susanna to remember him to Mrs. Crespin (James Crespin's mother) when she next visited her in London. He told his sister he was considering returning to England, if only for a visit; saying that he did not like the idea that he was not again to make one with them, at least for a time, but that it depended on the Indiana situation.

Daniel stayed in New York during the spring and early summer of 1823. In late June he spent a week on Long Island, which he much enjoyed. He described his trip in a letter to Susanna:

> Went to the best taverns, always sheets not slept in. Spent two nights quartered at private houses, farmers, as nicely clean as the best of your Dames; about such a room and arrangement as Mrs. Mansell would give her guest, with ewers and hand basin, etc., but more carpets about the house. In the kitchen live the coloured folk, sometimes little, naked negroes crawling about.

The whole week cost him $4.90 and he walked 200 miles. He also wrote:

> Near the head of the Island I was induced to stay the whole Sunday, from the great niceness and comfort of a little tavern. Here was a fine pond; I boated, swam and went to Meeting and what do you think, Susan, up at this wild end of Long Island was a congregation of smart, spruce, dressed up folk, that would leave all your Horley, Burstow and Charlwood church folk entirely in the background. Open clock stockings, reticules, parasols, silk dresses, leghorn bonnets, etc.

Daniel went on to say that he thought he might bring Mildred and Emma to New York, leaving John James Purse to finalise things in Evansville.

Daniel left New York for Pittsford in August 1823. He travelled up the Hudson River to Troy, retracing the steps of his and William's original journey to Buffalo. En route he stayed with Thos. and Ann Billinghurst in Pittsford where he found the farm greatly improved and the family in high spirits. Ann Billinghurst, née Browne, knew Daniel well from his youth, although it was William who worked for her brother, Henry, in Lewes. They had built a fine new brick house to replace the original log cabin portrayed by William in 1806. Perhaps it was at this moment that he decided Pittsford might well be the right place for the Purse family to live. Thomas and Ann Billinghurst had become respected inhabitants of their community. Ann had started a school while Thomas had become an elder of the church.

From Buffalo Daniel wrote to William telling that the Cohoes Falls near Troy were little changed owing to the poverty of the soil and that, for this reason, he thought they would remain nearly unchanged during the next few generations. He told how he found the Little Falls of the Mohawk delightful with a handsome stone aqueduct carrying the canal across the river. He took passage on a boat along the newly dug canal and passed on through Utica, where he described a thistle nearly 12 feet high, through Onondaya to Montezuma near the Seneca Lake. Here he called on Col. Tyler (of the Burr Conspiracy and one of their companions at Beaver Falls). He found him most hospitable and little changed: 'a hardy good looking man, fuller limbed and wider faced than when a fellow at Natchez called him a damned, long, yellow-faced, blue Yankee'. Daniel wrote that there were

Mandrakes or Mayapples in abundance, a luscious, tart, pulpy fruit growing upon a plant with a single stem. He was amazed at the growth of Rochester and told William that the canal crossed the Genessee River in a gigantic aquaduct right through the city. He took a steamboat up the Genessee River and along Lake Ontario to the Niagara Falls, which he also found much changed with spacious hotels either side of the Falls. William must have been fascinated by this account of places so well remembered, although with a young wife and a busy working life to occupy him he seemed well satisfied with life in England.

Daniel took passage in a boat to Detroit across the lake. However, when a big storm blew up at Erie he was, as always, intensely seasick so decided to put ashore at Sandusky City, a much shorter voyage. From here he took to his feet again and walked east to the head of the Muskingam River through some of the tall prairie grass of which they had so often heard spoken, which grew so high it could hide men and horses. He stopped awhile here, having abandoned his idea of floating a wagon down the river, while he had a skiff built to order. He then floated down the Muskingam to its junction with the Ohio River, and thence to Evansville, arriving at the end of November. This solitary journey took two and a half months:

> The greatest part of this time I was entirely alone, the fineness of an American autumn in these regions, with the little adventures daily happening, made this journey to me very pleasant. To the leisure man no mode of travelling can equal this skiff navigation for independence and ease.

As mentioned Daniel spent the winter with the Purse family, during which time they managed to let Volney Farm. In September the party was able to set off on its 800-mile journey to Pittsford. Daniel wrote to Matilda, James's elder daughter, now sixteen years old, recounting their experiences:

Take our final departure from Volney and find the waggon chock full though the weight did not exceed 15 cwt. Soon after starting our leader horse jerked out of her geers [sic] (the traces breaking) and scampered into the woods at full speed. Next, in descending a hill, the skid chain tore away the side of the waggon. These things at the beginning of a journey of 800 miles were very discouraging. We got on tolerably well after this and encamped in the woods for the night. A rattle snake was close under our waggon – a pole was shouted for – and he was soon killed.

Second Day: Proceeded about three miles when our team made a dead stand at a little stone bank. Our waggoner could not get them up this. Some travellers came along and we shouldered the wheels but all was unavailing. We now were all in a sad dilemma and I believe all wished themselves under the roof of Volney and had the house not been occupied, perhaps should have returned. The nearest house was then three miles ahead, from thence we got a span of horses and, after counselling sometime what could be done, I proposed to stay behind, take out the plunder [baggage] and proceed up the Ohio when and how I could. This was about 12 miles from Volney and 20 from Evansville. I was sorry and disappointed at this arrangement as I had anticipated some pleasure and adventure in this overland journey, as my routes in this country had always been down rivers. To leave the things at Evansville to be sent on would have caused considerable uneasiness and risk.

Third Day: The waggon now very light and we move on without any difficulty.

Fourth Day: Go on about 12 miles when I return to Princeton. I now find myself lame from sore feet and ankles and was unable to travel for three weeks. The accursed seed ticks, which you have heard of before, in our letters, had caused me to scratch the skin and the poison dews from some vines or plants caused these places to fester and whenever I walked a little, soon became painful. This poisoning, as they call it, is not an uncommon thing here. When in their country before I was in the same scrape. None of these plagues assail me east of the Allegheny.

27th September: Leave Mr. Phillip's at Princeton, stay a night at Squire Barker's at Volney.

28th September: Arrive at Evansville and take up my abode at Major Warner's tavern, who is also High Sheriff of the County. For my board and a handsome room to myself, with a well found bed and as much wood as I like to burn, I pay $2.50 per day. At the table board judges, councillors, doctors, shoemakers and merchants, shopkeepers. The Mail Stage from Vincennes puts up here. Poultry, fruit, honey and all the substantial dishes.

22nd October: Start down the river to Henderson, 12 miles lower, having been three weeks at Evansville, without the chance of a boat, the keels generally going up on the opposite shore and the river being broad I have no chance of hailing them.

24th October: A Keel boat hove in sight. The Captain lands, his boat bound to Pittsburgh, distance 900 mile, agree with him to take me as a passenger for $8 and my freight at

$1 per cwt.

Matilda, I shall give you some perticulars [sic] of the voyage of this Keel boat, as it will give you and your cousins, boys and girls, an idea of the vast magnitude of this broad country and its powerful rivers. Tho you are such a potent and daring people, all the world knows you cannot get much more than 50 miles from the ocean that encircles your little, foggy, Bull island and yet 'tis a nice, tight, little island and thronged with heaps of clever bipeds. But to the Keel boat: she took her departure from Pittsburgh in August, laden with dry goods (that is, cases of drapery etc.), bound to Florence, State of Alabama – 1,350 miles, 1,020 miles down the Ohio and 330 miles up the Tennessee River. Your maps will show you through what States these magnificent streams shape their mighty courses. The cargo they take back is a freight of Cane, from the shores of the Tennessee River, for reed-makers and fishing rods; some of the latter 40 feet long. One of your great men defined angling thus: A long pole, with a bit of twine, a worm at one end and a fool at the other.

The greatest of my misery arose from cold. I had a bag of straw, some carpeting, a large wolfskin and extra clothing (undressing out of the question) but with all my scheming I could not be warm. At Cincinnati I gave $6 for a buffalo robe, extra large, dressed and Indian painted. This settled the matter and gave me all the comfort as to warmth from the crown of my head to the sole of my foot that I could wish for. Its ample and glowing folds set wind and frost at defiance. It was worth more to me than the Holy Ghost or even the whole Trinity, all of a heap. (By the bye, has your brother, Charles, yet made out what the Holy Ghost is – it used to perplex him.)

You perhaps may wonder at why I chose this mode of

travelling, when you hear so much about American steamboats. The waters are too low for them and we are now in some danger of being frozen up before we reach Pittsburgh.

13th December, Pittsburgh: Landed here today after a passage of 50 days up the Ohio. Here I stay 15 days, hesitating about the best way of getting along the ton of baggage to Rochester. I, at last, decide on taking it onto Philadelphia, freight per waggon $1.00, 290 miles, Philadelphia, by sea to New York, up the North River and along the Canal. I have engaged to stand by these things, in all their wandering, so you see I have got a job. It may be April before the Canal opens.

20th December: Attend to getting all the matters well packed in a well. Found a horse waggon, tyres of the wheel $1^1/_2$" thick, an honest waggoner – the owner.

30th December: See the horses in the waggon and with my bag on my shoulder and a full trimmed western hunting shirt, commence my march once more over the Blue Mountains

15th January: Arrived at Philadelphia after sixteen days from Pittsburgh. The roads were bad and I had considerable deal of stormy, bad weather in the mountains, a rick of an ankle laid me up one day and retarded my headway several others. Now all well and snugly fixed in a handsome little parlour with a pile of blazing pine at my elbow and feel fixed for three or four weeks' enjoyment, after which I shall proceed to New York and as soon as the Canal opens, take the things on to Mildred.

Matilda, now aged seventeen, and her brothers and sister, must have been amazed at this account of a journey in the wilderness of western America. They lived in a large, comfortable house among the verdant Sussex lanes, surrounded by green hedges and ancient oak trees.

In January 1825, Daniel wrote to his brother, Charles. He was anxious to hear news from home, particularly whether anyone had got married: 'I love folks should increase their happiness by getting good husbands and wives; if there are such schemes afloat tell me now, there's a good man and that quickly too.' This was probably a reference to his sister, Susanna. Charles was apparently still talking of visiting America but Daniel warned him of the penalties, disadvantages, etc. Subsequently, however, he went on to plan a route for him, up the Hudson River, along the canal to Pittsford, on to Niagara Falls, Lake Erie, down the Allegheny and the Ohio Rivers then down the Mississippi to New Orleans and back overland to New York. This was much the same route as that taken by Daniel and William during the early part of the 1800s but made much faster by the advent of better roads and steamships. Daniel thought this would take a year to fifteen months, and would probably cost around £100.

Daniel enclosed a parcel for Richard Carlile, containing Noak's *National Advocate*, which included the account of the celebration of Thomas Paine's birthday. Daniel asked Charles to make his kind remembrance to Mr. and Mrs. Carlile, with 'best wishes for their health and prosperity, and that their future usefulness may continue uninterrupted by the officious and cowardly combination of bigots and tyrants'. He also said that many people in New York felt interested in Carlile, that his daring and boldness surprised the citizens, and from it they concluded the press was pretty free in England.

Daniel was at pains to convince his family in England that all was well in his life. He admitted sometimes feeling the lack of an interesting occupation, at the same time stating that he generally had some project in train.

James, by his own admission no great man of letters, wrote to Daniel assuring him that all was well with the family, pleased with life and his acquisition of property. Daniel was still concerned that their father had not yet arranged his affairs and he wished his brothers could manage this between them; James Constable Sr. was by now seventy-five years old.

While Daniel was staying in Pittsford General Lafayette passed along the canal on his way to a reception at Rochester. Le Marquis de Lafayette, soldier and politician, fought in the American War of Independence (1777-1802) and became a hero to the young George Washington. On returning to France he presented a draft of the Declaration of the Rights of Man to the French National Assembly. However, during the French Revolution he became disliked because of his moderation and finally had to flee his native country. He was arrested by the Austrians and imprisoned until 1797. He later became the radical leader of the Opposition party and then leader of the National Guard in the 1830 revolution. Daniel recounts:

> having never seen this justly celebrated soldier and daring and always active asserter of the rights of man, I fixed out

to do this thing completely. Arriving sometime before the gay and enthusiastic cavalcade and lines of boats and barges I sauntered up the canal alone, as I like to be at such times, individualising always does best. By a little management, that is a lookout for a chance to step on board the packet in which was the hero; which I accomplished and had the satisfaction of being one of the little groups by his side for some distance. This was a chance but few had as the Militia Companies, on his arrival at Rochester, kept the admiring crowds at a distance. But I, being on the barge, went uninterruptedly to the Arch. I took the opportunity of taking him by the hand, with a short say. He thanked me, said he was glad to see me, in such English as would have given no suspicion of his being a Frenchman. Some of your papers have sneered at all this and called it affectation and vanity but they cannot feel like us Americans. The history of his life and actions prove his value in that contest which gave birth to freedom on our earth and was the first link ever knocked out of the chain that has always bound nations to the will of Kings, Priests and Ignobles.

Daniel planned to visit Canada once he had reunited the Purse family with their possessions. He thought he might visit Charles Claude Grece from Redstone Hill, near Reigate, who was farming part of his father's land on the Ottawa River. He asked Charles to find out if Mr. Grece was still in Canada, or if he had returned to England (it was into the Grece family that Susanna was to marry). However, Daniel did not go to Canada as planned as, by the time he was ready to leave, the weather was closing in. He left Mount Volney at Christmas time, 1825, having spent three months helping John Purse paint his house and glaze the windows. He travelled to Albany along the canal, before continuing on to New York. In a postscript he added to a letter home, written by Mildred, he said that although the prospect of the Purse family was that of a tranquil, quiet life, they had no chance of getting rich. He wrote that he planned to travel on to Philadelphia, Baltimore and Washington almost immediately, an area where he had not been for a while, although he also mentioned the possibility of returning to England, if only for a visit.

In a letter to Susanna Daniel observed that he had seen by the papers the grand celebration on commencing the new London Bridge. He asked that Charles be reminded to send him a set of views and plans of the Thames Tunnel works (the Rotherhithe Tunnel built by Marc Isambard Brunel). Daniel stayed in New York until after the celebrations for Independence Day in July 1826, then travelled back to Pittsford. He had been wandering around the local country, by Canandaigua, Rochester, Henrietta, etc., observing people and scenes, as was his wont. He had planned to go to Canada but again had been trapped by the weather, as Lake Ontario was too stormy and the canal had just begun to freeze. Because of this he decided to spend the winter in Pittsford and descend the St. Lawrence as soon as the weather was more kindly in the spring.

In the spring he wrote home to say the weather had been so severe that the peach trees, laden with blossom, were covered with snow. He noted how busy the area of Rochester had become, remembering that when he and William were there in 1806, nineteen years earlier, there was nothing but a log cabin and a mill, with a pair of two-and-a-half-foot stones. This was very small compared to the several pairs of four-foot stones at Horley Mill.

Daniel did not descend the St. Lawrence River but instead in June 1827 set off by canal to Buffalo, where he took a steamboat for Detroit, crossing Lake Erie into Lake St. Clair upon which Detroit is situated. He continued across Lake Huron through the Straits of Mackinac into Lake Michigan (the largest of the U.S. lakes) into Green Bay, a lake of that name famed for its scenery. This was not his planned route but he had heard that Governor Cass, the Secretary of State, Henry Clay, and some Indian agents were going to form new treaties with several Indian Nations, whose representatives were to be assembled in these regions. So, out of interest he travelled on the same boat with them. This was typical of Daniel. He was very much an observer of life, and permanently fascinated by the goings on around him. It is probable that he also had a strong sense that he was witnessing something historical. In the autumn he returned to Pittsford.

Once again Daniel did not return to England. Instead he bought a farm, adjoining that of Mildred, and let the land to John Purse. He felt himself a true American and planned to take out U.S. citizenship; perhaps, by now, even the restless Daniel felt the need for some roots. Daniel did not stay in Pittsford long. He was off again that winter, back to New York for a while, and then on to Philadelphia, Baltimore and Washington where he intended to call on General Jackson.

From Pittsford Ann Billinghurst wrote to her brother, James

Browne, in Sussex, describing Daniel:

> I wish you could have Mr. Daniel Constable with you a week. He could tell you more than I can write in 40 letters. He has travelled so much about America and he is a man that takes such perticular [sic] pains to inform himself about all sorts of business and what progress is going on here. He always carries his pencil in his pocket and writes down what he wants to remember. He will travel from one township to another all round about for his amusement and find all the fresh manufactories that are set up and every new work or old work that is going on and go into people's houses where he is an entire stranger and ask for a little water to drink, or to sit down to rest him a little. Then he will entertain them with many little tales and anecdotes of his travels and excursions which is very pleasing and ask them a great many questions all about their business and prosperity and everything he wants to know. He makes himself so agreeable they always want him to come again. I am always glad to see him. He has always something new to tell us and if he can do us any good any way, he is always ready and willing.

This is a lovely description of Daniel, who seemed to be everyone's friend.

CHAPTER FOURTEEN

Susanna

SUSANNA WAS SEVENTEEN years old when her brothers, Daniel and William, returned from America. They must have been surprised to find a young lady in the place of the child they had left behind. She was quite small and very attractive, with fine, regular features. She must have been very pleased to have her brothers at home, particularly William, who was always so kind to her.

In December of 1808 Susanna went to stay in Storrington to help her brother James, and Sophia, with their new baby, Matilda. She spent some months with James and his family before returning home. There were to be eight more nephews and nieces born within the next six years, and no doubt Susanna was dispatched from pillar to post to help. In between times she helped her mother in the house and her father in the shop.

In June 1814 Daniel gave her a book called *The Cry of Nature* in the flyleaf of which he inscribed: 'D. Constable to Susan, a barter for her Ear-Rings, a barbarism she for ever renounces, her understanding the folly of torturing the body to make it fine.' Susanna had obviously had her ears pierced, much to Daniel's disapproval. She was now twenty-three years old.

Susanna was probably in great demand from her brothers to help out in their schoolrooms as the children grew older. A notebook of hers survives for the year 1817, in which long tracts by Henry Bolingbroke, amongst others, are copied. Susanna's corrections are in black ink throughout the book.

As we have seen when Daniel returned to America in 1820, after the death of their mother, he was very keen that his father and Susanna should think seriously about leaving England. Although Susanna may have considered this possibility, she cared for her elderly father and it is unlikely that he would ever have considered emigrating.

It is probable that Susanna met Henry Grece through his family being customers at her father's shop, although he was also a personal friend of her brothers James, William and Charles. They had become well acquainted because Henry travelled to London in his gig every Monday morning, and the spare seat was available for family and friends on the unspoken understandiing that they paid the toll fees. Apparently a flag went up from Chart Lodge at a stated hour, visible for miles around with the aid of a spy glass, red being for 'Go' and white for 'No Go'. James, William and Charles all regularly availed themselves of this service and often accompanied Henry.

By 1823 Henry knew the family well enough to spend Christmas with them. That particular Christmas there was quite a gathering at The Old Mill House, including Clio Rickman and Susan Jordan, a cousin of the Constables through their mother.

She had been housekeeping for Charles and his father and became good friends with Susanna. (In the spring of 1825 Susan married a Mr. Pugh, a farmer, and went to live in Shropshire. The two Susans conducted a lively correspondence over the years.) Susanna and Henry's courtship must have proceeded in a rather slow fashion as in November 1828, Daniel wrote to Susanna, from Pittsford, when he was still urging her to think of settling in America:

> James said in his letter that you had a perticular [sic] friend in one of the Messrs. Grece, that is all I know about the matter except James expressed a wish that you were settled. My acquaintance with that family was slight and I only knew the person of one of the young men and his name I have forgot. One, I think, was a lawyer, who I think was farming in Canada when I came away and I guess your friend must be the one I continually saw at Reigate, a hale, young, practical farmer?
>
> Has it ever come athwart your mind to come to this country? I have lately thought a good deal on that subject. A small capital stands for so much here and we have now the knowledge that would enable people to steer their course aright, at least I think so. I would, by no means, persuade you to come right away to this land. I could not take such a responsibility upon myself.

It was, indeed, Henry Grece who was Susanna's 'perticular' friend. He was an extremely handsome, intelligent and amusing man. His mother was reputed to be directly descended from the infamous

James Whitney, a notorious highwayman hanged at Smithfield. Henry's father, John William Grece, was of Hanoverian extraction; he had made a fortune in various merchant adventures. He and his wife were painted by Thomas Lawrence, the famous portraitist, and these paintings were left as heirlooms in his will. During the French naval blockade of 1801 John William Grece had obtained a wayleave from the Government, and had imported a large quantity of wheat from the Prussian ports; for this the king granted him a township of 10,000 acres on the banks of the Ottawa River in Canada, which was named Grece's Point. He also owned a large farm on Canvey Island with its own landing, fronting onto the estuary of the River Thames.

In 1806 John William and Ann Grece were living in the Surrey village of Brixton. According to their eldest son, Charles Claude:

> One day, while strolling about, John William from curiosity entered an auction shop; the auctioneer was expatiating on the beauty, fertility and great value of a piece of land he had just put up. There were very few present and the bidding at first was confined chiefly to the auctioneer himself. Becoming interested, however, Mr. Grece began to bid and the competition was lively for a time between the auctioneer and himself until, most unexpectedly to Mr. Grece, it was struck off to him at £150.
>
> A few days after this he set out to view his newly acquired property which was located at some distance from the place where he resided. This was Father's first visit to the Chart. We had walked from Godstone and I remember he was

puzzled to find the place at all. And what a wild place then. Just at nightfall he reached an Inn in a rural hamlet and made some enquiries of the landlord respecting his property. Without giving him the required information the landlord quietly advised him to wait till morning when he could see it and judge of its value himself. He accepted the advice and early the next morning, in high spirits, walked out to view his purchase.

Some little time after his return the landlord asked him how he liked his property and his only reply was that he wished he could blow it and all recollection of it into oblivion.

This same property, however, developing its hidden treasures of Fullers Earth, paid the owner £2,300 and, in 1862, it sold at public auction for £10,050.

Thus John William Grece became a fuller's earth merchant. In 1828 Henry's elder brother, Charles Claude, and his younger brother, Horatio, were already farmng in Canada and it had been the elder Mr. Grece's intention that the whole family should move there. However, he was still engaged in a lawsuit with the British and Canadian Governments over land they had requisitioned, without his permission, for a canal which cut through his land.

As mentioned earlier the Constable family received a severe blow at the end of January 1829, when John and Elizabeth Constable died within days of each other. Early in February Clio Rickman, staying at Pillar Cottage, wrote a note to Susanna, asking for a stock to wear at the funeral:

My dear Susan,

I am distrest [sic] for a black stock. I know your great
goodness will not let me remain so. I pray to George to send
me a decent shaving brush as I left mine at Brighton.

Best love and regards and wishes among you,

Yours, dear Susan, for ever and ever.

Clio.

In April 1829 Clio, back in London, returned a cake box to
Susanna, with some verses as a thank you for a cake she had
evidently made for him. In the verse he refers to John and
Elizabeth's death, and to Susanna's wedding plans:

My dear Susan,

> *A cake from her I've loved so long*
> *And shall not this awake the song?*
> *The past, the golden hours of yore*
> *And days, that can return no more;*
> *Tho gone, the souls of truest worth,*
> *And flown each bliss I knew on earth,*
> *Some little comfort still is left,*
> *I'm not of every good bereft,*
> *And Susan, ever good and kind,*
> *Still bears poor Clio in her mind.*

> *Thanks, dearest girl! May the next be*
> *Thy wedding cake! and I with glee*
> *Will quaff thy health and this my prayer*
> *May'st thou be heaven's peculiar care.*

> *All things are not quite what they seem*
> *So, this same box not empty deem;*

Naught visible indeed 'tis true
Of solid form appears to view;
But 'tis full, Susan! to the brim,
Of countless thanks − of prayers from him.
That every blessing yours may be,
And those attached to thine and thee.

Farewell! Whene'er it please your grace,
Solids within the box to place,
It will be grateful to the bard,
Provided they are not very hard,
For all his lockers (full of yore)
Are empty now − and out of store.

To those around you who still care,
If well, or ill, the bard may face,
Present my love − and wishes best,
And may no ills betide the rest.

Clio

P.S. Since writing this letter I have been severely confined to my bed but am again downstairs.

Henry Grece and Susanna were now betrothed, but there were serious problems in the way of their marriage. Henry had been left in charge of the fuller's earth pits and the farms when his father departed for Canada to oversee his estate on the Ottawa River. He was also left in charge of his numerous younger brothers and sisters, some of whom were still at school. Although John William Grece had now returned to England, his health was causing grave concern. He was still fighting the British Government over his claim for compensation. Either he was very confident of his success or he was too ill to be aware of his deteriorating financial situation.

Eventually the marriage was arranged for December 1829. However, Susanna was stood up, practically at the altar. On the appointed day Susanna waited and waited but Henry never appeared. She was obviously distraught and William immediately rode over to Redstone Hill to find out what was happening. Lucy Browne from Baltimore (Henry Browne's niece) was on a visit to England with her mother and was supposed to be the bridesmaid. Years later she explained to Henry and Susanna's son some of what happened on that day:

> The last day that Dec., Mother and I were at Dovers Green, it was on a Sunday and your father was there all the evening and that was a most sorrowful day for your poor mother which I did not know until afterwards. The next day my mother and I left for London on our way home and very much to my surprise your Uncle William came, I think the day after, to bring me back to be bridesmaid to your mother.
>
> I learned from my sister, when I got back, how it all happened. Your mother expected your father at Horley the Sunday before and as he did not come, she was greatly distressed. That week her marriage license would run out and she was in such great trouble that your Uncle William went to your father to ask him what his intentions were. What passed between them we never knew, only that your father consented to be married. He then went to your mother and told her she must decide. She was in great distress and took counsel of my sister, Mary. She could not

decide for herself and she told sister she must decide for her and she would abide by it. So sister told her to marry. I asked her how she could so decide. Because, she said, she knew Susan was so devoted to him that she would be perfectly miserable if she did not have him. I told her I thought it would be better to be miserable for a while than to run the risk of being so the remainder of her life.

When we got to the church the clergyman was not there. We waited a long time and he only came just in time to perform the ceremony before twelve o'clock. Your father and mother and I got into a post chaise and went to London and in a few days my mother and I sailed for home.

We shall never know exactly why Henry stayed away on the day he was due to marry. It must have been obvious by now that his father was dying and he must have known that his family were in money difficulties. He probably felt unequal to the task of providing for a wife as well but that does not excuse his behaviour. Upon their marriage Susanna moved in with Henry's family who lived at Chart Lodge, Redstone Hill (later abbreviated to Redhill). Unfortunately John William Grece died just three weeks later and his financial affairs were, indeed, to prove a great burden to Henry. There were twelve children altogether, and the youngest was thirteen and still at school. As Henry's elder brother was in Canada, the responsibility for his mother and the younger children fell on Henry.

In April 1830, Clio again wrote to Susanna:

My dear Susan,
I write to you for the first time by the name of Grece. God

bless it to you. But I address by the old, endearing name of Susan and I hope I shall hear well of you and your dear Henry.

I have been very, very ill but live in hopes as the winter wears away all will be better. Alas, I have a winter about me, much worse than the season.

I write now a begging letter. My chamber towels are all rags and I want a few coarse unbound handkerchiefs, stuff for pillowcases, anything is good enough if they wear, in both the articles, but I am in a great need of them! I owe something at your shop and tho' I am now actually in want, the winding up of my affairs, after my death, will leave enough for all debts.

God bless you all. I am in great pain. When shall I see Henry with you, dear Susan?

Clio

It is quite possible that Clio's various spells in gaol had injured his health. He lived alone in Marylebone now his children had all grown and left.

Susanna went home to Horley in August 1831, where she gave birth to a son, Clair James, the youngest of the Constable grandchildren. She was now forty-one years old, which was relatively elderly to embark on pregnancy and childbirth for the first time. All was well, however, and Clair James was to prove a tower of strength to his mother, helping to assuage the misery of what seems to have been an unhappy marriage. As Lucy Browne was to write to Clair James many years later:

> All that my sisters could tell me was that it turned out a very unhappy marriage. If her married life was miserable I

suppose it did not last long and she must have felt great pride and pleasure in you and the many happy years you have spent together must have compensated her for her unhappy wedded life which I should like to know as much about as you like to tell me. If it is not too painful for you to write about you may write freely.

Neither Lucy nor Mary Browne ever married. Mary remained in Lewes where she opened a school and was much loved by all her pupils. In later years Henry Browne (William's ertswhile employer in Lewes) was to say that she had proved a tower of strength to all, and was very like her mother.

CHAPTER FIFTEEN

Charles The Miller

CHARLES WAS THE YOUNGEST surviving son of the family, born in 1786. Photographs show him to be tall, with prominent craggy features. Daniel described him as: 'that broad round limbed miller man'. He was the only son to remain in the milling business for all his working life, a pillar of the local community. Was this perhaps a relic of the old Sussex law that declared the youngest son the heir of his father, rather than the eldest?

In a letter to Susanna in 1823 Daniel is clearly concerned about Clio, who had been taken prisoner for non-payment of debts. He is worried, too, that Clio has too big an influence on their brother, Charles, as he has heard that he is often a visitor at the Mill: 'Don't let him get too much footing among you, nor advance him money in consequence of this legacy business.' Clio has written down the side of the letter: 'This is malappreciation of my character. It is most unfeeling, false and unjust!'

Although Daniel often urged Charles to visit America he procrastinated and in May 1826 he married Jane Charman, from Lee Farm in Clapham. Although Jane was living in Clapham at the time of their marriage the Charman family were from

Sussex. For many years they lived at Lyminster Court in Lyminster, which they leased from Thomas Knight of Chawton (Jane Austen's brother was adopted by the Knight family). After their marriage Charles and Jane made The Mill House their home.

In 1821 James Sr. had obtained consent to enclose a circular area of the heath around the windmill. This was ratified in April 1827. The windmill was now let. This was presumably done after the big watermill was working at full strength and Charles had more than enough to do. In 1827 the tenant, Mr. Parker, became extremely worried that the precious wind he needed for milling would be reduced by the new building taking place on the heath. Apparently this building also took the sun and the view from the windmill. Presumably with the backing of the Constable family he tried to bring an injunction against the project. The *Morning Advertiser* for 2 April 1827 produced a drawing of the windmill showing the sunrise eclipsed by the offending house. Underneath was the caption:

The Great White House and the Windmill. An Eclogue.
Scene: Lowfield Heath, -The Mill, -Time, Sunrise.
First Miller: Curse on that great white house, say I
Rearing its saucy front so high
Our prospects how it does impede,
It is a nuisance vile indeed
See how it shades the rising beam
Of the bright sun that here should gleam
What shall we do, my fellows civil
To rid us of this crying evil.

Second Miller:
You have not stated half our wrong.
You have only named small ills; ere long
What with the buildings – fences – trees,
We soon shall want the eastern breeze,
And that White House with all its clutter
Will rid us – of our bread and butter.

First Miller:
I know the way to do the deed.
We will Injunction wise proceed!!!
The Chancellor surely will not cavil
To help us in this hour of evil,
And though His Honour calmly bears
To see the people cross the squares,
He will not let the White House, here
Rob us of wind, view, sunny cheer
But quick will order all away,
Open, enlarge, our prospect gay.
Then spite of all the great White House can say,
We'll cheerily work our mill by night and day.

All the Millers:
Let's give three hearty cheers, my boys, to show
That we the bouncing White House folks can do!
Huzza – Huzza – Huzza! my boys so clever!
The windmill and the Chancellor for ever!!!

The article read:

The Chancellor's Court, Saturday, Injunctions
Mr. Parker applied this morning for an Injunction to restrain

a Mr. Woodbridge from enclosing a Common called Lowfield Heath, situate in the parish of Charlwood in the county of Surrey. The Learned Gentleman was proceeding to read the affidavits in support of the application when he was interrupted by the Vice-Chancellor, who inquired what irreparable injury would result from the enclosure which is sought to prevent.

Mr. Parker confessed that he did not think that the injury would be irreparable. The Vice-Chancellor. – We shall soon have injunctions to prevent a party from crossing a Square, – injunctions are now applied for upon every occasion as matters of course. This is going much beyond the principle upon which the jurisdiction of this Court is exercised. The injury apprehended must be irreparable or the Court ought not to interfere. I must refuse this application.

The Constable family and their tenant, Mr. Parker, must have been disappointed in the verdict, particularly as a windmill bereft of wind must have seemed an irreparable injury to them.

A daughter was born to Charles and Jane in 1828, whom they named Lavinia Sara Jane. A second daughter, Frances, to be known as Fanny, was born in 1830.

The Mill business was steady, although times were not easy. However, it was a big mill and custom came from a large area. Charles had become a pillar of local society and was as well known at Reigate Market as he was at the annual Market Dinner. He became a member of the Crawley Society, formed for the apprehension of felons and thieves. This society offered rewards ranging from 20gns for anyone convicted of murdering any member of the society, to 1gn for anyone assaulting any member of the society on the highway. Charles was also one of the surveyors for the parish of Horley and in 1829 he was involved in a skirmish with the governors of Christ's Hospital. This apparently came about because Christ's Hospital had failed to pay maintenance costs for the local highway. A summons was issued against Christ's Hospital which William delivered to them on 30 April.

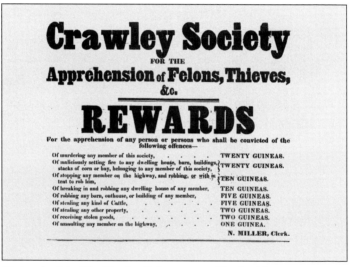

Poster advertising The Crawley Society, courtesy Crawley Museum

Early in 1831 Charles was appointed High Constable for the Reigate Hundred. This was a position of great responsibility involving, as it did, being a Conservator of the Peace, reporting all offences which 'tend to the corruption of morals or to the promotion of idleness – such as profanations of the Lord's Day, Gaming, Drunkenness, profane Cursing and Swearing, the keeping of Alehouses by Persons who have no License from the Magistrates, or who being licenced, permit Tippling at late hours or during Divine Service on the Lord's Day, Gaming and other irregularities therein, the keeping of Houses of ill fame'. Charles would also have been responsible for the superintendence of the Petty Constables and Headboroughs in the hundred as well as being on the lookout for any tradesman who used defective weights or measures. He also had to be aware of any maintenance needed on the roads or bridges in his care. Needless to say he had the authority to apprehend any offenders in order to present them to a Magistrate; this included uncovering any planned treasonable or seditious meetings. One wonders how Charles equated this last obligation with his own family's political views.

There were ongoing problems with the bridge over the river Mole adjacent to the watermill. Charles must have found himself in a difficult situation being both the occupier of the mill and the local surveyor. No doubt Charles felt that the parish should contribute towards the repairs of the bridge but as a local resident, William Comber, wrote:

> There never was such a thing mentioned for the parish of Horley to have anything to do with the footbridge up the pond bay at Horley Mills. I have seen Mr. Daniel Constable take his horse over that bridge up the fields to Hookwood Common to go to Cuckfield Market upwards of fifty years ago, also the aforesaid bridge was frequently used in high water to take over grists etc. for the use of the mill.

I fully believe the parishes of Horley nor Charlwood never had anything to do with it, were it a Parish concern Charlwood must have the same wright (sic) to there (sic) half of it, as it is over the stream which parts the parishes, were it there wright it must be a Joint Concern but I fully believe the Parishes have nothing to do with it Whatsoever.

Although Charles probably had to pay for repairs on this occasion times were improving. By 1833 he felt financially secure enough to spend a large amount of money making improvements to the Mill House. Then as soon as Lavinia and Fanny were old enough for their lessons Charles and Jane decided to employ a governess. Their obvious choice was William's ward, Emily Blundell, who was just eighteen years old. Emily's grandfather, George Blundell, had leased both the watermill and windmill from Daniel Sr. Emily had grown up at Benhams, just along the lane from the mill but her father, Richard, had died in 1824 when she was very young. William was not only trustee but guardian to Richard's three children (it may be remembered that William and Richard were in the militia together in 1812). No doubt Richard's widow, Mary, relied on William's advice. It was William's name on young Robert's apprenticeship papers when he began his training with the well known surveyor, John Hosmer, in 1837.

Lavinia and Fanny, known as the 'mill girls', were much of an age with their cousin, Clair James Grece. He often visited with his mother and father and the trio bowled their hoops and played tag for amusement. Clair James sometimes joined the two girls in their schoolroom although he, himself, did not have formal lessons at home.

CHAPTER SIXTEEN

Daniel in England

DANIEL MUST HAVE BEEN horrified to learn of John and Elizabeth's deaths, early in 1829. He had little time to recover from this shock before the news of Jemima's ill health took a serious turn, culminating in her death in November. However, there was good news to follow, of Susanna's marriage to Henry in January 1830, although William must have written to him about Henry's extraordinary behaviour.

Daniel may well have felt that his presence in England would be welcome at this time, or he may have just felt it was high time for a visit. Before he left, however, he signed the declaration that he wished to become an American citizen.

He wrote to his father in July saying that he had been detained in New York, as he wanted to hear the lectures of a certain Miss Frances Wright, who had recently returned from Haiti. Miss Wright was the celebrated Scottish social reformer who, in 1821, had written *Views of Society and Manners in America*. In 1824 she had accompanied the Marquis de Lafayette on a tour of the U.S. and on a subsequent visit had established an experimental community in Tennessee designed to prepare slaves for emancipation. This experiment, however, was not a success, so she travelled to Haiti to settle the freed slaves from her community. Later, when living in Indiana, she became coeditor, with R. D. Owen, of the *New Harmony Gazette*. When they decided life in Indiana was not for them they founded the *Free Enquirer* in New York.

Daniel also told his family that he had had a small growth on his chest for many years, which had recently begun to tingle, and he was undecided as to whether to have it removed or not. Having weighed up the pros and cons he decided against an operation and booked his passage to England. In the summer of 1830 there must have been great rejoicing in the family when Daniel arrived home after an absence of ten years. His father, particularly, must have been overjoyed to see him. He found the old man very fit and active for a man of his age. In a letter to her sister, Ann Billinghurst, Mary Browne (Susanna's great friend) observed: 'Mr. Constable Sr. is very well indeed – he is 83 and runs about like a young man.'

In March 1831, Lord Russell proposed the first Reform Bill to the House of Commons. It was mooted that over one hundred Rotten Boroughs should be abolished and replaced with new constituencies. (A Rotten Borough was a sham borough, e.g. the Borough of Gatton, near Reigate, which had a mock Town Hall built in the grounds of Gatton Park, probably better described as a folly.) The Reform Bill was an affront to the Tories of the day, who firmly believed that the landed classes had a right to rule, and that seats should be bought and sold like any other piece of property. There was great agitation throughout the country and the bill was defeated. This provoked an uproar; the king, William IV, was under great pressure and the Whigs gained a majority of over a hundred in the House of Commons. However, although the peers themselves were divided in their opinions in the House of Lords, the twenty-one Bishops in the Lords voted against reform and the bill was defeated. It is unfortunately not recorded what Daniel and his friends thought of this, but they were certainly bitterly disappointed.

Daniel did not stay in Horley for long. By the middle of August 1831 he was off again on his travels through England, carrying with him various tracts and papers brought from America to show newspaper editors and fellow reformers in the clubs and newsrooms of the provincial towns and cities. The Industrial Revolution had arrived, together with general unrest and rioting across the land. Much of this manifested itself in rick burnings and deliberate damage to threshing machines and factory machinery (seen as the evil force behind unemployment). In September Daniel wrote to William and Charles; the letter is headed from Birmingham, Worcester, Bristol, etc. He was obviously fascinated by the changes that had been wrought in England during his ten years absence in America:

Dear Broth's,
Your gazateers [sic] will always tell better about places than a wanderer like me can but some things it may not tell you. I got along the canal well enough, baggage and all for 1/- to Birmingham and the next day fixed myself in a snug, little lodging and have been cruising around in all directions.

The whole country, as far as the eye can reach, presents one continued scene of blazing furnaces, roaring bellows, steam engines with their lofty chimneys almost darkening the sun with thick clouds of smoke and continued mounds of fires burning coal into coke for the iron furnaces.

Bull Baiting is the all and all attractive persuit [sic]. I think you have no idea of these shocking exhibitions, 'tis far more devilish than any of you can think. These Wakes last four or five days; it was the second at 7.00 a.m. when I got there. I did not know of any such amusement, as it is called, of Bull Baiting being in operation. There are five bulls this year but some years it exceeds that number. These are chained round in the different suburbs and always surrounded by a savage mob and their dogs. They go round with a hat and collect copper for a dog owner, 6d seems to do; a dog is then let loose at the poor animal. The first bull I saw was, as they term it, a good deal down, his horns were favourably fixed to defend himself, his nose, face and throat were horridly lacerated and swelled. Even in this state he cantered and threw the dogs about with much courage; one dog he threw quite over a house. I wished much to have seen some of the poor thing's two legged tormentors killed. As long as the animals can stand, day after day, do these fiends continue the bloody work of cruelty and then gorge his flesh at about 2d or $2^1/_2$d per pound, for they are all ultimately killed as food for their tormenting devils. The very climax of savage exultation is when a dog fixes the poor beast and he cannot shake him off; the pain then is so excruciating that his moans and bellowing are heart rending. What a damned infernal system of despotism and villainy, where the laws do not put down such savage barbarity as this, a nursery for murder, crime and cruelty. And how vigilant and fierce to fine and imprison people for selling 1d unstamped papers, of a very equivocal character as to the meaning of the law regarding them.

The Birmingham Political Union numbers about 10,000. They have a vigilant council of 40 who meet weekly. At some of these meetings have I been and have some acquaintance among them.

Worcester, 13th Sept. I arrived here two days since, a fine walk of 25 miles from Birmingham, the Malvern and Clay hills in full view often. Saw a good deal of barley uncut and wheat standing out through Bromsgrove, the great hobnail town, and Droitwich, famous for its salt works.

I am so nicely and happily fixed in a pretty, little dandy parlour with people so kind and civil, at the easy rent of 5/- per week, to do all I want in the shape of cooking, etc., and had I asked would have found me fuel but I felt in conscience I had enough for my money; coal 10d. per cwt. I believe, Charles, you know Worcester pretty well. My location is in a quiet sort of square, very near the big, grand Judge's office and the Head Juggler's Palace, but you know he is just gone to the Kingdom but if to the Upper one or the Lower one, we don't know. The quiet and cleanliness of this place contrasts finely with the din, fire and smoke of Birmingham.

In Bristol, with its ships, interesting situations and local beauties, I can make myself content and happy. I have kept myself pretty busy, interestingly so, among radicals, infidels, etc., walks round the country and in storms in newsrooms. At Birmingham they have a splendid one and here a very handsome structure built expressly for that purpose. As for words, hey dey, what a quantity I have got. Perkins sent me a copy of work by that talented R. D. Owen, upon the

subject of Carlile's *Everywoman's Book*, most discreetly
managed. It is termed *Moral Physiology*; it has been read at
Birmingham by some of the best informed Unitarians, who
approve of it much and will import some.

Well, now, if I can be of any use I will make one among you
at any time. Should anything be about to be done in the
arrangements of our father's affairs, or any other matters, a
few days will bring me along. I have an idea I shall like to
take up my abode in Bristol; its climate is better than yours.
For one week while at Birmingham I was right bad, weak
as a rat, hot and cold fits, night perspiration, hideous dreams
and did, indeed, think I was going to the Kingdom but,
mind me, I was not frightened about that. I made some
enquiry for a curing man and dreaded to be in the hands of
physic. I trusted to honest nature and her good disposition
to put all wrongs right. I never was better and had I gone to
the Gallipots they would most assuredly have had all the
credit and poor honest nature lost all the praise for her
energies.

Affectionately,

D.C.

Note: The Gallipots were the small earthware vessels used
for potions and salves.

After the defeat of the Reform Bill rioting broke out in the
Midlands and by November 1831 when Daniel had reached
Bath, Bristol was a scene of chaos. Amidst mounting unrest the
city recorder, Sir Charles Weatherall, had insisted on the usual
Parade, with full regalia, through the city to open the Assises, in
spite of advice to the contrary. Almost inevitably fierce rioting

began. Daniel wrote to Matilda (Tilly) and Clara (Titsey), James's daughters, now aged twenty-two and seventeen:

Dear Tilly and Titsey and all,

Well, here I am in the very focus of fire, fury and vengeance, plunder, blood and desecration. Episcopal Palaces, Custom House, Mansions, etc., wreck, ruin and misery and all through the obstinacy of one silly old dotard of an incorrigible incendiary Tory, Sir C. Weatherall. Yesterday (Tuesday) I mounted the coach and was in Bristol soon after 9.00 a.m., being as soon as I thought I could safely go. I had been two weeks at Bristol so the scene of destruction was familiar to my eye. All was under martial law and had, what I suppose, the appearance of a city sacked. I returned at night, the shops generally shut, the Military and innumerable Special Constables thronged the streets. The Exchange was thrown open for the reception of goods of every kind recovered from thieves, of which I think it quite likely 50 waggon loads were deposited during the day besides what streams of Constables kept bringing in by hand, such as mirrors, china, etc. In some of the streets guards were placed at each end permitting no person to pass in or out while every house was searched. When I left about 4.00 p.m. upwards of 200 thieves had been made prisoner. The number of lives lost can as yet be only known by conjecture, many of whom are no loss to the earth. Many innocent people are known to have been shot and sabered; a pretty good lot got roasted to death in a drunken state. The jails, bridges and public buildings which I saw a few days before so neat and trim, now masses of smoking and flaming ruins, for the flames were not extinguished.

The intense anxiety here, for the two preceding days, by the groups and runnings about after intelligence from Bristol put everything in the greatest confusion in our stone city. All sorts of reports were flying about, sometimes 10,000 colliers were in full march upon Bath. There was no peace and quiet anywhere. General indignation, loud and spiteful, is uttered against the vile old Tory with wishes that he and his carriage had been thrown over Bristol Bridge into the Avon. Doubtless the upholders of pious frauds and tyranny will lay all this at the door of the Reformers and bellow about it, as a foretaste of what will be the result of any Reform. Among my folks here there is no sympathy for that haughty Prelate's loss of his Palace, plate, wine and books of lies by which he carried on his fraudulent craft. I am right glad these knaves voted as they have done. It has forced the people, all about, into a train of investigating into their lofty claims of pretended knowledge about other worlds and other existences, fudging people out of their wits and cash. Oh! the Holy Fathers in God, how the rascals are terror struck. This Holy Ghost man of Bath and Wells is a cruel, immoral chap, does not pay his just debts; persons who have felt his injustice have told me so.

On Sunday night when all was so terrific at Bristol, we had here what in ordinary times would have been called a terrible destructive mob. Of this I saw the rise, progress and finish. About dusk on Sunday, expresses arrived here from the Bristol authorities for aid. The Bath Yeoman Cavalry made an attempt to assemble; this, the people would not permit. The Captain retreated to the splendid hotel, The White Hart, for personal safety, from which he attempted to harangue them but he would not be heard. The Inn doors were then shut and volleys of stones soon broke in all the windows and shutters and some persons entered and injured much furniture. The next day many best shops shut and Specials, as they say here, paraded the street in groups, keeping everybody on the move; by night it was pretty much over. They are keeping this as quiet as they can, fearing the aristocrats will not feel themselves safe here either; they have retreated from Clifton to Bath in considerable numbers, poor devils. You will see plenty about all this in the newspapers, so I will quit this subject and tell you a little about my mortal self.

While I think of it, I must tell you of a just rebuke I met with at Birmingham. Walking in the street and feeling saucy after a good breakfast I met a very good-looking girl, her face very black. I observed it was a pity such a pretty girl as she did not keep her face cleaner. She turned round, perfectly good natured and with confidence observed 'Sir, if you had to work as hard as I have in a gun factory for a living, perhaps you would not keep your face much cleaner than I do' and passed on. Poor wretch, I thought, you are helping to make muskets for some King or Emperor, to cause better men than themselves to be shot. I ran and overtook her, begged her pardon for the thoughtless rudeness I had been guilty of and hoped she would forgive me. I gave her the price of a day's work; she was very thankful and we parted right good friends.

Next put myself, bag and baggage, on board a barge and four days brought me to Bristol. This, you know, is an old, smoky, commercial city with some whole streets of such houses as you sometimes see a solitary one in London. In one place you might truly shake hands across the street with your opposite neighbours but among all this was much that I liked. There were streets terraced one above the other, with clean stone passages so steep that carriages could not get up. In one of these streets I had my abiding place. But Clifton, ah that is a fine place. Here you know are Hot Wells and Palace-like houses and gangs of aristocrats, the blind, lame and halt and surprising bold and beautiful scenes. Bath has 65,000 people (Brighton 40,000). Bath is the finest general built place I have ever been in. Its squares, circles, crescents and long, fine streets are magnificent but some of them so steep that carriages can hardly get up them. So entirely is this a stone city that I have not seen a single brick. The stone is a nice, clean buff colour. The grand salon, at the Pump Room, where assemble the gay and healthy, the helpless and cripples and invalids of all shapes; some in Sedans (which I thought had been quite out of fashion) and wheelchairs which put me in mind of a National Hospital. The shops and their contents are of the first order.

I am most delightfully located in a snug cottage within a stone's throw of the finest rows of Palace-like houses, commanding a bird's eye view of a great part of the city and the bold, finely cultivated hills above. For a great part of Bath lies in a valley with the Avon winding through it. From my window at night the gas lights are as pretty as Vauxhall. I am rather more than pleased, I am charmed and delighted with my fixings and pursuits. I find many folks here that suit me. Here is a Mechanics Institute, open every evening, fires, books, newspapers, etc., attached to which is a Lectures Room. To all this I am a free man. Many things I have with me about America delight them much. Oh! What hordes of good Infidels I meet with. In London, when I took my departure, I found a parcel of books, newspapers, etc. These have been a source of much interest to the Reformers and Infidels. I keep them well in circulation, loaning them to Editors of newspapers, libraries, newsrooms, Institutes and private persons. They give me full credit for my industry, zeal and usefulness. This, you know, must help to make me pleased with myself and contented. I believe I am a very good missionary man, in a very good and holy cause.

Now I hope this will find you all, every one, as well physically and mentally as I am and have been.

Affectionately,

D.C.

Reform was in the air and Daniel's progression through the towns and cities of middle England, armed with American pamphlets and other information that he had with him from the New World, spreading the word, was obviously highly satisfying. Daniel's letters are so vivid that the scenes are painted before our eyes.

CHAPTER SEVENTEEN

The New Generation

James's children were growing up fast. Matilda, his eldest child, was now twenty-one. She took her mother's place in the household although she found enough time to make long visits to her Uncle William and her Cobham cousins: William and Matilda shared an interest in painting and geology. William dedicated one of his lithographs: 'To my fair friend and cousin, Matilda'. Charles Jr., James's elder son, now aged nineteen, was studying law with Messrs. Gell & Roberts in London. William had arranged the articles through his friendship with Francis Gell, whom he had known in Lewes, where they had been fellow actors in the amateur dramatic society. The Gell family had long been associated with the law. Charles lodged with the family as was the usual practice at that time. Jemmy, now seventeen, had gone to work for his Uncle John in Cobham when he had left school the year before, the idea being that he would eventually take over his father's business. However, he did not take well to his new life:

> There was only one shopman besides myself; here I was
> called upon to open and shut up shop, sweep and dust out

and to do any thing in addition to waiting on customers; up at 6 a.m. and closing the store at 9 p.m. I had always been a very active boy, the first at all sorts of games; this great change and close confinement soon told on my health and in about two years I was considered to be in rapid consumption.

After the sudden death of his uncle and aunt Jemmy returned to Storrington, thankful to be free of these onerous duties. Whilst recovering his health and strength he spent some months ostensibly helping his father, although he actually spent the greater part of his time riding his horse on the Downs. James was very keen that his younger son should stay in Storrington and eventually take over his business. However, Jemmy had other ideas and, after some debate, he eventually took a post with Hall & Allen of St. Paul's Churchyard. The Halls were old family friends, so he was well treated and began to enjoy life more. Clara, the youngest, now aged fifteen, was still at school. She was a general favourite with her childless uncles, Daniel and William. She was delicately made with button bright dark eyes and rosy cheeks.

After the death of John and Elizabeth Constable in February 1829, their four children, Caroline twenty-five, Benjamin twenty-three, Eliza twenty-one and Daniel nineteen considered their future. They had been well educated. Caroline was a music teacher and Eliza a school teacher. They had all been taught to speak French and the boys had been trained as surveyors. Meantime it is probable that the boys took over running the shop while Caroline ran the household. Eliza was living with William at Doversgreen where she had been since the onset of Jemima's illness. The era of bad luck that seemed to dog the young family was not yet over. In November 1831, William wrote to his brother, James, with the news that their nephew, young Daniel, was seriously ill. This letter was written from Cobham where William had been summoned the night before:

Dear James,

I am very sorry to have a piece of very unfortunate news to communicate to you. Our little friend, Daniel, at this place is very ill indeed. He returned home from Dovers Green to this place a week ago today and the next day was seized with inflammation of the chest.

We were informed of it the day before yesterday by letter but we did not then apprehend there was much reason for alarm. The disease has since made rapid progress and I was called up at midnight by an express messenger who brought me the intelligence that the case was one of great and immediate danger.

I called Eliza from her bed, procured a post chaise and came away immediately and arrived here at half past four this morning and greatly regret to say I find the case without the least hope. You will easily imagine the distress that at present exists here. Caroline is pretty well but of course is much worn out with constant watching. I shall leave Eliza here for the present but she is considerably unwell and I should not consent to her quitting her warm quarters at Dovers Green at present except in the case of a pressing emergency.

The Shop department suffers for want of assistance. Have you a hand that you could spare for the present. Caroline has been in constant attendance on the shop during Daniel's holiday but now, of course, that assistance is withdrawn. I think the taking a hand from Horley would occasion great inconvenience there, as much perhaps as is now felt here. I am going away again almost immediately and leave this to be forwarded by tonight's post. I fear some important addition will be made to it before it is despatched.

7.30 p.m. Mr. Brown has just been here. He perceives no symptom of improvement. I feel quite satisfied that the malady has been attacked by a vigorous and decided mode of treatment and we may console ourselves that no advantage has been lost or neglected although the issue is likely to be so unfortunate.

We send our joint love to you all.

Yours affectionately,

William Constable.

A postscript was added by Daniel's elder brother, Benjamin:

P.S. Half past nine Wednesday evening: I am glad to say Daniel is no worse than he was in the morning, perhaps he is a trifle better but Mr. Brown says there is no hope. Benjamin Constable.

Happily, young Daniel made a miraculous recovery, seemingly against all odds.

Daniel Sr. was presently staying in Bath. He was not yet aware of young Daniel's recovery when he wrote to Matilda and Clara telling them that he had inspected the property in Bath that would be part of their Mansell inheritance:

> Poor Dan. I hope the poor chap will soon get well. I have nothing from Horley since yours. Three days since I have a letter from Yeend and when I move from hence I shall sojourn with him since he gives me such a hearty invitation.
>
> Tilly, I tell you more about this place as I hope among you you have got a good stake in it. The Avon, you know, winds through the town, its bed being a stone trough, being wharved up on each side. And Titsey, you elegant little Christian and fine-minded and fine-moulded little creature, here is such a superb Temple for you to worship in. Don't be mad with me, that's a dear little creature, you know I must have a queer say and a joke when I am in the humour and so I pray you to forgive my levity.
>
> Here are some snug, little, terraced rows of houses with gardens upon Avonside, that rent for £8 per year. When you come to take possession of your estates in these regions of health and fashion and it should so happen that I am upon this star of ours, I can have a canoe and fish for you and squat in one of these stone tenements. They have a bedroom, a parlour and kitchen, perpendicular, one right above the other and £10 would furnish them with enough for all the purposes of happiness, ease and security from the elements.

Clara had become a keen churchgoer so Daniel found it quite irresistible to tease her. She had acquired a suitor by the name of

William Maybury, a Protestant Irish surgeon, from Kenmare in Co. Kerry, who was building up a successful practice in Islington.

William wrote to Matilda in Storrington in December 1833, giving her the latest news about her Mansell grandfather, now aged seventy-seven;

> My dear Matilda,
> I write chiefly to inform you how poor grandpapa Mansell gets on. You will not be surprised to learn that he does not improve. I think the certainty has been established for some time that he will not rally again from this attack.
> He is declining slowly but very gradually and he is now greatly reduced in strength and substance from what he was when you last saw him. He has taken nothing whatever of the nature of food since last Tuesday when he sipped a small quantity of mutton broth. He, of course, now and for some time past keeps his bed entirely. I had a message from Mrs. Hunter this morning, stating that he had been yesterday much worse and she had apprehended at one time that his death was very near. I went over very soon after and saw him. He was then considerably recovered from the attack, talked to me cheerfully and sensibly for some time but says he finds his head apt to run sadly. He still complains of suffering a good deal from the uneasiness of his stomach but otherwise he has no pain. He is removed into the other front room for the benefit of a fire. The first bedroom he was in, I think, had no grate or was on some account unfit for a fire.
> I am grieved to have so much of disaster to talk about but the cat that you gave to Mrs. Penfold has been dispatched

for misdemeanours among the chickens. Our old game cock, too, is dead; he never recovered from the attempt that Flora made upon him of dragging him through the hedge. Perhaps you would like to hear more about the burning of the office. It is a bad story but the best of it is there was but little damage done. Nothing suffered but the deal boards that formed the front of the fireplace but they suffered considerably from the devouring element (I believe it is so called). When I came to this house and put in a low grate, it became necessary to depress the front of the fireplace and I, with great sagacity, had a piece of wooden timber put into the breast. I thought to make it fireproof by casing it with tin and it stood very well 13 years but 14 were too many for it. So, one evening last week, there having been a good fire in the morning, though but little in the afternoon, it broke out in a bright flame. Nobody had been in the room for a good while for I was from home and the housekeeper was busied with a long job upstairs but her nostril scented the conflagration and when she came downstairs to enquire into it, she saw the work that was going on. She did not faint, nor yet go into fits but she got some water and got the maid to help and between them put it out and then sent for Master Rozell to come and pull down the timber work and see if any slippery fragment of fire had escaped their vengeance. The only damage has been in the necessity of an entirely new frontispiece and the deprivation of the use of the room for a week or two. We hope to see it refitted tomorrow then a coat or two of paint and then we shall resume our wonted quarters.

I have got your dahlia root from Gilliam; if I do not see any opportunity of sending it soon I shall stow it away among my own for the winter.

Tom and the maid do not seem much to improve; they are under sharper discipline that they have been used to but nothing will make them good for much.

Eliza sends her love to you and Papa, of course and I am, of course as ever, affectionately thine,

William C.

Tom was probably the gardener-cum-odd-job-man. Both William and Matilda were keen botanists and often exchanged plant cuttings and roots. They enjoyed a close companionship for many years.

Ambrose Mansell died at the beginning of January 1834 and left his not inconsiderable estate to his four grandchildren. Jemmy was still not really decided about his future but now he felt he might look around for a business of his own.

William wrote to Matilda one evening telling of his dahlia losses over the winter. He was also still concerned about Eliza's health:

Mine dear Matilda,

It is so late and I am so tired that I should hardly be tempted to write even to you, dear coz, upon any subject less important than that of flowers. But anon to business; the failures among our Dahlias are: Well's Dwarf Yellow, Glove Crimson, Niobe, Scarlet Tonbene (which we shall easily replace from our neighbours at The Mill), Neptune, Lord Liverpool, Guttata, Mutabile Crimson, Chiswick Donna Maria. Car. writes that you can give us a Niobe; we shall be very glad of it. You can only have had it among the half roots you had in the autumn. We have potted off more than

170; they are all looking remarkably well and we think there will hardly one fail.

You have heard of our very fine seedling Polyanthus, one of the progeny of the favourite that last year grew in the three cornered plat, close to the hedge. Even John Sharp says it is the finest he ever saw, therefore 'tis certainly something. I have named it the Meridian, in honour of a line that runs from the North Pole of the world to the South and is of great use to Geographers.

Poor Eliza has been pretty bad for some days. She is much better now than she was two days ago but I am not sure she will get well without some more doctoring. Mr. Martin has taken some blood from the arm and hinted today that it may yet be necessary to apply leeches or a blister but he is watching the case and I hope such proceedings may not be necessary. She is strictly confined to her bed. She sends her love to you and all of you. I charge you to present my love to Car. and Papa.

Dear Matilda, thine now and always,

William C.

Matilda's brother known as 'Little Charles' to differentiate him from his Uncle Charles, was actually 6 feet, 1 inch tall. His articles with Gell & Roberts had come to an end and he was now working in Cheapside. He, too, often visited his uncles, and one day while with William, wrote crosswise on his uncle's letter to his sister Matilda:

My dear Matilda,

I have just taken a chop with Uncle W., and he has given

me this letter. It is now only a quarter of an hour of our postman's calling, therefore I must be brief.

Reigate Races are on Wednesday and Thursday next. I think of going down with Uncle Wm., tomorrow evening to stay the first day of the Races. If Father could send Jane up there tomorrow, she might make her appearance on the course (I understand that Reigate Races are not thought a little of now). There may be a good many people there, as the country is full of them, far and near. I think this will be a very good plan of getting her along to this great city. I think she is very likely to fetch a good price and the sooner she is here the better. I told Father some time ago that if he thought of sending her up, he ought to lose no time. I should have been very glad to have had the opportunity of shewing (sic) her off at The Derby.

Rogers knows a gent., who wants a horse to ride and go in a cab. He is a tall, thin fellow, something like myself, and I think she would be about the thing for him. It is almost a pity that she stands so high; it would be an objection with many. The Worthing Coach runs by Dovers Green now (I believe this is the first day), and therefore if the mare were to be sent up to Dovers Green, there is a good conveyance back.

I do not know that you know that that very nice, little creature, Miss Fanny Wirgman is staying at Mrs. Penfold's. She has sent me a letter for you which I shall enclose in my box on Thursday next. It is enquiring, I believe, when you can receive her. Geo. Charman is going out to America; he intends to start by the ship on the 27th, if he can get a berth. The postman has come and gone, therefore I must conclude in haste with love to all.

Your very affectionate brother,

C. Constable.

P.S. The mare should be sent off tomorrow, to be ready for Reigate Races.

Note: The practice of writing between the lines of a letter, only running the other way, makes it extremely hard to decipher. George Charman was Jane Constable's brother, Charles's brother-in-law, who was emigrating to Pittsford to work with John Purse. Chas. Jr. was going to compete in the Reigate Races which enjoyed a brief notoriety on Reigate Heath, and the Jane to whom he refers was one of their horses. Fanny Wirgman was the daughter of Thomas Wirgman and lived at Povey Cross, near the mill at Horley.

All these young people seemed to get on very well with each other and with their uncles, Daniel and William.

CHAPTER EIGHTEEN

The Cobham Young

IN THE SPRING OF 1832 John and Elizabeth's four children decided to sell their parents' house and business. Their plan was to emigrate to America where they would start a new life. Particulars of a later sale describe the property: 'A brick and tiled dwelling house and shop in Cobham Street, with two front parlours and six bedrooms, with a large garden containing a bake house with flour chamber over and a two stalled stable, loft, cart shed, piggery and two cottages adjoining.' A prospective purchaser was soon found, a Mr. Burberry.

During the summer of 1832 a good friend of Daniel's called Hartwell Carver stayed with the Constables at Horley Mill. It was he, among others, who encouraged young Daniel to emigrate, offering to help find him a suitable position. Dr. Carver had a thriving medical practice in Pittsford, New York, and among his patients were John, Mildred and Emma Purse. He also ran several stores in the area. He had spent a year in New Orleans in 1825 and liked the winter climate so much that he subsequently spent his summers in Pittsford and his winters in the south. Hartwell Carver may well be called the father of the transcontinenal

Lithograph of W. Constable's suspension bridge, Reigate Hill 1825

Benjamin Constable
(1804-1878) c. 1841

Eliza (1807-1873) and Caroline Constable (1803-1883) daguerreotype c. 1850

courtesy P. Garner

Painting on tin tray of Horley Mill after rebuilding
courtesy R. Olmsted

The Surrey Iron Railway, a water colour by G.B. Wollaston
courtesy of Croydon Art Collection, Croydon Clocktower c.1838

Lavinia Jane Constable (1828-1905)
daguerreotype c.1841

Fanny Constable (1830-1924)
daguerreotype c.1841

courtesy of Photographic History Collection, National Museum of American History,
Smithsonian Institution

Beachy Head, painting by W. Constable, 1833

Charles Constable Jr. (1810-1884)

Jemmy (1812-!900), daguerreotype c. 1841

courtesy R. Olmsted

Beechy Head

Chart Lodge, Redstone Hill, today

John William Grece (1769-1830) painted by Sir Thomas Lawrence c.1820

Henry Grece (1799-1851) daguerreotype

*Ann Whitney Grece
(1780-1845)
painted by Sir
Thomas Lawrence
c. 1820*

*Clair James Grece (1831-1905)
daguerreotype, 1841*

Susanna Constable (1790-1879)

Box probably made by Daniel, undoubtedly illustrated by William c. 1812

HORLEY MILLS, SURRY,
D. CONSTABLE,
MEALMAN.

Daniel's business card c. 1812

railroad: 'after a trip up the Missouri in 1837 the propriety and the practicality of running a railroad across the Rocky Mountains burst upon my mind with perfect correctness and has ever since been the idol of my heart!' He subsequently published several articles in the *New York Courier* and *Enquirer* proposing a transcontinental railroad line. Although this was not to be built until several years later it was Carver who brought this plan before the public. He had a memorial before Congress in 1849 asking for a charter, in which he said:

> This railroad will be the great political and commercial artery of our Union, through which will circulate the golden treasures of California, of all the Pacific and Asiatic millions of people, throwing off its numerous branches as it sweeps through the whole body of this great Republic to all parts, whose life and vitality is democracy, liberty, and universal freedom and equal rights to all.

He campaigned until 1862 when at last, in spite of the Civil War, the enterprise began to get off the ground. Eventually Dr. Carver was not only able to witness the consummation of his wishes but also to ride on the new railroad to San Francisco and back.

During the spring of 1833, Ann Browne of Shipley, who was married to Henry Browne's nephew, described a visit from Dr. Carver in a letter to her sister-in-law, Ann Billinghurst:

> Your neighbour Dr. Carver favoured us with a visit last summer. We were much pleased with his visit, he was all life and animation and appeared to have the highest enjoyment

of existence but I should expect the account which he gave you of this country to be far too flattering; he was not domesticated with the poor and his visits to other classes were too short to find out about their difficulties. Please to give him our kind respects and tell him I have not forgotten the trick Mr. D. Constable played on him, in taking him for so long a walk and how his poor feet suffered for it.

The negotiations for the sale of the Cobham shop were nearly completed but, although William was still arguing on their behalf, the sale unfortunately fell through at the last moment:

Have you heard of the affair we have had at Cobham? We found a chapman for the business who agreed to give £100 Premium and take the things at valuation. The Treaty was some time in hand and was settled to everybody's satisfaction. The taker, Burberry, went to Cobham to assist in preparing the stock for valuation; he measured goods and put his own private mark upon them. Then, after he had been at work a day, withdrew from the concern and having taken a few days to quibble, in order to give some grace to his retreat, declared he would have nothing to do with it. We called on him immediately to arbitrate the damage sustained from his conduct but we cannot yet get him into it. We are enquiring also if the law will not compel his fulfillment of the engagement but have not yet been answered. We believe he is fully committed to the contract and, if so, we shall get what damages we can, as we feel what we deem just offence at his proceedings.

There can be no doubt also that Daniel Sr. encouraged his young namesake, promising introductions and other assistance. The plan was that young Daniel would settle in New York, and once he was established his brother and sisters could join him. Now that the Cobham business was being sold, there was nothing to hinder the twenty-three year old, so in the winter of 1832 he set sail for America, armed with an introduction to Mr. Joseph Perkins, a printer, of New York:

My dear Sir,

In the first place I must make you a little acquainted with the bearer of this, his views and objects in transporting himself across the great deep. He is my nephew and namesake, Daniel Constable, a good and unsophisticated young man, whose object is to become a citizen of your wide domain. The Dr. Carver who has been sojourning with us and to whom I gave a hasty introduction to you (I presume before this you have seen him) is from Rochester and who, I think, may have made some arrangement as to a situation for our young friend and perhaps may be yet in New York.

The aforesaid D. Constable is a general storekeeper, a little of a draughtsman, surveyor and he speaks the French language and plays the violin. He is a temperance man but have not heard that he has joined any society, is in every case to be depended upon and, I think, is as good a subject as appertains to King William's family. It has cost a good many dollars to make him what he is and that, of course, is so much added to the wealth of the Republic.

Should there be no clerkship provided for him he will proceed on to Rochester, after having spent a few days in looking over New York City, as a youth like him has much awakened curiosity to gratify in seeing and learning how things look in the new world. He is but little of a traveller and in a new world of strangers may have some diffidence to correct. Upon the whole I felt satisfied that I could not introduce him to a kinder, better informed man than yourself, to aid and assist him with such information as his predicament may require. But I fear you will think me intrusive by continually pestering you with application of this kind, valuable as your time is.

How I am pleased to find you have so many things to give you pleasure; such a house as yours, the garden, vineyard, children and, above all, so good a wife. Thank you again for your advice and good wishes upon that vastly important subject of getting a wife!

You ask me if I expect to return to the U.S.? I do but just when I do not know. I shall take especial good care not to take any permanent rooting on this sod but should like to help root up Palaces, Thrones and Altars, of all which, I fear, there is little chance; to be at such a grand work as this would induce me to stay and see the finish of so glorious a deed.

D. Constable.

Was it Dr. Carver who knew Aaron Arnold, a dry goods merchant in New York? Almost immediately after Daniel's arrival he was offered a job as a clerk with Messrs. Arnold and Hearn. At the end of February 1833, Daniel travelled to Pittsford to see the Purse family and to take various letters and packages that he had brought for them from England. Upon his return to New York he started work. Tragically, he was suddenly taken seriously ill with fever and died only a few weeks later. He was buried in July 1833 in Holy Trinity Church, New York. A note from L. Cox, M.D., Attending Physician, New York reads:

> January 25th, 1834.
> This may certify that Daniel Constable of Cobham, England, was interred in the Cemetery belonging to the parish of Trinity Church, on Friday, July 19th, 1833.

Eliza, Daniel's sister, now aged twenty-five, had also left England in the spring of 1833, to take up a teaching post in a school in Bruges. Coincidentally, she was taken seriously ill in June and William rushed to Bruges, leaving Matilda in charge at Doversgreen. He wrote to her upon his arrival:

> My dear Matilda,
> I had an excellent passage over the salt sea, being from Dover to Ostend no more than seven hours; sea running high and a very stiff wind right abaft. Left Dover at 10.00 a.m. arrived at Ostend at 5.00 p.m. but could not get to Bruges 'till next morn.
> I had the high satisfaction to find our little friend here almost recovered from the indisposition which had so much alarmed us. She followed the directions given by Mr. Van Beesbrook, which Mr. Martin said were the opposite of those he should have given and is got well under them. I am very glad now that she has been restored by a different treatment from that which Mr. Martin would have pursued because she is now restored at once to health and strength and Mr. Martin's method would have taken her to health

and weakness and then she would have had to linger slowly into strength. Her indisposition has been pretty severe and her improvement is now rapid. The school is, I think, going on very well. The children are very happy and are, I hope, improving well. Here is a very jolly Parisian dame to teach them French, a very well mannered lady and very handsome, even now at 60 or thereabout. I am sure you will be pleased to hear this good account.

I shall add to your pleasure by telling you that the plants came in as handsome order and keeping as when they left your skilful hands. They were perfectly fresh and there was not the slightest disarrangement or damage. I have just bargained for a barrowload of manure to plant them in the garden. They were very gratefully received here and have considerably enhanced your reputation for skill and kindness. The houses here abound in handsome and well kept potted plants. Fine cactuses are seen commonly now in the windows; fine specimens of Speciocissima may be bought in the streets for 1 franc or less and beautiful Neriums Splendums or Oleander, in full and fine flower, for 6d sterling, including pots.

I am going to treat Eliza with a trip tomorrow to Ghent by the Canal Boat. This is a very easy, interesting and inexpensive trip and I am sure will give her pleasure and help her forward in her health and will perhaps be the only opportunity she will have of seeing a little more of Flanders. I shall not be quite ready to return home with the next return of packets but I shall certainly travel by the one next after. It will leave Ostend either in the night of Friday or early on Saturday morning and shall be in London on Sunday morning. You will please say to Charles that if it will be more agreeable to him I will remain in London and do the marketing on Monday. I shall be governed in this matter by any instructions I may receive from him which he will please to address to me at The Artichoke. These should be sent up by Friday's post as, if I do not find them on my arrival on Sunday, I shall come right home.

We are having some very slight but frequent showers; enough, I fear, to check your haymaking but not to benefit your floral charges. Strawberries and cherries are very abundant here and are our daily fare. Bruges is as clean and pleasant and, I think, even duller than ever. There is a Bruges letter from Eliza to me which you have full liberty to peruse. I hope that you are going on comfortably and particularly that you are not in want of work. Eliza presents her love to you, it is to be followed by a letter on my return.

Dear Matilda, very affectionately thine,

William C.

Had the news of young Daniel's death reached England by September? Was this why William returned to Bruges, to break the news to Eliza and to fetch her home? He wrote to Matilda, who was again holding the fort for him in Doversgreen, although this time Clara was keeping her sister company:

Dear Matilda,

No doubt, long before this you have been expecting my letter and today, instead of the letter, you are probably expecting our return. However, my return must be delayed about three days longer. I have been cruising on the Meuse from Namur to Liege with Eliza and we are returned only today.

We are cogitating on the propriety of abandoning the route by Calais and should certainly do so if there were a steamboat direct for London on Saturday from Ostend but we are informed that there is now no such arrangement, there being no boat appointed in the place of the late unlucky Talbot which, you know, was wrecked in the late storm, the regular service of which was from Ostend to London every Saturday. I think I can safely say we shall certainly be at home on Tuesday night and, I hope, on Monday as I begin to be uneasy at a stay so much exceeding my appointment. I shall say to you nothing about our excursion further than that it has been a very pleasant one and that the Meuse has exhibited to our view by far the finest and most magnificent river scenery I have ever beheld, excepting of course Niagara and some other cataracts. To my surprise I found, for a length of 20 miles, the banks wherever they were culturable [sic] covered with vineyards. It is the region, too, of coals, iron and the rocks which accompany the coal in England.

I found Eliza and the children [Eliza's pupils] in excellent health, the latter grown and in all respects improved. I had a good voyage over, as you may have concluded from the state of the atmosphere and we have been pretty lucky in the weather ever since. We came home today, having travelled all last night and have been very busy ever since, enquiring into the most proper means of taking our departure hence.

I am just warned that it is approaching the close of the mail. I am quite ashamed that you should have to pay postage for so short and shabby a letter but I cannot help it. I would enclose the money but I am afraid the rogues of the Post Office will steal it. I hope I shall be in a situation to tell you

a longer story for nothing soon. I assure you I am anxious
to have the means of doing so as speedily as possible.
Pray, accept Eliza's and my best love and share it between
Tit and yourself. The children send their love to you.
Dear Matilda, thine affectionately as ever,
William C.

Whenever the news of Daniel's death finally reached Caroline,
Eliza and Benjamin they must have been very shocked and
grieved.

Joseph Perkins, with whom young Daniel had boarded,
wrote to Daniel telling of the young man's short-lived life in
New York and urging that Benjamin should come to New York
as soon as possible:

> He had become a real American in heart and had also taken
> the usual step by declaring his intention of becoming one
> in legal form. Considering his age and the short time he
> had been in this country, his prospects were truly very
> flattering. In a very short time, by close application, he had
> become well acquainted with the manner of transacting
> business although it is quite different from what he had
> been accustomed to in old England. After he had been with
> the Messrs. Arnold & Hearn a few weeks on trial they
> appeared to have become very much attached to him and
> he often made mention to us of the friendly treatment and
> kindly familiarity they constantly manifested towards him,
> unlike that experienced by clerks in England. Since his
> death I have scarcely seen Mr. Arnold or Mr. Hearn without
> their speaking of him as a remarkable man in whose death

they had sustained irreparable loss. They have, formerly, told me that with the exception of James Hearn, Mr. H.'s brother, Daniel was the best clerk they had, although they had a goodly number of fine, active fellows. Mr. A. has spoken to me several times respecting Daniel's brother, Benjamin; that he would reserve a situation for him if he were sure of his coming to New York in the spring and since I received your letter I have seen him but once. He appeared pleased that Benjamin talked of coming. I let him take your letter but have not seen him since; from what he said I think he will write you on the subject.

Daniel's great friend, Hartwell Carver, the doctor from Pittsford, also wrote:

The fate of poor Daniel awakens our feeling of sensibility on behalf of Benjamin. I do assure you and the sisters of Daniel that I hardly knew how to reconcile myself to his death. Never had a young man better prospects before him than he had. Fortune seemed to hover around him, on every side, with her sweetest smiles. If he had lived, wealth and eminence would very shortly have been in his possession and he would have paved the way for his brother and sisters in this country, to the same inheritance.

Benjamin set sail for New York at the end of January 1834. His Uncle Daniel was also planning to cross the Atlantic, but as he suffered badly from seasickness, would delay his departure until the summer months arrived. William, too, as already stated, had a plan to return to America, in order to present a *Panorama of*

Niagara Falls and to market a microscope he had invented. The idea was that Caroline and Eliza would accompany their uncles.

Benjamin had a long and difficult voyage across the Atlantic and then found he had arrived at a moment of crisis in American history. He wrote to Daniel at the beginning of April:

My dear Uncle,

I arrived here on the 30th March, 59 days passage. The first 17 or 18 days we had light southerly breezes and were nearly half way, the remaining part of our passage we had continual head wind, calm and severe gales. I was straightened for provisions and, owing to the long passage, the Captain and cabin passengers were put on an allowance of grub and the last fortnight we had water that had salt water with it. This was worst than all. The Mate had not secured the tanks properly in London. At last New York was in sight, 9.00 a.m. Saturday.

I went to Arnold & Hearn directly and then to Mr. Perkins and was well received at both places. I have been introduced to most of your acquaintances who were particularly anxious in their enquiries after you, and wish to know when you would return to America. I told them it was likely you would come over in the course of the summer.

On the 2nd instant was held at the Concert Hall a Ball in honour of Jefferson. I went to it with Mr. and Mrs. Perkins and Mr. Jacob Perkins. It was respectfully attended though not so numerous as the one held in memory of Paine. But that is accounted for by the lateness of the season and the stormy weather, besides it being the first time. It is expected it will be more numerously attended next year. We passed a very pleasant evening.

I have spent one evening with the Misses Belcher of your acquaintance and am well pleased with my reception in this city. I am staying at Mr. P.'s at present on the same terms that poor Dan'l. agreed to. In attending to the accounts of my brother I find the surgeon's bill is $90 and the physician's $70, besides the apothecary's which I have not had yet which I believe is not much. An a/c owing to Mr. P. for some little bill which he has paid and something due to him for board and lodging, altogether at a guess, perhaps $190 to sell. Against this there is $150 in Mr. Arnold's hands with $200 in Mr. Keeler's, together $350 with interest. I will send $120 on to my Aunt Purse which will be in about a week. The Rochester merchants will be here in that time where the package I brought from you will go.

Mr. Couzens has been to Mr. P.'s in my absence and seen the Sulphate of Byrates Uncle W. sent him and is much pleased with it. He has some specimens of stones from Staten Island which he is going to send to Uncle W.

Upon my arrival here I found the city in a panic in consequence of Jackson having moved the deposits from the U.S. Bank. Credit is destroyed, business is entirely at a stand and politics is the universal theme of conversation. Jackson has behaved despotically and it is considered as an unlimited stretch of power but not unconstitutional. It has split the people in two parties, one for the Bank, the other for Jackson. It remains to be seen whether this measure of Jackson's will not prove of ultimate good to the State. I believe the majority of the people are of the opinion that it will. Amongst those are some that were not of Jackson's party before. Of course, the capitalists and merchants who feel it in their pockets are of the Bank party.

The election for Mayor for this city begins this day. The

candidates are Laurence of Jackson's party and Ver Plantz of the Bank party; the excitement is very great, no-one is neutral. There have been political meetings every evening for the last week. I went to an anti-Jackson meeting last evening and am going tonight to the Masonic Hall to a Jackson meeting – likely I shall go every evening this week. The election lasts three days.

I was not so successful as I wished in bringing over the geraniums. Two of the best are dead, the others are sickly but will recover. Mr. Arnold exonerates me from blame; he says that they should have been larger and more healthy plants and that Dennis ought to have known that they could not have lived. The passage was so long cold and it was impossible to bring them over better. We were for three or four days and nights under close hatches in foul and offensive air at one time and frequently so for one or two days and nights during the passage, so that the plants for want of air and light made long slender shoots and then withered.

The ship suffered a little damage to the bulwarks on the starboard side; from the bows to the quarter deck were all stove in. Everything of the livestock, but a pig, was drowned in the longboat. The cookhouse on deck was smashed to pieces, the steerage hatch was carried away, the cabin windows were broken, the ship laid nearly on her beam end. This was done by one tremendous sea in the middle of the night of the 6th of March which came pouring into the steerage in a terrific manner, the cabins the same. Lack of grub and the probability of being much longer at sea made us rather dejected but a south east wind sprang up on the 26th March and continued two or three days, quite a breeze.

We sailed 10 or 12 miles an hour, in style, our starboard gunnel almost in the water, cutting through the sea and the spray dashing all over the deck. We were now in good spirits and I don't recollect that I ever felt more joy than I did when sailing into the harbour of New York; the finest ports in the world up along each side with its ships, brigs, schooners and steamers unequalled by anything I ever saw in England.

I have enquired of Mr. Perkins his opinion of the painting of The Falls for Uncle Wm. and he thinks that it is a subject that will not be attractive here and this is likewise the opinion of Mr. Arnold, as well as other persons of competent judgement that Mr. P. has conversed with. It is also the decided opinion of the Messrs. Godfrey that it would not take here. They say they have seen since some pictures of engravings of The Falls which were superior to that in London. Mr. P. says that the Microscope would be very likely to please the people of America and would prove highly attractive if firstly shown at New York and then at other cities of the State and after that again at New York, as it would be quite novel. There was a person had something of the sort exhibiting which he could only shew [sic] in the middle of fine days, which attracted the attention of the people in this city and made some stir and this is one reason which inclined Mr. P. to think favourably of the Microscope.

I believe I said in my letter from Portsmouth that the invoice of my plants was lost. I forgot that it was put away securely and found it the next day after I wrote to you. Please tell Caroline and Eliza I will write to them shortly, perhaps in two weeks or thereabouts.

I have not made any particular arrangements with Messrs. A. & H.; that is, we have not agreed upon any particular salary.

Trade is very flat; the spring trade has not yet commenced if
it will while this panic is the cause.

With best love to Caroline and Eliza and all my friends, I
remain,

Affectionately yours,

Benj'n. Constable.

Benjamin was musical and perhaps less worldly than his younger
brother. Was that why Daniel had emigrated first?

CHAPTER NINETEEN

Daniel's Last Years

DANIEL PLANNED TO RETURN to America in the summer of 1834, close on the heels of young Benjamin, who had sailed in January to take his brother's place in New York. Meanwhile he received a letter from John Purse, dated January 1834, discussing family affairs and the letting of Daniel's farm:

> Dear Sir,
>
> We fear the unfortunate circumstance of the loss of poor Daniel will derange the hopes and plans of the other branches of that family in their contemplated removal to this country. Ourselves had been forming fairy visions that they might conduct the Pittsford business profitably to themselves and pleasantly to us, for so deep an interest did we feel in that fine young man. His amiable disposition and engaging manners had so won our affection during the short time he sojourned with us that we looked forward with pleasure to the possibility of his residence in our neighbourhood. His loss must be long and severely felt by those who knew him best, for he had only to be known to be beloved.

I do not know but I have exceeded my authority in what I have done about your possessions here. When I last wrote to you True had taken it for another year at a rent of $40 and to build a certain length of stone fence. Before half the time had elapsed his father (Jonathan True) had bought a farm in Pennsylvania, near Meadville, on the road between Pittsburgh and Erie; a considerable tract of land in that quarter has recently come onto the market very cheap and many of our neighbours have purchased there. William (True) and his wife among the rest could think of nothing else than going and at the end of the half year threw up the farm and moved off – he had built a considerable length of fence but not the quantity agreed on. He never cultivated the farm as it ought to have been and of course never made the crops it was capable of producing. He was too easy a man and his wife was a discontented woman. On the whole, perhaps, it is no great loss they are gone. Several applications were made for the place but they were mostly poor wretches who owned nothing. Among others, a Mr. Akers who came from England last August, by trade a shoemaker, made proposals. I thought at the time he was possessed of some property but find it is but little. He seems very industrious, earns a great deal of money shoemaking, has an apprentice he brought with him that has a year to serve and who is a good workman and sticks close to the seat. Has a wife much younger than himself and a servant girl related to his wife; this composes the family. He is not much used to farming but seems very fond of it. To this man I have given a lease of five years; if I have done wrong I hope for forgiveness. I know it is a considerable stretch of authority.

During Mr. True's stay I had the ceiling of the lower room lathed and plastered and on Akers taking the place, had the upper storey done the same. It is now divided into two chambers. It was, before this was done, miserably cold for decent people to sleep in in winter. True was to have drywalled the cellar and deducted it out of the rent. He got it about half done and so it remained at his departure. It is since finished digging but not yet walled. You, of course, recollect the shape of your farm. The five acres to be cleared is progressing, you see from the diagram.

Should there be a chance of getting sent a few grafts of the apples I spoke of, from the Crowhurst orchard, I should be much pleased to get them. John Robinson brought over a great number of grafts but owing to his remaining so long in Duchess County they dried up and only one (a Nutmeg Pippin) lived. He brought them stuck in potatoes, which I believe is a very good way.

Emma wishes to know from what time she is to date the commencement of your kind donation to her?

On Sunday morning last, a most destructive fire broke out in a grocery under the Market House at Rochester. The wind was very high at the time. It burnt down the Market, swept the whole range of buildings along the bridge away and completely destroyed that fine edifice, The Globe Building, with all the machinery and factories it contained and the well stocked store in its basement. The spread of the flames was so rapid, very little was saved. Rochester has not met with such a loss since its foundation. Have had some very tempestuous weather, which has blown down many chimneys and stripped the roofs off buildings.

Sincerely yours,

J. Purse.

Perhaps aware that Emma did not have the same advantages as her English cousins, and not much in the way of expectations, Daniel had made over to her the rent he received from his little farm.

By 1834 John Purse was finally finding his feet. As well as his farm he had speculated on a sawmill, locating a good site on a small stream locally and building the mill, complete with miller's house. As soon as this was completed he sold the going concern at an exceedingly good profit. He now speculated again in sawmill property, made another excellent profit, and soon became the talk of the neighbourhood.

Hartwell Carver, Daniel's good friend from Pittsford, returning home after a prolonged stay in Europe, wrote to Daniel in that spring:

> Dear Sir,
>
> I saw Mr. Purse on Tuesday, who told me he was going to forward a package to England on Saturday and asked me if I wished to send. I told him if I could get time I should like to write you. I have only half an hour, sir, but as I am in the habit of doing whatever I do offhand, it will be in character to write hastily. My only cares are that so hasty an epistle will not be gratifying to you and I am again at a loss what subjects to include as I have not time fully to explain anyone particular subject.
>
> But, as we Americans say, I will go ahead and say to you, that our politics and the affairs of our government was the last year and still are this year, very much confused. Much

litigation and highly agitated feeling exists in consequence. As they say in North Carolina, we are in a mighty bad fix. Times have not been so hard and money so scarce since my remembrance. Can and do let out all the money I can share, for 30% and 40% interest with good and safe security.

The commencement of this hostility between the Administration and the United States Bank commenced shortly before I left England, in the vetoing of the bill, which passes both Houses of Congress, by a large majority for renewing the Charter of the United States Bank by the President, General Jackson. The present Charter expires March 1836. In short, my opinion is that our present Administration is corrupt and bad in every sense of the word and that the first cause of all this hostility arose from a refusal of the Bank to become a tool of the government and use its influence to strengthen and perpetuate the present Administration. I was in the first place a strong Jackson man and continued to be so up to the time of my departure from this country for Europe. On my return to this country, I found things and principles strangely perverted and I am now as unswerving in trying to pull down the man, Jackson, as I was in building him up. I think I did much towards building him and the Party up and I know I am doing at present much to pull and break the would-be-tyrant and the present corrupt party in power down. I hope and trust there is a moral virtue in the American people which will save our country and still perpetuate blessings and valuable privileges.

Now sir, permit me to speak of myself and say to you that I still enjoy the blessings of a single life. As you are a brother bachelor I hope you will indulge me in stating perticulars [sic].

On my return from Europe I went directly into my practice and had a full ride immediately. My business, in my profession, has been more lucrative since my return than it was before I left and is rapidly extending in every direction for twenty, thirty and forty miles, through twenty towns. I was absent a few weeks in August at Saratoga Springs, which is the Brighton of the United States. I intend to go there again the ensuing summer, with my own horses and carriage. The Saratoga Springs have become a great and fashionable watering place, hardly exceeded by any in the world at the present day. Last season I met there many of my acquaintances from Paris, Switzerland, Italy, etc. etc.

I keep house, live well and have as much sport as any other fellow (as the Yankees would say). I keep two or three domestics, five horses, no dogs nor cats. I intend to spend half my income, at all events let it be more or less. Bachelors cannot live always, you know, and therefore they should not lay up too much money but always keep a shot in the locker sufficiently to meet the vicissitudes of life. I am very busy, at the moment, building me a very fine horse and carriage barn.

Mr. Purse tells me he got letters from you last week. We both were much surprised to learn that Benjamin left England last January and that we have not heard anything from him yet. The fate of poor Daniel awakens our feeling of sensibility on behalf of Benjamin. I do assure you and the sisters of Daniel that I hardly knew how to reconcile myself to his death.

I learn that Miss Matilda has poor health, which I am very sorry for. She is certainly a fine young lady, possessing a good mind and fine general talents. Tell her if she would only come to this country and consent to marry an American she would be perfectly healthy. The celebrated Miss Fanny Kemble is in love with an American and will be married to him. Miss Fanny and her father called on me last summer on their way to Niagara Falls; she is a talented woman. I shall expect to see Caroline in this country and I hope to see Eliza, whose health I understand is not good. They are both fine ladies and if they come out will do honour to our country. But there is Miss Clara Constable I have a strong partiality for; I think her one of the best-hearted girls living. I often think of her red cheeks, which calls forth all the best wishes for her welfare and good health imaginable. I am glad to hear she is not yet married; tell her not to be in a hurry.

Now, my good friend, will you be so good as not to forget the good times we have had together and will you give my love to the four young ladies and Mrs. Charles Constable, to your honoured father and sister, to your brothers, Charles, William and James, to his sons, Charles and young James, and all others of my acquaintance in your neighbourhood.

Write me.

Hartwell Carver.

Note: Fanny Kemble was the famous English actress. She was travelling through the United States with her father, Charles Kemble, also an actor. She married a southern planter, but the marriage was not a success and the couple subsequently divorced.

Daniel had not been well, but Mildred was more concerned over the health of their father, and said as much in a letter to her brother accompanying that of Dr. Carver:

Dear Daniel,

Your letter, which we so long thought lost, did come at last and rejoiced enough we were to receive it. The neglect I felt I was subject to made my trouble heavier. I was sorry indeed for our dear father's illness and long confinement but made very comfortable to know he was restored before your letter came off.

Your own unpleasant situation threw a damp upon my spirits but your not mentioning them in your last gives me reason to hope your complaints are on the mend. I was in hopes we should have seen our D'n'l. come here soon but the Panorama Scheme is discouraged and all pleasurable expectation of that kind is, for the present, abandoned.

Getting no account of Benjamin's having arrived fidgets me and not having time to get an answer to my enquiries from New York before this must be sent off is unpleasant in the extreme. I would be willing to persuade myself if it is at all probable that he is arrived but has not had sufficient time to write here. I hope the poor fellow has not had a three months passage.

Susan, I find, has left the Shop. I hope she will not think I neglect her but I fear I shall not have the opportunity of scribbling to her this time. I am pleased her darling is such a fine fellow. Does she like that you should teach him to nickname himself? Charles' girls too, I learn, are clever, nice children. Well, I suppose I shall never see any of them without I come home. It gives me pleasure that our young friends at Storrington are put into possession of such handsome fortunes. I wish them all health and long life to enjoy it. With steady perseverance I trust George, too, will make good headway; I wish him every success.

We have had a most extraordinary winter, almost entirely dry frost. We had no rain for a great number of weeks and not snow enough to sleigh one whole day. April came in so warm all vegetation came on at an astonishing rate, peach trees all blown, etc. but since that time April has out April'd April. We have had all the changes of the seasons daily and with more rain and snow falling freely and several mornings ice more than half an inch thick. We expect peaches and plums are cut off, apples were not forward enough. I hope you have escaped this on your side.

You may depend upon it, there is no mistake when I tell you I am failing in my health. I find more of it this spring that I have heretofore done. Doctor Carver has greatly restored the health of Mrs. Billinghurst and I am to have some of the same kind of medicine.

Our most affectionate remembrance to you all.

Yours most truly, M. Purse

Mildred must have heard from Benjamin very shortly after she wrote this letter. A letter to England often took sixty days or more to reach its destination.

Emma, now twenty-four, added a short letter to that of her mother:

Dear Uncle,

You call upon me for the gossiping news of the neighbourhood but really the great political excitement that agitates the nation seems to have set every other topic and all kinds of business at rest for the moment.

The great scarcity of money caused by the Bank refusing to

discount has prevented the sale of all sorts of farm produce. Those who have been obliged to sell have done so at considerable loss. The spirits of the people appear dull in proportion to the hardness of the times and I have, therefore, very little to communicate. Of the few occurrences worth mentioning I will give you the best account I can.

I attended William Marsh's wedding at Scottsville, on the 26th of March. There was a large party of the most respectable of the young people of the neighbourhood assembled on the occasion. Mr. Marsh says he is very pleased with his new daughter. She is an American. Mrs. M. is not expected to last much longer.

Mr. and Mrs. J. Hawkins passed two nights with us about three weeks since, the first time we had seen him since his return from England. He, with his niece, Sophia and her husband, are keeping a tavern at Ithaca, at the head of the Seneca Lake. He describes the scenery around them as very beautiful and romantic and invites me to come and view it this summer, as I hope I shall, for I have not been in York State. The rest of the folk are going on about as usual, very little stirring among any of them. Many English continue to settle around us.

Mr. Hoath furnishes the good folk of our town with a capital subject of merriment. He has been trying, since he purchased his farm, to get him a wife also and has, I believe, had rather poor success among the girls here as they make considerable sport of him. But not a word of this as I think I am something of a favourite. His sister has sent me a present of a pair of bracelets and an invite to visit them if I should ever go to England.

Yours affectionately,

Emma Purse.

Daniel's health did not improve, however, and by the autumn he had moved back to Horley. Susanna, accompanied by Clair James, moved home to nurse him. He had brought an iron sprung bedstead from America on his return in 1830 which was supremely comfortable. Mildred wrote to him in November 1834:

> My dear brother,
> I am much grieved for your sufferings but hope they are gradually diminishing. Am happy indeed you have a couch so comfortable as the bed you describe. I wish you had one of those very easy but well constructed rocking chairs that are in some of the houses here. Your crook legged chair and work table get the admiration of every stranger. The sofa chair is yet a very comfortable seat when put under the shade of that little clump of trees opposite the end of the woodhouse, and the oak at the corner of the same building is a very thriving tree. The big windmill stands well but is now the worse for wear. The thorns round the lawn are getting to a good height.
> I am amazed at the transportation of a cooking stove from New York to Horley Mill. It would put my little machine quite in the shade if I had come and brought it, although quite a clever contrivance, bakes, roasts, made of tin with cast cylinders for the fire, and burns nothing but charcoal.
> When Mr. Richardson refused to buy our wheat and said we had better let the rats eat it the expression was caused by strong feelings of excitement against the President's party because he could not, at that time, sell wheat. We had a hot, dry summer, thermometer for some time steady at 86 degrees in the shade. Many people's wells and springs dry but you have a never failing spring, almost at the door of

Mr. Akers [Daniel's farm adjoining that of the Purse family].
All your old friends are much concerned for your illness.
We are all better, Purse in particular.
Yours with the truest affection,
M. Purse.

Note: The crooked leg chair and table to which Mildred
refers were probably made from the crooked hazel shrub
that grows so abundantly in America. Daniel was no mean
carpenter, among his other talents, and had often occupied
his spare time in making furniture for Mildred.

Mildred had long been considering a visit, with Emma, to
England. John Purse was agreeable to their making the long trip
home and had promised to look after things while they were
away. However, even by the time Mildred wrote, it was obvious
that Daniel was dying. She was in a torment at being so far away:

Had I been aware of such a stroke as this I might have gone
to England let the trial have cost me what it might. I had
the sad presentiment that his unfortunate case would thus
terminate. It comforts me very much that he is in the centre
of his friends and that he bears his heavy affliction with
such patience and fortitude.

In October, John Purse took Emma on a trip to Niagara Falls, a
distance of about 80 miles. They travelled by stagecoach. This
journey was obviously a great treat for Emma. Daniel, in spite of
his ill health, had teased Emma about Mr. Hoath and his search
for a wife. Emma wrote:

Travelling at the rate of 12 miles an hour in a crowded coach and the rain descending heavily all day is no joke over roads such as ours but we arrived safe. I went behind the great sheet of the cataract to Termination Rock, a feat that required some heroism, I can assure you. Uncle, I wish it to be understood that I have not taken any particular fancy to Mr. H. His awkward and unsuccessful attempts to get a wife has caused much sport among the girls here.

Note: John Hoath was a cousin of the Robinson family. He was successful in his search as Mary Robinson wrote to her sister in September 1837: 'We were indeed very much pleased with John's wife, she is quite an industrious little body. John did not choose her for beauty but she has other qualities which make her far more valuable to him'.

Daniel's health deteriorated still further, and early in February 1835 he died in Horley, much mourned by all who had known him, family and friends alike. This event must have been immensely traumatic, particularly so for James Sr. William, too, had not only lost Jemima a few years earlier, but now Daniel with whom he had shared many happy adventures. Mildred must have felt a sense of desolation. There is little doubt that without the enthusiasm of her adored elder brother she would not have managed to survive those early years in the wilderness of Indiana, trying to wrest a living from a seemingly inhospitable land.

Barely two years after Daniel's death *The Times* reported a serious fire at Messrs. Constable & Findon, Chymists and Druggists. Presumably William Butler had retired by now but the

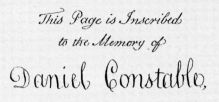

This Page is Inscribed
to the Memory of

Daniel Constable,

one of the Three Companions
of this Travel; who Died in
1835;

Leaving no Effigy of his material appearance save
two slight sketches of his general outline preserved
in these Volumes; — one of them as standing on the
Table Rock, at Niagara, page 44; the other seated on
a Rock, the right-hand figure, in the representation
of Cucumber Run, page 288.

Memorial to Daniel from Notes of a Travel in North America in the Years 1806, 7 and 8 by a Company of Three *by W. Constable*

Constable name was still on the door. The fire was discovered by police but, unfortunately, considerable damage was done before it could be contained.

CHAPTER TWENTY

Jemmy The Entrepreneur

IN THE SUMMER OF 1835 Charles, perhaps jolted by his brother's death, decided at last to visit America. Daniel had often urged him to go but he had always prevaricated. Now Caroline, joining her brother Benjamin, needed an escort. Charles's plan was to visit as many American mills as possible to see how Horley Mill might be improved. William was still living locally, and had generously offered to run the business while he was away.

At the last minute, before they sailed in early May 1835, Charles suggested to his nephew, Jemmy, that he should make one of the party. This was on a Wednesday and Charles had booked passage for the following Saturday. Although Jemmy was still working in London, he was immediately enthusiastic and asked his father if he could go. His father agreed, thinking the trip would be excellent for Jemmy's health, which was still considered 'somewhat precarious' after his time at Cobham. The plan was to spend some six months away, three months travelling across the ocean and three months seeing the country.

Charles and Jemmy arrived in New York on 18 June and spent a week or so in New York City, where they stayed with

Benjamin. They then accompanied Caroline to Pittsford, where they remained for some weeks before travelling to Philadelphia and Baltimore. In Baltimore they called on the Browne family; much to their amusement, Eliza Browne did not recognise Charles or Jemmy at first. They also visited Niagara, which was still, at that time, considered well west.

By September they were back in New York. Just two days before they were due to sail for England, Charles reported that Mr. Arnold had said to Jemmy: 'Mr. Constable, you had better not return, but come and live with us.' Jemmy talked the matter over with his uncle and then agreed with Mr. Arnold that he would stay for six months to see how he liked the country. So Charles returned to England alone, much impressed with all that he had seen and able to convince his brother that Jemmy had been given a tremendous opportunity. Thus it was that Jemmy became the third of the Constable cousins to be employed in the Arnold & Hearn business, which was growing apace.

Six months later Jemmy had completed his six months trial. Mr. Arnold was very pleased with him and increased his salary to $500 per annum, the highest salary paid to anyone in the store. It seemed as though he had found his métier. However Jemmy, with the arrogance of youth, thought he might start up a business on his own. His cousin, Benjamin, who was also still working for Arnold and Hearn, agreed to join him. Although Jemmy had inherited money from his Mansell grandparents, and Benjamin had his share of the Cobham estate, it was agreed that they needed a third partner. Also Jemmy had some reservations as he 'did not consider Benjamin a first class businessman', although the cousins were good friends. They finally agreed terms with a Mr. Van Eps, who was considered to have some business acumen. The plan was to conduct a wholesale ready-to-wear business. It was agreed that Jemmy and Benjamin put in a certain amount, and Mr. Van Eps, who was already in business, put in stock to the same value.

The enterprise started in January 1837 and then, unfortunately for the young men, April saw monetary panic spiral out of control, causing one-third of all the dry goods stores in New York to fail. As Van Eps and Young (his former partner) still had outstanding debts, their firm was one of those to fail. Jemmy had put in about $7,000 by this time, but the new money had become so tied up with the old firm that he was advised to stop all future payments from Van Eps and Young. Mr. Van Eps objected to this, and would not agree to a dissolution of the firm, so Jemmy advertised it under his own name. Van Eps then agreed to make an assignment to Jemmy to protect, as much as possible, the money he had invested. The creditors soon demanded payment, as most of them had failed themselves, and Jemmy paid them all off at a discount.

Jemmy and Benjamin were now free from debt, but left with $15,000 worth of goods. They decided to pack it all in large cases and ship it north to Buffalo, New York, along the Erie Canal, as soon as the weather permitted. In order to recoup their losses the idea was naturally to sell the goods for as high a price as possible.

In the spring of 1838 they journeyed to Buffalo. Here they met up with John Purse and George Charman (Charles Constable's brother-in-law), who had agreed to help. They decided to divide the shipment. Benjamin took his share to

Milwaukee in Wisconsin, where he shipped it via the Great Lakes to Michigan. He endeavoured to sell his stock but was not successful and ended up trading it for land. He then continued on to Texas, no doubt lured by the prospect of the far west of the country, which was now being opened up.

With the assistance of John Purse and George Charman the share belonging to Jemmy was shipped to Erie, Pennsylvania, on the shores of Lake Erie. Here, they hired a store for two weeks and managed to sell some of the stock. The remainder was then carted to Meadville and on to French Creek, at the head of the Allegheny River. Once there, they commissioned a flatboat, or ark, much the same as the one used by Daniel and William some thirty years before.

John Purse was keen that Jemmy join him in his sawmill ventures. It may be remembered that land was available in this area at a highly competitive price. While they were at Meadville, awaiting the construction of the boat, John Purse looked around for sawmill property and found a site on nearby Muddy Creek, which he bought. He then built a dam on the property, followed by a sawmill and house. This enterprise was financed jointly by the three of them, and when it was completed they appointed a manager. Once the ark was built there was nothing to detain them and, as soon as a freshet (high water caused by a flood or melting snow) came, they set off down the river. Jemmy describes this in his memoirs:

> As soon as the water was high enough we made a start from
> Meadville, entering the Allegheny river at Franklin and

proceeded down the river to Pittsburgh; the river was very low and we frequently grounded on the rocks, when ever we would jump with our shoes and stockings off, swing the boat round into deep water and off we went. We floated with the current about three miles an hour; at this season of the year the Allegheny was most beautiful, the river meandering between high hills which in many places were white with azaleas in bloom.

Jemmy describes the boat:

The gunnels were about 6" wide, by 8" high, tapered at each end and bottomed with plank 3" thick; staunchions 7' high were morticed into three gunnels, about 2' apart. The boat sided and roofed with a door at each end, so as to leave a passage through the boat. A rudder was arranged at each end so when the boat got aground, which frequently happens, she could be the more readily turned around and pushed off in deep water. A small room was partitioned off to be used as a kitchen, in which was a fireplace for cooking, etc.

The remaining stock was re-sorted so that the different kinds of clothing were easily accessible and placed in large cases, arranged along each side of the boat with a clear passage between.

At Pittsburgh John Purse left them to return to Pittsford, and George Charman and Jemmy spent a fruitless few days trying to make sales. They then decided to travel down the Ohio, trading where they could. This they did, tying the boat to a tree on the riverbank at night, if possible. They were their own cooks, and supplying themselves with provisions was no easy matter. If they were not near enough to a town to procure food, they went to a farmhouse. They even baked their own bread.

Jemmy went down with an attack of ague, which he thought was probably due to the change from city life to the exposure he was now experiencing. His symptoms were 'the shakes and a heavy fever', which alternated day by day, so by the fourth day of shakes he consulted a doctor, whose house was a mile from the riverbank. He was so weak he felt he would never manage to get there alive, and unfortunately the doctor was not at home when he finally staggered in. The doctor's wife allowed him to lie down until her husband returned; the doctor then dosed him with jalap (a purgative drug obtained from the roots of Ipomaea), followed by quinine every second day for three days. He was then instructed, on the day the shakes were due to arrive, to take a strong drink of hot whisky and walk it off. This might seem a 'kill or cure' remedy, but luckily it did not kill Jemmy.

In his memoir Jemmy writes; 'This was the first time I had tasted the common whisky of the country and I thought it the most abominable stuff I had ever tasted but use soon brought me to like it and before I returned to civilisation I could drink raw whisky with anybody; so much for habit.' This treatment broke the ague for a while, but eventually it returned, so we can assume the jalap and whisky cure had done no lasting good. This unfortunate state of affairs lasted until the cold weather set in, when his general good health reasserted itself.

Upon arriving at Cincinnati, Jemmy sent all the money they

had taken back to New York. They tried to make sales in Cincinnati, but once again were largely unsuccessful. They set off down river, finding that they were more successful in the smaller places, and in this way reached the head of the Mississippi River, at Cairo. At this time the town of Cairo was simply a wharf and a warehouse for freight. Having heard so much of the dangers of the Mississippi, they debated whether to abandon the boat, pack up the goods and return to St Louis, but in the end decided to take the risk and proceed down the Mississippi. Because of the great river's reputation for lawlessness, they determined to take every precaution. With this always in mind, they never took off all their clothes, the doors were strongly barricaded, a gun lay on either side of each young man and they had with them a fierce and powerful dog. They also decided that, whatever passed, they would never open a door after they had closed up for the night; apparently they kept to this decision.

According to Jemmy's memoir:

> In those days trading on the Ohio and Mississippi was a regular business. There were regular floating stores, equipped with dry goods, groceries, hardware, crockery and they were looked forward to, at certain intervals throughout the year when the surrounding planters would come to trade. These floating merchants had their wives and children on board; their boats were frequently 60' or 70' long. Upon reaching their destination they would either sell out their entire stock or pack up what was left, return to one of the large towns on the Ohio, buy a new boat, stock up and start afresh.

At that time counterfeiters abounded on the Mississippi, and large counterfeit bills were regularly offered to them in unfrequented places. They were afraid to challenge these bills, but instead countered that they were sorry not to be able to change such large sums, as at the last town they had sent all their money back East. In 1837, towns on the Mississippi were few and far between, but what were called 'landings' were frequent. These generally consisted of a country store, and a storehouse for the receipt of cotton and the landing of freight. They frequently stayed for two or three days at these places, selling not only to the store but also to the planters who passed by. They deposited their money with the Brandon Bank at Vicksburgh, and travelled on in this way until they reached Natchez, where they made a final sale of their stock. At this stage they probably thought they had done the best they could to recoup their losses but further financial disaster was to follow.

They had arranged to meet Benjamin, now on his return from Rockdale in Texas, in Natchez. George was anxious to get back to Muddy Creek, to see how the sawmill was progressing, so Benjamin took his place on the ark. At this stage, as Jemmy writes: 'The great speculation that had been going on throughout the whole country culminated in the great panic.' The country area in which they were was filled with all kinds of depreciated bank paper called 'wildcat', ranging in discount from 5% to 50%. This was the kind of money they had been obliged to take in their trading, and the further they were from New York the worse it became. Most of their money was in the Brandon Bank, which had a capital of $100,000.00. Brandon was a small town in the woods, about 100 miles east of Vicksburgh on the Mississippi River, and it was reported that this bank was checking on New York at a discount of 25%. Faced with financial ruin, Jemmy decided to ride to Vicksburgh immediately, to see what could be salvaged:

> I hired a horse and rode the distance in three days in the middle of July 1838. I had to cross the Pearl River but the ferry boat was on the opposite side so I dashed my horse into the water and he swam across. I was wet to the seat but the warm July sun soon dried me off. I arrived at Brandon just before the bank closed for the day which was Saturday, only to find they had no more New York funds to draw against. The President of the Bank promised me if I would deposit this money he would send me a cheque on New York shortly. This promise he never fulfilled, the bank ultimately failed, the President cut his throat, and I lost all my money, about ten thousand dollars.

This frantic ride, of around 200 miles, was over rough terrain and in the searing heat of a southern summer, but Jemmy's childhood astride a pony on the South Downs clearly stood him in good stead.

Jemmy rode back to Natchez with news of this fresh disaster. The two young men decided to cut their losses and return to New York. This they did by various means – canal, steamboat and railroad – finally reaching New York in September 1838. One wonders whether it crossed their minds to compare the ease of this journey with that of their uncles over the same route three decades earlier.

Benjamin decided to remain in New York, and was warmly welcomed back by Mr. Arnold. Jemmy, however, made the decision to go home to England, although he vowed to return.

CHAPTER TWENTY-ONE

Henry, Susanna & Clair James

IN WILLIAM RIDGEWAY'S MANUSCRIPT history of Reigate (undated) he describes the Grece's home, Chart Lodge: 'About a quarter of a mile beyond Redstone is a genteel house belonging to Mr. Grece.' Susanna's husband, Henry, as well as being a fuller's earth merchant and farmer, was high constable of the Reigate

Henry Grece
(1799–1851)

Clair James Grece
(1831–1905)

Silhouettes by Mary Robinson 1837

Hundred. His duties included attending the quarter sessions at Guildford and Kingston, serving precepts and collecting the county rates; on these occasions he was wont to take Susanna and Clair James with him in his gig.

Henry employed three teams of horses to transport the fuller's earth, using a sunken track behind Chart Lodge as a road to the railway at Merstham. Henry prided himself on his fine teams of matched grey horses. The railway was constructed of iron rails, over which horses pulled trains of wagons; this increased the power of the horse many times, as it was said that a horse could pull twelve wagons loaded with stones. Before the railway was built this same load would have required fifty men. At the time the Merstham railway opened in 1803, people thought the limit of power had been reached.

Henry's mother, Ann Whitney Grece, still lived at Chart Lodge, as did his two younger unmarried sisters, Octavia and Maria, and his three younger brothers, Julian, Septimus and Felix. It is clear that not only Henry but his whole family were good friends of the Constable family. At the Horley shop they purchased all sorts of necessities including: 'a new frock for Felix, a new bonnet for Susanna, furniture and food'.

In October 1835, Susanna began one of her many journals. At this time the family were still at Chart Lodge and her son, Clair James, was four years old.

Early in November, Susanna writes in her journal: 'The King gone to Brighton today. Clair James and I went to Reigate thinking to see him and his entourage, were ten minutes too late; did not care much about it. Met in Reigate W.C. [William

Constable] and Eliza, in his chaise.' A few days later she records: 'Myself determined, with the little, dear cherub, Clair James, to walk to Horley to see Grandpapa. We started at a quarter past three and reached Horley about a quarter before six o'clock; this, the first time of his walking to Horley, the distance nearly six miles and think the longest direct walk he has taken. He held in nicely, appeared not in the least tired. Found Father in good health and glad to see us.' Clair was not yet five years old.

The family ate well; dinner was often a goose or a hare and once, Susanna records: 'an old hen for dinner by mistake for a fowl'.

A typical day in her journal of 1836 reads:

East Grinstead Fair is today. Henry made up his mind to go; Clair and I bustled about to get a ride a short distance with him. He took us on to the Fair, did not remain there long, not finding much amusement but walked back to where the horse was put up, a mile and a half from Grinstead. Henry purchased six swine, the motive of his going and got an invite from Mr. Searle to dine at his house, where we arrived a little past five o'clock and met with a kind reception, a good fire and dinner. Left Horne Court about nine and got home soon after ten. Henry drove the swine nearly as far as Blindley Heath, where he got them taken in for the night. The weather bright but very cold, freezing sharp all day.

The Searles were a local family where Maria Grece, Henry's sister, was employed as governess. They lived at Horne Court, near Smallfield, and from here Maria often rode home, on horseback, on Sundays to spend the day with her family.

Susanna often visited her father and enjoyed a close relationship with her three brothers, James, William and Charles, all of whom were living locally. Maria and Octavia Grece, Henry's sisters, often walked to Doversgreen to visit William and Eliza, about three miles away.

George Constable was now running the shop at Horley, but whenever he was away Susanna would go down to take his place for a few days, taking Clair James with her. Septimus Grece, Henry's brother, aged seventeen, was now also apprenticed in the Horley shop, alongside John Maple, who was coming to the end of his apprenticeship.

In the spring of 1836 James Sr., by now nearly eighty-five, again had his portrait painted. Susanna, Eliza and Maria Grece went down to see it and found it 'much improved' since they saw it before. The artist was C. Dowley and the portrait showing James Constable's head and shoulders, depicts him dressed in a fine velvet coat with a snowy stock at his neck. It seems probable that James of Storrington commissioned this portrait of his father. His own portrait, by the same artist at about the same period, is a large, full-length painting illustrating him shooting on his land near Storrington, and surrounded by his beloved dogs. William had recorded, rather sadly, that after Daniel's death there was no pictorial record with which to remember his brother, which was probably also true of John and his wife. Perhaps this had spurred the portraits, although it was also a growing fashion of the day.

In the beginning of May, Julian Grece, yet another of Henry's brothers, was taken seriously ill:

> Poor Julian much, much worse. His case now is hopeless. He had between twenty and thirty leeches on this morning and was put into a hip bath. The bath made him feel quite comfortable and he remained in it about half an hour but poor fellow, on taking him out he was convulsed and we dreadfully feared he would never be restored again. He did come to and we had thought of putting him in again in the evening when the Doctor should be with us but it was not done, everything appearing useless. Every drop of liquid he took and he has taken nothing but liquid since Sunday night last, was vomited up with offensive matter all the day. With this sickness he has been tormented often through his very painful illness, preceded by a troublesome hiccough.

He died, aged only twenty-two, possibly because of a ruptured appendix. Susanna observed in her journal: 'Julian's coffin was neatly made entirely without ornament, a brass plate to tell his name and age engraved, by the instruction of W.C., was all that adorned it and the handles were of wood.'

It is worth mentioning here that Julian was attended by the family doctors, Dr. Thomas Martin and his son, Peter. Dr. Martin was bailiff to the Reigate Hundred and was much concerned at the state of lawlessness that prevailed in Reigate, which he attributed to the lack of facilities for the young. To this end he started the Mechanics Institute, which provided a library and reading room and lectures (this later became the Reigate Literary

Institution). Henry and Susanna, William and Eliza and many of their friends frequently attended these lectures.

William now exerted his considerable talents to build a steam engine capable of driving the mill wheel at Horley. Early in 1836 Susanna, together with Henry and Clair James, drove to the Mill to dine and to see the steam engine operate. There was quite a large party, which included the Robinsons, Penfolds and Blundells, as well as Charles and his family. This must have been a very exciting occasion for them all, but especially for a five-year-old boy – a taste of the mechanical age to come.

On another occasion Susanna records in her journal:

> Clair James and self went to London with Henry. When we got there Henry left us to pursue his business and Clair and I walked to the Surrey Zoological Gardens, were much amused there, the number of people surprised me, till I learn the cause. It was a Fete and what they call a Fancy Fair for some Charity, I forget what. There was plenty of music and plenty to please any person who went to be pleased. This was our case and I suppose most of those who were there.

In August 1836, James Constable Sr. went to stay for some weeks with his son, James, in Storrington and no doubt was royally entertained by his two lively grandaughters, Matilda and Clara, now twenty-eight and twenty-two years old. Despite his years he was still hale and hearty. Susanna mentions his walking from Horley to visit her one Sunday, accompanied by Septimus, Henry's brother (who worked in the Horley shop). Susanna regularly walked to Horley. She cut her father's hair and noted, on one occasion, cutting out a new cover for his easy chair. Susanna and Clair James moved to Horley to nurse him whenever he was unwell. Susanna wrote one day whilst staying with her father: 'We walked to Hookwood Common, hoping to see the King and Queen, who were going to Brighton; were fortunate enough to meet them on the Common and just caught sight of them. I saw only the King.'

By 1837 the railway age had arrived; it was to change the old way of life more than anyone could imagine. A company called the London and Brighton Railway Company planned to build a line from London to Brighton, incorporating the Old Surrey Iron Railroad which ran from Merstham to Wandsworth. As mentioned Henry Grece used this horse-drawn railroad nearly every working day for the transportation of his fuller's earth, and he was extremely concerned about the Merstham Gap.

Poor Henry was also still engaged in sorting out his father's affairs. As Susanna wrote in her diary: 'Mr. Bell [a mortgagor] walked from the Somers Arms to our house in all the rain and staid [sic] about half an hour. A stout, short man with a mild countenance and gentlemanly mild manners. He gave Clair James a silver fourpenny piece.'

It seems that Clair James was a precocious reader. His mother remarked in her journal that the two of them were kept inside by a fierce snowstorm and that he read to her, sometimes from *Shakespeare* and sometimes Baxter's *The History of England*. [The dedication in this book reads: 'To the people at large, to the London Corresponding Society in particular, and to the Political Societies of Great Britain in General, associated for Parliamentary Reform and the promotion of constitutional information, this new and impartial History of England (a work peculiarly calculated to accelerate their exertions in the glorious cause of liberty) is inscribed, with due respect, by their fellow citizen, John Baxter.] This book was given to Clair James by his Constable grandfather. Only a few weeks later his grandfather gave him a Latin Grammar. He apparently taught himself Greek in the evenings, by the aid of his rush lamp. He was at this time not yet six years old.

Susanna's entry for Wednesday, 12 July 1837 reads:

This day fortnight Henry took Clair James and self to Horley to nurse Grandpapa a little, he being poorly. We remained with him 'till last Sunday when Papa fetched us home again, Grandpapa being much improved. Mr. Martin is now his doctor. The first Saturday we were there the dear Clair James was much out of health and did not quite recover 'till the following Wednesday. He had much fever and on Tuesday a faint eruption all over his body. Mr. Martin gave the dear little thing some medicine. He has now a small cold and is gone to bed, being tired. Matilda called to say goodbye to me today, she being returning to Storrington tomorrow. The weather has been dry this last fortnight, some days rather warm and some of the evenings chilly. This day has been rather gloomy but warm and pleasant.

A month later:

> Went to Horley three weeks ago last Friday and remained
> there 15 days. Father was very much out of health when I got
> there but I left him pretty much restored again. During our
> stay there, the dear boy, of course, was with me. We had
> several showery days and some few exceeding warm ones
> and since our return no rain and upon the whole the
> weather has been just such as must suit all. On the 28th July
> the cherub had his Profile taken by Mary Robinson to go
> with my own and others to America for my sister. Mary
> Robinson, with her father and two brothers are now on their
> passage to that country of freedom and prosperity. Last
> Sunday, self, boy and Grandmama went to Uncle Wm.'s to
> look at the moon through his telescope; too cloudy to see it
> so Papa, self and boy went again on Friday and had a
> beautiful view of it and did not get home 'till near eleven
> o'clock, the little chap pretty tired. The dear little fellow
> walked nearly to Smitham Bottom on Monday evening, to
> meet Papa on his return from London. Intended to have
> gone much further but we walked slow and started too late.
> Grandpapa went to Reigate to vote for Mr. Locke-King. He
> had a post chaise and so treated self, Clair James, Fanny and
> Trotty with a ride with him. The first Election I ever saw, the
> hubbub and row amused me for once in my life and we all
> spent a pleasant day and got home nicely to tea. This has been
> a most delightful day and the dear child and self have
> wandered over the hill twice, 5 miles.

Henry's sister, Octavia, had a suitor called Dr. Gustav Eberty, a
Prussian professor. He visited Chart Lodge where he was much

struck not only by Octavia, but also by the little boy, Clair James. He wrote to him, in the autumn of 1837, enclosing a present of some toy soldiers:

> My dear little friend,
>
> I cannot leave this country without having fulfilled my promise to complete your army. You receive with these Frenchmen, those with the white waistcoats are it, two bodies of Prussians. You may now play with them The Battle of Waterloo, which we call that of 'La Belle Alliance'. The sense of these French words will, I hope, once become a true one for us. I made for this purpose the power of the Prussians stronger and I am sure they will conquer the French, which separate from your true countrymen.
>
> I have also, I hope you will excuse here this also, added a little remainder of my own, which perhaps your Aunt will accept of your hands.
>
> Believe me, my dear fellow, that there remains something more of me with you. I think I will never forget neither you, my dear little fellow, nor your Octavia.
>
> I am affrayed [sic] it will not be possible for me to call upon you before my departure, my plan of voyage being altered but I will carry the image of you all, engraved in my head, with me over sea and land and nobody loves you more than your friend.
>
> Gustav Eberty.
>
> *Note:* It should be remembered that the Prussians were our allies at this time.

Henry attended church regularly, either the parish church of

Nutfield or that of Bletchingly. Sometimes he took Clair James and occasionally Susanna accompanied him, but not often. She probably shared the views on organised religion of the rest of her family, but appeared happy for their son to make his own decision.

In 1837 William gave Susanna a copy of a lithograph of the bridge he had designed at the top of Reigate Hill. She took Clair James to see the bridge on one of their walks.

Susanna and Clair James spent most of the autumn with James Sr. Susanna recorded on 5 December:

> Last Wednesday the cherub and self returned from Grandpapa's where we have been staying excepting about one fortnight from Sep. 17th. Much of the time Grandpapa poorly and nearly a month ago he was so unfortunate as to have another fall and sprained his right wrist sadly. This accident also disarranged his general health which was got pretty well and when I left him he was pretty well, though not yet able to dress and undress himself. Last Monday he had the children to make merry on his birthday, being his 88th. He was much pleased to see the little things jumping around a large dish of snapdragons etc. etc. Grandpapa has received from Mildred a very, very nice looking rocking chair. It was purchased at New York and taken care of to England by John Risbridger.
>
> *Note:* This rocking chair is indeed a most comfortable, bentwood rocking chair with caned seat and back, and remains in the family to this day.

CHAPTER TWENTY-TWO

William in Maturity

ALTHOUGH WILLIAM MUST have been devastated at the death of his brother Daniel in February 1835, he was not one to indulge in maudlin reminiscences. He was still living at Doversgreen with his niece Eliza but was also running the watermill during Charles's absence in America. He records making a survey of the late Mr. Charrington's land during July (Mr. Charrington had lived in the manor house whose land stood between the mill and the church. The Charrington and Jordan families had intermarried). In November he wrote to Matilda regarding a small commission he had executed on her behalf (meticulously recorded in his notebook under '300 Garden tallies for Matilda'):

> Dear Matilda,
> At length behold 300 iron tallies. I dare say you think and perhaps say that I have been devilishly negligent about them and I do not know how I can convince you to the contrary, unless I give you a journal of every day's transactions with me since I had the honour to receive your commission. I must try, however, a shorter way and that is I have kept the memorandum on my London Minutes ever since.

I was not able to attend to the matter on the first week or two and, since Charles returned I have not once visited the metropolis. Yesterday week, the case becoming hopeless with respect to myself, I requested Charles to execute the commission and instructed him to forward them in the way you directed but he happened to recollect something about a box to be sent from Horley, brought them hither to be enclosed, instead of sending them as instructed. The whole quantity could not be got. I wanted 400 for myself and I have divided them fairly between us.

I am stopped suddenly and can no more. Very much indeed yours and all of yours,

William C

P.S. I've not found time to dig up a single Dahlia yet. I mean to put all in a pit. Eliza's best love to you.

At this time William was commissioned to draw up plans for a railway in Jamaica. This task kept him busy although the project seemed to blow hot and cold. He planned to travel through America on his way to Jamaica, both to revisit places he remembered from his earlier trip and to visit the young Constables, as well as his sister, Mildred, and her family. He wrote to Matilda in the spring of 1836, regarding a new watch:

My dear Matilda,

I shall execute your commands with respect to the watches with much pleasure; under so unrestricted a commission I shall be at no loss what to do. I shall go to Mr. Pascal, the person who procured my very excellent watch for me and shall have no fear that he will treat me fairly and shall have confidence that he will give me very good watches.

You know, perhaps, that the projected Jamaican railway has latterly very much occupied me. It is still engaging my attention and time and I have felt, and do feel, at a loss how to appoint with your Papa. Nevertheless, I am anxious to make progress and will hold myself engaged to him for Saturday, the fourth of June and hope it will be convenient to him to be at Dovers Green on that day. If the fates should overmatch me with any insurmountable difficulty I will give due notice but I hope they will not be so uncivil.

Dahlias: we have a tidy little lot, in spite of mischances. The worst of it is that we have scarcely any duplicates worth the acceptance of an amateur and therefore can make no return just now for the civility of your offer. From among those you kindly propose to give I should like to accept from you the following: Miss Ramsden, Commander-in-Chief, Waterloo and a Widnal's Perfection if you have them in plenty, not otherwise, as we received one from Gilliam. With respect to your unnamed, I think I would rather give you no trouble, unless you should have two or three to spare with perfect convenience and that might come in conveniently to fill the waste corners of a basket or what else you might pack in. I have bought several lots this year at the auction mart. How well they keep faith with the catalogue I know not but many of them are grown into fine strong plants and ought decidedly to be now in the ground and shall be there as soon as this confounded north easter abates his spite.

Dear Matilda, very much indeed yours, Clara's and Papa's also.

William C.

P.S. Eliza sends her love to all of you.

In July William again wrote to Matilda, from Horley Mill:

Mine dear Matilda,

At length I have had the opportunity of taking Mrs. Ingram's watch to Mr. Pascal. I left it with him a day or two so that he has had an opportunity of conning it well. He returned it to me last night, with a letter in which he states he can make two watches like, and in all respects equal to the pattern, for a price not more than 25 guineas each, to include an improvement in the means of setting the hands which consists in performing the operation at the back instead of at the face. You are most likely aware that the silver face is a very delicate affair. If exposed much to the air it tarnishes and the slipping of the key upon it, in setting inevitably disfigures it. Eliza had the face of hers totally spoiled by a clumsy watch maker at Bruges; the best in that eminent city, who had it to cleanse. Therefore a scheme that obviates the necessity of exposing the face is certainly an improvement.

I do not know whether you may want any advice in this matter and shall therefore not offer any, because people do not like to have their counsel, which of course they always deem valuable, thanklessly received. I will, nevertheless, offer a suggestion or two that may be worth thinking about when you set about judging for yourselves, thus: a good watch is far less costly to keep in repair than an inferior one. My own excellent one never costs me anything but for cleansing once in three or four years and is never out of order or out of time. A bad watch is a deceiver and if put into a good case and has some pretence about it, is a gay deceiver, a sort of commodity that prudent young women regularly eschew. A watch lasts long and if both good and handsome, will always inspire a judicious wearer with a sentiment akin to friendship; such a friendship is always safely placed. If bad, it is a mere hanger on from which a wearer commonly endures much and finally finds it necessary to rid himself of by a rough shake off.

When you have determined on the course you will take, do me the favour to write and continue me in my agency of this affair. I shall attend to it with much pleasure.

I enclose a Jamaica Railway Prospectus, which has a look of progress. Nevertheless, I consider it to be safely settled that I shall take my next Christmas cheer in our own 'tight little island'. These papers are printed solely for circulation in Jamaica and no further step will be taken here 'till 'tis ascertained how the project is received there. The papers were sent off last week and a return is not expected 'till towards the end of October. If it proceeds further arrangements will take two, three or four months in England. I may then perhaps cross the Atlantic with the easterly winds of February or March, make some necessary traverses in the States and then down the Mississippi and on to Jamaica. This is as I should like it to turn out. I am very glad that the business has arrived at a temporary settlement. I have now a little clear look ahead and think I may perhaps manage seven or ten days of holiday keeping. How stands your purse? Can you afford from £5 to £7 for a real exploration of the Isle of Wight or the coast of Lyme Regis or of Whitby? I am thinking of treating Eliza in this way but you are too wealthy to be thought of in that way. Nevertheless, I should much want to have you and should not want to have anybody else, unless some good soul should offer and confess to a decided penchant for poring into rocks and clay beds. I shall enquire very shortly into the charges that will be incurred in travelling to either of these places. In the meantime I should be glad to know what you are thinking about it and shall not grumble to obtain this knowledge at the expense of postage.

Dahlias are growing away very well; they drink a vast deal of water. Half a score or so have flowered but there has been no eminent beauty among them yet. One that I had from the auction mart has come false and of course we are afraid of more deceits.

Mrs. Charles begs me to present her love and say that when the haying is over, Charles will be ready very soon to take Papa to Horsham on his way to you, or it may be that he will go to Findon Fair and take him so far but no certain arrangement is yet made.

I am very fully engaged with Surveying business up to the 12th of August and therefore think of no excursion 'till that time.

Pray give my best love to Tit and say to her that we understand distinctly that we shall be favoured with her visit and a good long one, too, in the autumn. Love to Papa, of course.

My dear Matilda, very much indeed yours, now and evermore.

William

P.S. I write this unexpectedly from the Mill and have therefore nothing to say from Eliza. Final settlement of Mr. Mansell's affairs as speedily as possible.

Note: Mrs. Ingram was the late Elizabeth Constable's sister.

At the beginning of August 1836, William wrote to Matilda once more, outlining their plans for a trip to Yorkshire:

Mine dear Matilda,

I have done nothing about the watch yet. I went to Mr. Pascal's last Monday, intending to tell him the terms on which you could be supplied at Porterhouse's and to hear what he had to say but he was out of London and would not return 'till three weeks are elapsed. While I remain in commission I shall not hesitate if the opportunity occurs of buying such watches as Mrs. Ingram's at $22^1/_2$ guineas, to make that purchase on your behalf. You are right in your recollection that I do not think much of the contrivance of Mr. Porterhouse's which dispenses with the use of a key. I dare say it may be clever enough but I apprehend it is but a small piece of cleverness when placed in comparison with the vast accumulation of ingenuity which is exhibited in a well made watch. The inconvenience of a key is a mere trifle and, if its use will dispense with a single moveable piece in the keyless watch, I should prefer the more simple machine with the key. Nevertheless, the sight of it might make me change my mind about it. I shall endeavour to call on Mr. Porterhouse and see it. I have no care at all about buying the watches off Mr. Pascal other than that, knowing him, I could better depend on him than on another that I do not know. The experience that I have had with my own watch further recommends Mr. Pascal to me.

Now, for journeying to the north. Steam passage from London to Hull is 4/-, best cabin. From Hull there is no doubt steamwork to Scarborough and Whitby or to Pickering somehow and from thence to Whitby there is a railroad, opened a month or two ago. Pickering is on weald clay, so is Scarborough. I told you when I wrote before that I could not be disengaged 'till after the 12th. A move on the part of the Turnpike Trustees has, since that time, confined me here 'till the 26th. After that I think we shall be ready for you when it suits your convenience and shall be very glad indeed to have you. I think, under the circumstances, Yorkshire must be the best. What think you? The west of England is much less accessible and the White Island is hardly more so. Now, contrive about your guests as you best may. Eliza and I will wait upon your convenience. You will be sure to consider the first part of September better than the last but other circumstances, as well as time, must be considered.

Dahlias go on so-so. Many of them I bought in London turned out cheats, as you call them but they were bought vastly cheap and they, for the most part, come true and those that I bought by auction are certainly bargains. The first flowers of several of the good kinds are but sad concerns; the seedlings fall very far below those of last year. Only three have yet flowered that we deemed worth saving. Chief business: Papa comes to see you next Wednesday. Charles will take him to Horsham on that day at 11 o'clock and will expect some of you there, to take him on.

My very best love to Tit, also Eliza's to all of you and to Papa. All blessings be upon you.

Yours very much,

William C

P.S. Eliza will write by Granpapa about travelling equipments.

William's interests were so wide ranging that it is perhaps not surprising that he was so knowledgeable about both watches and garden matters, particularly his beloved dahlias.

They had a successful trip to Yorkshire and Derbyshire; and not only did Matilda accompany William and Eliza, but so also did her sister, Clara. William and Eliza both drew the hills and valleys which captivated them, and these drawings, a delightful souvenir to bring back with them, are still extant, as is the Derbyshire spar egg, mentioned in Susanna's journal:

> Matilda, Eliza and Clara came to see us, expressed themselves much pleased with their late trip into Yorkshire, etc., from which they returned last Tuesday. William brought for Clair a pretty egg, made from Derbyshire spars and Matilda gave me an exceedingly pretty little Pestle & Mortar of the same. Uncle William 'sent his compliments to Clair James', which made us laugh.

William, now aged fifty-three, spent the first two weeks of October surveying the local route of the South Eastern Brighton Railway. He had been employed to find the line, to survey and plot it. Being of a mechanical turn of mind, he must have been fascinated by the railway mania. No less than five lines were suggested from London to Brighton.

Did anyone foresee quite how the arrival of the 'iron horse' would affect everyone's lives? Large numbers of people who had scarcely ever left their villages would begin to use the railway and to travel about freely. Within just a few years the coaching trade collapsed, especially when the mail was put onto the railways in 1838. When the coaching trade declined, all the industries connected with it suffered: inns closed, the market in horses declined, as did all the jobs associated with the horse, such as grooms, postboys, stable lads, blacksmiths, etc. In addition, produce and milk was transported quickly, which, as this was before the days of refrigeration, must have improved the quality of food.

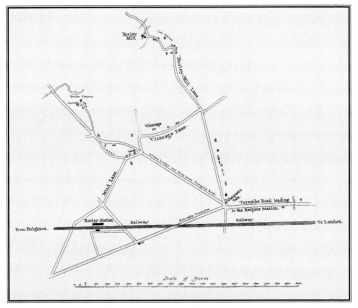

Map of Ley Street and Horley, W. Constable 1837

In the spring of 1837 William wrote to Matilda, who had recently returned from a visit to London. The plans for the Jamaican railway had run into trouble:

Mine dear Matilda,
Many thanks for the very handsome stone with spiral shells and the more than handsome, or even superb, Nautile [sic] that came along with it. I prize them both very highly, more

especially the latter which has taken me entirely by surprise as I did not think the London clay contained anything half so beautiful. I think I shall hereafter look upon our great city with unwonted respect, now that I know it to have for its foundations such magnificent relics bearing testimony of the life that existed in that remote time which preceded, by long enduring ages, the fable of the six days' labour and shall tolerate the lies that are preached within its walls for the sake of the splendid reputations presented by the earth, by which those walls are supported.

I don't know how to repay you in this way. My only hope is to send you over one of the Catskill Mountains, if I can find a ship large enough to take it.

I have got your watch back again from Mr. Pascal and send it herewith. It was found that a minute hair had got into it and was entangled with the machinery and it was that, that occasioned it to stop. I hope it will be now found to go well. I have not had an opportunity of seeing to its movements since I got it back because Mr. Cannaneo has broken the second hand of my clock and without that no regular comparison can be made. Good as my own watch is, I do not depend upon it for correcting another watch by. Many persons do not know how to regulate their watches and perhaps you may be such a one. If you are, please to observe that the moving the little index towards the letter F will make the watch go faster or will correct the error of too much fastness, either of which may be supposed with probability.

The Jamaica Railway sleeps and I have now but little expectation that it will awaken in my time, that is within the next three months. I do not care much about it when I think of the blue tops of the Alleghenies and the Whip-Poor-Wills of the valleys.

I believe my Dahlia roots are doing what it is said the Parsley seeds always do, make nine journeys to the devil before they send their plants above ground and my only hope is that they may be near their last stages but not a bud yet has shown itself above the surface. I have had the bed taken to pieces once, about 14 days ago, and the bark dried and returned to the Pit, with a good layer of fresh stable dung underneath but it is still as cold as Lapland and that perhaps is a good excuse for the peregrinations I am proposing them to be making. I have had much thought myself all through this spring, by the Almanac, of going that way to look for a better climate but I saw three swallows yesterday and think now of not going before next winter.

Pray give my best love to Tit. I hope the malady of her heart is somewhat abated. This is decidedly one of the cases where the doctor does more harm than good. If she would but take her tea and bread and butter and dismiss from her mind thoughts of all things connected with physic, she will find herself cooler and better.

I had just got to this place as your father's letter came in, by the Crawley postman, announcing that the wheat waggon would not pass between your country and this before Monday. I therefore take the watch again into my possession and will observe it as well as I can before that time.

My dear Matilda, yours indeed and in truth,
William C

Note: The reference to Tit's malady of the heart referred to her relationship with the Irish doctor, William Maybury, which was obviously not going as smoothly as she might have liked.

In August William pencilled in, on the Manorial Plan of the borough of Reigate, the course of the proposed London/Brighton railway: 'shewing the various demesnes and copyhold lands and making a schedule thereof, that will be intersected or touched by the said line'. By October he had decided to sail to America before the winter closed in. He was to accompany Eliza, now well enough to join her brother and sister. They embarked from London and stopped at Portsmouth for a short time. Susanna recorded that the weather was sad and rough, and towards evening blew quite a hurricane, but that luckily the travellers sustained no injury.

It was not until 12 January 1838 that the family heard that William and Eliza had landed safely in New York. William sent Clair James a newspaper from that city where they would have stayed some time with Benjamin. With the advent of the railways they no longer had to wait for the canal to thaw before travelling to Pittsford. No doubt Caroline and Eliza were delighted to see each other again but no more so than Mildred and William. In the spring William left Pittsford and travelled on down the Ohio and Mississippi rivers revisiting many of the scenes he and Daniel had first described in their journals of 1806 and 1807:

...found such change in the condition and aspect of the country as may justify the extravagance of my surmise as to what may happen in a few centuries. This, at the Falls of the river Genessee where there was a succession of noble cataracts shrouded on every side by a dense, unbroken, forest, hiding within its dark recesses one little cabin, the only shelter within many miles, I found on my last visit a busy city of 20,000 inhabitants, twenty large and powerful mills manufacturing flour, which found its way into most of the markets of the old world, the West Indies and South America, manufactories of other kinds, printing presses, churches, chapels and merchants' stores and warehouses filled with the products of all the manufacturing countries of the earth. But the native charm of the scenery as I had known it and drawn it were entirely swept away, the once delightful banks of the whole river were shorn of their sylvan beauty and the vanished forest replaced by obtrusive buildings of all sorts of unsightly figures. The upper fall, or rapid, was so obliterated by the havoc of civilisation that I could not discover where it formerly had been. Changes such as these I found going on everywhere, though not always to so striking an extent. Buffalo, from a few cabins, was grown into an important city.

William continued his travels by steamboat but found that: '...the river banks had been deprived of their magnificent solitude by hordes of invading men and the snorting steamboat had frightened away the swans, the cranes and pelicans which I had formerly seen in multitudes adorning the solitary shores of these magnificent streams'. At the Passaic Falls he encountered a turnpike road and: 'oh barbarous intrusion, within 20 yards a tollgate exhibiting all the usual sordid features of advertisements and so forth in front of the waterfall'.

He despatched a newspaper home from Natchez, before continuing on to New Orleans. While he was travelling he heard that the Jamaica Railway plan had been shelved, although he was probably not that surprised. He was back in Pittsford by the summer of 1838, where, again, he must have been warmly welcomed by his sister, Mildred, and her family. In the autumn he persuaded Mildred and Emma to accompany him back to England for their long-planned visit. Mildred had been talking of such a trip since 1834 and this seemed a good opportunity. Jemmy, James's younger son, was also returning home after his failed business venture, and agreed to make one of the party. The four of them, William, Jemmy, Mildred and Emma travelled to England on Isambard Kingdom Brunel's steamship, *The Great Western*, making the journey in twelve-and-a-half days. This was only the third time a steamship had crossed the Atlantic. They each paid £35.0s.0d. for their passage, a fantastic amount in 1838 (equivalent to £1800 today), and must have been amazed at their speed of travel. Indeed their journey was so rapid that their arrival preceded the news that they were on their way.

CHAPTER TWENTY-THREE

End of an Era

By THE SUMMER OF 1838 Matilda had a serious suitor, a young lawyer from an established Petworth legal family, named Arthur Daintrey (Petworth was a neighbouring village to Storrington). At the same time any problems that Clara had experienced in her love life appear to have been solved as on 4 July she married Dr. William Augustus Maybury, from Kenmare, County Kerry. Early in September Susanna and Clair went to visit Clara and William Maybury in their new Islington home. Susanna wrote: 'Henry took Clair James and self to London to see Cousin Clara, spent a most pleasant day with her and her little man. They seem very, very comfortable and their house is exceeding nice. Very late home, near twelve o'clock.'

Clair James had just passed his seventh birthday and Susanna gave him a miniature of his father. She recorded in her journal that he was overwhelmed and refused at first to accept the present, saying he would not deprive his mother of it and that something not so valuable would do as well.

A few days later Henry appealed against his window tax. He was too late to see the Magistrates, and in any case was told that even if he had, there was no chance of getting off. The window tax was most unpopular. Evidence of it is still commonly seen in the many bricked-in window spaces in villages and towns the length and breadth of England.

Early in October Henry attended the sessions at Kingston as high constable. He took Susanna and Clair James in the gig with him. It was quite late when they returned home over Epsom Downs and they had some difficulty in finding the road in the dark. Two days later while Clair James was having two baby teeth removed by Mr. Martin, they learned that Mildred and Emma were coming to England for a visit. Susanna must have been astonished as well as delighted. Neither William nor Mildred would have had time to write, since the mail from North America often took several months.

However, George, who was still running the Horley shop, had been confined to bed for several weeks with an inflammation of the liver. Susanna had been extremely worried that her father would overdo things while George was ill. Now she was even more worried about the excitement caused by Mildred's and Emma's arrival.

On 20 October William, Mildred, Emma and Jemmy landed in England and travelled to Horley Mill, where there was no doubt a great welcome. Henry had taken Susanna and Clair to the Mill for the occasion, and Susanna found her father: 'poorly but very excited'. We can imagine the old man's response to the safe arrival of Mildred and Emma, neither of whom he had seen for nearly twenty years, not to mention the relief he must have felt to have William home again. Mildred and Susanna, too, must have been intrigued to meet each other after all these years, not to mention Emma and little Clair.

As Susanna had feared, it was all too much for the old man, now nearly eighty-nine. Apart from all the flurry caused by Mildred's arrival, the chimney caught fire. He took to his bed on 25 October with Mildred and Susanna acting as his nurses. Both Clair James's grandmother, Ann Grece, and his aunt, Octavia Grece, wrote to offer their congratulations on the old man's approaching birthday:

> My dear Clair James,
> I should have answered your letter before this but I thought I would wait until this day, when I could congratulate your good Grandpapa on the 89th anniversary of his birth. Will you tell him that Aunt Octavia and myself would pay our respects to him this day but that we are both invalids, she with the toothache and I with my chough [sic].
> James Peat was clearing up the rubbish the other day, when he found your dial plate. He brought it to me and I shall take care of it until you come home. We want you to come home to eat the bread crusts, for your Papa takes all the crumb to make his toast.
> The shrubs are cut down and we can see Gatton Park quite plain from the door.
> Now I did mind and kept the doors shut but the rogues did not mind that; they broke them open and stole the beans in spite of me and the locks. Poor Chloe [Clair's dog] is come home but she is very ill and very thin. I think if she had

been here they would not have got in, unless it was somebody that knew her.

We have had the chimney swept or we should have had a fire, as well as you; they got four bushels of soot.

Give my respects to your Aunt Purse and love to your Mama and ask her to kiss your soft cheek for me, and believe me to be, my dear Clair James,

Your affectionate,

A.G.

Octavia wrote:

My dear little Clair,

Many thanks for your kind little note and for your kind wishes about my toothache. I do believe they did me good for I slept better on Sunday night than for three weeks past. I am very glad Uncle William is returned because I think you will be glad too.

You tell me George is downstairs again; that is a good thing. You have had a very sick house. I hope I shall go and see poor Grandpapa on Thursday, with Papa. I should have seen him and all of you before now if I had been better.

Grandmama sends her love to you and acknowledges the receiving of your note of Sunday. She is greatly obliged for your attention.

Now with kind remembrance to all of you I am,

Your affectionate Aunt,

Octavia

James Constable Sr. died on 24 December. Susanna wrote an account of her father's illness in her journal:

From this time 'till his death, Dec. 24th, I was almost wholly his nurse, sitting up with him each other night and attending to him much throughout the day. The first Sunday of his keeping his bed he had considerable pain in his chest which was relieved by a Blister and from that time 'till within about 24 hours of his death he might be said to have had no pain, gradually sinking 'till the before-mentioned 24 hours, when his right foot was seized up with spasm which soon extended all up the right side. Anodyne medicine was given and taken with some difficulty, which succeeded in giving relief and we had the consolation of knowing that he was freed from pain, from his own lips, for about an hour before his last. I thought I observed him a little rallied and I asked him if he was in pain. He distinctly answered, 'Not at all'. He had exhibited restlessness which induced me to put the question. Previous to when he answered me he did not appear conscious of being spoken to 'till the time he said, 'Not at all'. He bid the dear little Clair James goodnight on his last night with animation and affection, saying 'Goodnight, little dear'. He breathed his last about one, midday, but so tranquil was his departure we could not tell exactly when it happened. He kept his 90th birthday and had snapdragons in his bedroom, with which he was pleased.

James Constable's death notice published in the *Morning Chronicle* of 27 December 1838 read as follows: 'James Constable. He died at his house at Horley in Surrey. He closed his simple, unaffected and honourable life in the 90th year of his age.'

James Constable Sr. often wrote small verse and one in particular was attributed to him:

Life

The Past, what is it but a gleam
Which memory faintly throws?
The Future? 'Tis the faery dream
Which hopes and fears compose.
The Present is the lightning glance
Which comes and disappears.
Thus life is but a moment's trance
Of memories, hopes and fears.

During his grandfather's illness, Clair James spent most of his time with William in the Great Parlour, which William had taken as his study. Clair became much attached to William and 'wept sadly' at leaving him and Horley, which they did not do until early February. William taught Clair to make maps by copying from the globe, of which Susanna and Henry much approved since it taught their son geography. The time Clair and William spent together was to form the basis for an enduring relationship between the two of them.

The reason Susanna stayed so long in Horley was that Clair James developed measles, as did Emma. Charles's daughters, Lavinia and Fanny, had recently recovered from the disease so presumably he caught it from them. Fortunately, however, they both had it mildly, this was particularly fortunate in Emma's case, as childhood diseases are often serious illnesses for an adult, and she, at this time, was twenty-eight. Emma did not have a good reintroduction to England. First she was confronted with her grandfather's illness, followed by his death, and then she caught measles.

Mildred must have been very upset, particularly as she must have felt that the excitement of her homecoming had hastened her father's death. After Susanna's departure for home, Mildred and Emma went to stay with the Robinson family at Manor House, Lowfield Heath. Over and above their leasing the mill at Lowfield Heath, the two families were connected by marriage and had been neighbours and friends for many generations. In 1837 John Robinson Sr., his sons John and Joseph and his daughter, Mary, had sailed for the New World with the intention of finding somewhere to settle. In England farming and milling were both in the doldrums and John Jr., who had previously visited America, was no doubt most enthusiastic. They spent two years near Pittsford where they bought a farm. They often visited Mildred and her family but unfortunately family problems in England forced them to return. They were no doubt in an excellent position to comfort Mildred on the catastrophe occasioned by her first visit to England for nearly twenty years.

Meanwhile, James in Storrington was living well, spending much of his time out shooting with his friends. Snipe were still plentiful on the heaths and bogs around Storrington. William, although bereaved, had been very successful as surveyor to the Reigate Turnpike Trust, but was now considering a new career. He was carefully watching the news about the new invention of M. Daguerre, who claimed to catch images on glass. Charles, in spite of his conviction that life was difficult, certainly lived the good life. Mildred was at last financially secure, thanks to John Purse and his sawmill investments, and she had recovered from her earlier experience of hardship. Susanna, although finding her marriage more difficult than she had imagined, took great consolation in her son, and was also close to her brothers, particularly James and William.

By the time of his death James Constable Sr. had created an astonishingly prosperous business in Horley. He had also helped found three other companies that were to become extremely successful, Hanningtons of Brighton, Arnold Constable & Co. (previously Arnold & Hearn) in New York (with branches in Manchester, South America and Paris), and Maples of Tottenham Court Road. Two of his grandsons, Benjamin and Jemmy, and a great-grandson (Charles's son, Walter) were to settle permanently in America.

With the death of James Constable in 1838, barely a year into the reign of Victoria, came the end of an era. He had outlived four of his sons, Richard, who had died as a child; Benjamin, who had died as a young man; John, who had died in 1829, and Daniel, who had died three years before his father. Industrialisation had changed the face of the England he knew and loved, but the spirit of the old man lived on in his children and grandchildren.

Epilogue

MY GRANDPARENTS, LEWIS and Clara Grece, were both descended from the Constable family. Lewis was Susanna's grandson and Clara was James's great-granddaughter. Between the wars Lewis Grece had given a collection of his Great Uncle William's watercolours and drawings, original journals covering his and his brother, Daniel's, American travels, and a small table to the Corporation of Reigate. The table is historically important, because on it Thomas Paine wrote *The Rights of Man*, which so influenced the course of the American War of Independence. These were to furnish a small museum at the Town Hall with the idea that the local people would have access to some of their history. Sadly the museum closed down and the contents were taken to the Museum of Labour History in Bethnal Green. Even more sadly, this museum sold William's paintings and mislaid one of William's original journals.

In 1949 Lewis and Clara Grece gave the deeds of Tedhams to their son, Clair, as a wedding gift. A little later they gave Spikemead to their daughter, Clara Diana. In 1954 Clair was appointed Air Attaché in Washington D.C. He suggested that his parents move to Tedhams (now called The Old Mill House), a more manageable home than their large Victorian house in Redhill. Chas (as he was called) knew that it would be many years before he could contemplate living there himself. Unfortunately before Chas could take up his appointment he was killed in an air crash. His heir was Diana's fourteen-year-old son, David. It was agreed, on his behalf, that Lewis and Clara would still make the move. Christmas dinner always took place in the heavily beamed dining room of The Old Mill House. The big oil painting of Frank, the dog, hung on the wall and there were endless tales of the two brothers who, accompanied by this dog, walked around America.

In 1963 Lewis Grece died and two years later David married. Clara Grece, now seventy-four, moved to a flat nearby so that the young couple could move into their home. She left the house furnished, the family portraits and books still in place. The family were unaware that antique dealers called on her. Among the things she sold were two paintings of early American scenes. David Mitchell, from Sothebys, happened to see these paintings and enquired their provenance. He visited Clara who told him that there were several more paintings in the care of her grandson. David Mitchell was shown the family archive and was the first person outside the family to realise its importance. He purchased the collection and returned to Toronto.

Clara also sold some daguerreotypes which were seen by Philippe Garner, also of Sothebys. Philippe plans a book about William's photographic career and is responsible for his entry in the *Dictionary of National Biography*.

Blundells School in Tiverton were offered a bundle of papers called 'Blundell Family Papers' although it was discovered that they were mostly to do with someone called Daniel Constable. Brian Jenkins, Director of Studies, was so intrigued by Daniel's letters that he decided to edit and publish them (*Citizen Daniel and the Call of America*, 1999).

Both Philippe and Brian asked me if I knew the whereabouts of William Constable's book, written in the 1850s, which described the American adventures of his brother, Daniel, and himself. I had the great good fortune, on my first research trip to New York, to locate it on the first day. It lay in a vault in Connecticut, quite safe, still owned by a descendant of the Constable family.

It was not until 1995 that I found the time to catalogue my papers, planning to give the originals to a record office. By now my mother had produced a small sea-stained chest full of yet more family letters. It soon became apparent that there was a story to be told.

On my most recent trip to Canada, David Mitchell decided that I had amassed so much material that he bowed out, and generously agreed that I should write this story as he had always meant to do. He kindly allowed me to bring back to England the remainder of the family file.

Acknowledgements

First and foremost I should like to thank Philippe Garner, of Sothebys, who has encouraged me every inch of the way. I should also like to thank Brian Jenkins, firstly for tracking me down, and secondly for his help and encouragement. It is due to Brian, and the generosity of Blundells School, that the Blundell papers are being restored to the family. I should also like to thank David Mitchell both for his help and for his generosity in allowing me to retrieve family papers that had come his way. I should like to thank my long time travelling companion, Valerie Levine, for dropping everything to accompany me on research trips around the USA. I should like to thank all my American cousins for their help and hospitality, particularly Tom and Alexandra McCracken, Bob and Stephanie Olmsted and Mike and Polly Stanley. I am indebted to descendants of the Mott family on both sides of the Atlantic; also to Liz Butler, a descendant of the Robinson family. I should also like to thank the staff of the Brighton Library, British Library, Crowborough Library, Hastings Library, Horley Library, Lewes Library, Redhill Library, Surrey History Service, East and West Sussex Record Offices, Sussex Archeological Society, East and West Surrey

Family History Societies, Sussex Family History Society and the rector and churchwardens of Horley. In the USA I should like to thank the New Brighton Library, Pittsburgh Library, New York and Pittsford Historical Societies and the curator of the Photographic History Collection at the National Museum of American History, Smithsonian Institute. I am also deeply indebted to Sally Astridge and Christine Davis for their editing skills, to Monica Bratt for her design skills and Sue Wales for her artistic skills. If I have omitted to thank anyone I apologise.

Notes

249 *City under Fire* (G Amey 1979)

266 D. Taylor, Cobham

267 Dr. Hartwell Carver, Friends of Mt. Hope, Pittsford Hist. Soc.

267 *The Browne American Letters*, as above

307 *A History of the Fullers Earth Industry in Surrey* (J Greenwood 1941)

310 Martin Family Papers, SHS 325/4

317 W. Constable Notebook

325 W. Constable Notebook

329 W. Constable Notebook

338 Robinson Family Papers, private collection

Bibliography

IT WOULD BE IMPOSSIBLE to mention every book through which I have browsed. I mention here the ones that were most helpful to me. *A Geological, Historical and Topographical Description of the Borough of Reigate* by Robert Phillips (1885), *Old Watermills and Windmills* by R. Thurston Hopkins (date unknown), *The Free Men of Charlwood* by R. Sewill and E. Lane (1951), *Early Days in Horley, Sidlow and Salfords* by E. Lane (1958), *Shadrach Blundell His Family and Property 1580-1880* by Dorothea Teague (1985), *History of Brighthelmston* by J.A. Erredge (1862), *A Peep into the Past: Brighton in the Olden Time* by J.G. Bishop (1892), *Pioneer History of Indiana* by Col. W. M. Cockrum (1907), *The Romance of American Transportation* by F. M. Reck (1939), *The Age of Revolution* by Eric Hobsbawm (1962), *Britons, Forging the Nation 1707-1837* by Linda Colley (1992).

Index